'Dr Johnston's *Media Relations* text is a true asset for anyone wanting to learn more about the media relations world. It is filled with fantastic examples and helpful techniques that I continually find myself putting into practice on a daily basis in my career. Not only a great course book, but one I reference often in my day to day work.' **Ian Loughrey, Marketing Department, Google+, Chicago, USA**

'This text helped me to understand the very core of what we do in public relations, thus allowing me to excel in my tertiary studies. The benefit, however, did not stop there—media relations is a life-long skill for communications professionals, this text has also helped me excel in my career.' **Reis Maher, Cohn & Wolfe Global Communications and Public Relations, London, UK**

'Your textbook has been used as my working guideline. The first news that I wrote and distributed to media was published in two major publications in Thailand and a number of the minor ones—the secret of how I got the coverage can be found in your textbook.' **Panadda Sirisopapong, PTT Retail Management—a subsidiary of PTT, a state-owned oil and gas company in Bangkok, Thailand**

'You don't have to be a PR student to understand how important the media is. Students from fields as diverse as nursing and engineering are enrolling in media relations units and through Johnston's clear, insightful and contemporary work realise that everyone needs to be aware of the function and roles of media.' **Mark Sheehan, Course Director undergraduate PR, Deakin University, Melbourne**

'This was really the first serious textbook on media relations to be produced in either Australia or New Zealand, and I've been using it since the first edition. It covers in plain language the useable skills needed for an entry level media relations position, but makes sure these are contextualised in broader currents of research and theory.' **Dr Elspeth Tilley, School of Communication, Journalism & Marketing, Massey University, New Zealand**

Jane Johnston

media relations

issues & strategies

2ND EDITION

ALLEN&UNWIN
SYDNEY · MELBOURNE · AUCKLAND · LONDON

This second edition published in 2013
First published in Australia in 2007

Allen & Unwin
Sydney, Melbourne, Auckland, London

83 Alexander Street
Crows Nest NSW 2065
Australia
Phone: (61 2) 8425 0100
Fax: (61 2) 9906 2218
Email: info@allenandunwin.com
Web: www.allenandunwin.com

Cataloguing-in-Publication details are available from the
National Library of Australia
www.trove.nla.gov.au

ISBN 978 1 74237 644 8

Index by Russell Brooks
Typeset in 11/14 pt Galliard by Midland Typesetters, Australia
Printed by South Wind Productions, Singapore

10 9 8 7 6 5 4 3 2 1

CONTENTS

ACKNOWLEDGEMENTS

This edition required extensive primary and secondary research and I would like to thank the people and organisations who gave their time, expertise and materials to contribute. Some provided access to media and public relations workplaces in order for me to gain up-to-date insights into current best practice. Others gave permission for the use of illustrations and media materials which have contributed to a richer text. My thanks go to Director of News at ABC TV Brisbane Fiona Crawford, and the Brisbane ABC television, radio and online teams; Amanda Robson and the team at Brumfield, Bird and Sandford; Susan Boyd at Infront Communications; Wayne Hickson at HicksonMedia; Stephanie Edmond from the 'It's not OK' campaign, New Zealand; Tamara Morris from the 2018 Commonwealth Games bid; Anthony Hayes from Queensland Tourism; John Flannery from the AMA; and the team at Mindframe. Thanks also to the *Gold Coast Bulletin* and the *Caloundra Journal* and the other organisations throughout the book that provided copyright clearance to use stories and other materials including the Henley-on-Todd regatta and Mt Buller ski resort.

I would also like to thank talented Bond postgraduate and research assistant Soraya Klemenz and Bond adjunct staffer and former radio journalist Denise Raward for their important contributions to the new edition. I am grateful to my employer Bond University for allowing me the research time during 2011 to write the new edition; Allen &

Unwin's Elizabeth Weiss, ever encouraging and constructive in her approach to publishing; and book editor Christa Munns and copy editor Sue Jarvis for their valuable input.

And, finally, since I worked on Christmas Day and every other weekend and holiday during late 2011 and early 2012 in order to make deadline I thank my partner, Nigel, and daughter, Tess, for their unfailing patience, support and encouragement.

MEDIA RELATIONS IN CONTEXT 1

This book is about the working relationship between public relations (PR) and the media—the role of media relations. This is one of the best known segments of the public relations mix; its outcomes are often tangible and visible, whether printed in a newspaper, published on the internet or broadcast on radio or television. But achieving and managing media coverage is just the tip of the media relations iceberg. Media relations is also about establishing professional relationships, knowing the way your professional counterparts (in this case, the news media) operate, understanding the timeframes, deadlines, varied formats and practices of this profession, and using the media as a barometer for society, as well as a launching pad for your own initiatives.

As with any field of practice, it is important to know the environment in which you will be working. The book therefore investigates the shifting terrains of the modern media and introduces some key theoretical concepts that underpin contemporary media practice. It analyses the current state of play in the media environments of newspapers, radio and television, magazines, the web and the blogosphere, as well as sections of the entertainment media like reality TV, panel shows and lifestyle programs. It takes a look at trends and changes within contemporary media, including the impact and adoption of social media, and how public relations professionals working within these industries and platforms can best operate. Throughout, the book

1

aims to remain focused on the people who work within these media environments: journalists, editors, news producers and bloggers—the individuals with whom the media relations professional will engage to get their story published and heard. Finally, it presents a range of tools and techniques that may be employed in this practice—from preparing a media campaign to putting together the components of media kits, releases, conferences, events, social media and more.

While the field of media relations is a practical one, it requires research and reflection to grow and develop. This book works towards this goal, with a balance of analysis, policy, theory and practice to place media relations *in context* within the profession of public relations, the news (and sometimes entertainment) media and the changing patterns of society.

THE MEDIA AND CHANGE

The media are facing a time of massive change. With the emergence of the internet as one of the primary forms of communication, media commentators across the globe have begun questioning the news media's capacity to adapt: How have the news media reorganised themselves in the contemporary media environment? What other media channels are now the dominant forms of information in local, national and global contexts? Is glocal—a mix of local and global—the way forward? In Australia, Tony Moore (2010, p. vii) argues that the internet will be 'journalism's saviour. What will perish, however, is the 20th century's version of journalism'. The 'model' of journalism that has held since the introduction of the printing press is now outdated. Prophesies from all over the world predict massive change; book titles such as *Changing Journalism* (Lee-Wright, Phillips and Witschge, 2012) and *Will the Last Reporter Please Turn Out the Lights* (McChesney and Pickard, 2011) focus on significant shifts in the media, referring to it as being at best in a period of 'transition' (Lee-Wright et al., 2012, back cover) and at worst in a 'meltdown' and 'crisis' (McChesney and Pickard, 2011, back cover). In his book, *The Vanishing Newspaper*, Meyer predicts that the final copy of the final newspaper will appear on somebody's doorstep in 2043

(Meyer, 2004). However, many see change as a way to strengthen the news media: 'Citizen journalism will not make institutional journalism redundant or irrelevant ... it will make traditional journalism stronger, better, more responsive. Sceptics tend to make you lift your game' (McDonald, in Deitz, 2010, p. xii). However the change is articulated, the media are, as McChesney and Pickard (2011) explain, on a 'new and shifting terrain'.

In the few years since the first edition of this book was published in 2007, social media have changed the ways individuals, corporations, governments and the not-for-profit sector communicate—this includes how the media communicate to their audiences and how we, as media relations professionals, communicate with the media.

At the same time, social media and other digital technologies have also provided the means to circumvent the need for working with the news media, reaching niche audiences and publics via targeted alternative channels of communication such as Twitter, Facebook or YouTube. Communication choices have never been greater, but the issue is where to start, which to choose and how to make the best choices. This book is all about providing choices from the sea of news and entertainment media, and using the variety of communication channels now available to us.

News is still news, whether it's distributed in a 140-word tweet, a radio or newspaper story or TV panel show—or all of these. The important issue is whether the news reaches the audience it is intended to reach. Very often, if the story is interesting enough, one story or medium will lead to another. Take, for example, the 'Gasp gaffe' in which Melbourne clothing store Gasp became the focus of a major news story after a confrontation with a bride-to-be shopper in late 2011. An email response by Gasp to a complaint by the shopper went viral and the story began to trend in social media, on Twitter and Facebook, with 'Boycott Gasp' and 'We hate Gasp' social networking sites springing up immediately. At the same time, the story became mainstream news, with articles and interviews on Channel 7's *Sunrise*, Channel 10's *The Project*, newspapers *The Age*, the *Sydney Morning Herald*, the *Herald Sun*, radio station NovaFM and made international news in the *Daily Mail* and *Telegraph* in the United Kingdom. The story trended for days in both mainstream and social media, illustrating how news spreads like wildfire across all mediums and around the globe, and how both news and social media continue to fan each other's flames.

The choices available to the news media, including citizen-generated material, provide both opportunities and challenges to journalists and other media workers—opportunities because the choice of material available to the news gatherer is so huge, and challenges because these very choices now compete with the media for attention and audience share. The media relations professional, too, must work strategically if they are successfully to reach their audiences in the competitive and saturated ocean of media and information sources.

With this is mind, it seems logical that public relations professionals will shift more and more to specialising within the industry. As noted in Johnston and Zawawi (2009), just as other professions (such as doctors) include both general practitioners and specialists, public relations is now taking this specialised approach, too. Increasingly, organisations are employing social media experts to work alongside their traditional media experts—organisations like the Law Institute of Victoria and Bond University, which have adopted social media strategies with newly appointed social media coordinators. At the very least, media relations experts must also be social media savvy, able to work across platforms to maximise impact and reach, and to work collaboratively with others in the 360-degree media environment.

MEDIA RELATIONS IN THE PUBLIC RELATIONS MIX

But media relations is just part of the bigger picture of public relations, so it is useful to take a step back to look at that bigger picture. As outlined in Johnston and Zawawi (2009), confusion remains over just what public relations is because it is an inappropriately and over-used term—that is, people see great 'public relations' as being any behaviour that has a positive outcome. In addition, it encompasses such an array of roles, tasks and functions, as noted by Foster (1995), who found 74 different titles used in job advertisements for people performing public relations roles. One study found that, over a 70-year period, a total of 472 definitions for public relations had been developed (Harlow, in Lamme and Russell, 2010, p. 284). Indeed, public relations has been described as 'amoebic in its ease at changing shape to functionally conform to different situations and circumstances' (Cropp and Pincus, 2001, p. 194). A working definition sees public relations understanding and facilitating the needs of the various publics that surround and interact with an organisation or group. The media constitute one of these publics.

Media relations is among the best-known fields of public relations because its work can be seen in media outputs. Nevertheless, it is sometimes viewed as a 'soft' part of public relations—not as complex as issues management, or as urgent as crisis management, as personal as community relations or as specialised as financial relations. But since media relations often plays a part in each of these areas of public relations (and many others), it is more useful to recast it as providing important access points and communications options for the industry as a whole. A strong working relationship with journalists, bloggers and other members of the media translates into smoother practices right across the spectrum of public relations activities and functions.

Media relations is often classed as a technical area of public relations work associated with publicity. Much of media relations is indeed technical—writing and distributing media releases, media alerts and media kits, staging media conferences, maintaining up-to-date media distribution lists, photographs, video and audio materials, and updating online organisational information are all important parts of the role. These tools are outlined and described in later chapters. However, media relations comprises much more than compiling, writing, distributing and posting information for the media. It also requires skills that are more complex than 'using' the media simply to get a message out or control a story. Successful media relations is underpinned by knowing more than *what* to do to achieve your goals: it also requires that you consider *why* you do what you do in the first place and *how* you would best achieve it. By implementing some of the generic skills commonly associated with public relations—careful research, strategic planning and implementation, clear and succinct writing, and systematic evaluation—media relations practitioners can achieve the best possible outcomes for their clients, themselves and the media.

Media relations is one of the 20 or more primary roles and functions of the public relations practitioner, and is equally important in all three sectors of society: the political, corporate and 'third' (or not-for-profit) sectors. There are few definitions of media relations to help establish how we might best define the field. To provide us with some parameters, the following definition brings together its key elements:

> Media relations is the ongoing facilitation and coordination of communication and relationships between an individual, group or organisation and the media.

This definition suggests that the media relations practitioner holds a dual role with the media: both as a communicator but also as a relationship manager. It further identifies how media relations can be undertaken at many levels—within an organisation or group of people, or individually. This definition will resonate as you work your way through the book and learn more about the multi-faceted role of the media relations professional.

THE IMPACT OF MEDIA RELATIONS

Partly because of its great flexibility and adaptability, and partly because of the growing recognition that organisations need to communicate effectively in an increasingly complex information world, public relations has become a growth industry. In 1989, Australian political academic Rod Tiffen described public relations as 'one of the most spectacular growth industries in Australia' (1989, p. 71), noting how the number of public relations practitioners employed in the 1980s was ten times greater than the number employed in the 1960s (1989, p. 73). Since that time, those figures have continued to rise at exponential rates. In 2010, it was estimated that 822 public relations and marketing personnel were employed by the Victorian state government (Rolfe and Kearney, 2010). In 2008, Queensland Premier Anna Bligh said 320 media and public relations officers were employed in that state—compared with 46 such positions in Queensland less than 20 years earlier (EARC, 1993). Likewise, the industry has seen massive growth internationally. Davis (2000) notes that from 1979 to 1996, the number of information officers in the British government's

Central Office rose from 36 to 160. And, in 2005, *Fortune* magazine listed public relations as one of the top ten fastest growing professions in the United States (Fisher, 2005).

Accompanying this growth is a rise in information supplied to the media—through either media releases or other public relations-initiated materials. International studies show that the media have become more and more reliant on media relations materials. Lewis, Williams and Franklin (2008) studied 2207 newspaper stories from five newspapers in the United Kingdom and found that public relations and wire agency (such as the Press Association, see Chapter 2) copy represented 88 per cent of stories. They suggest a 'clear linear process in which PR material is reproduced by agency journalists whose copy is, in turn, reproduced in the news media' (2008, p. 15). Davies (2008, p. 74) confirms this, noting that news is based largely on 'two primary conveyor belts: the Press Association and public relations'.

In Australia, studies by journalism academics and public relations professionals have reached the same conclusion: that journalism relies heavily on media relations-generated material. Brisbane public relations firm Brumfield, Bird and Sandford's (BBS) 2007 *Media Survey* report found 55 per cent of journalists use press releases to create news (Edwards and Newbury, 2007, p. 3). Their 2011 media study, which focused on bloggers rather than mainstream journalists, found that 42 per cent of bloggers had used media releases or other PR material more than once (Edwards and Newbury, 2011, p. 17). In Sydney, the Centre for Independent Journalism (CIJ) and the independent news organisation Crikey.com found similar outcomes: nearly 55 per cent of stories were 'driven by some form of public relations—media release, public relations professional or some form of promotion' (Crikey, 2010).

An earlier Australian study found 31 per cent of press releases were used, either wholly or partly, in mainstream media, with far higher figures found in trade and specialist media (Macnamara, 2001). This trend had been developing for some time; in 1994, well over half of news in three daily papers was found to have been generated by public relations sources (Zawawi, 1994), while in 1993, other research found a heavy reliance by media outlets on government media releases, with 279 media releases resulting in 220 news stories that had been 'reproduced virtually unchanged' (EARC, 1993, p. 70). The trend has become known as 'media release journalism'.

But it is not just media releases that are used in media relations. Information made available to the news media has been called 'news subsidies' and 'information subsidies' (Gandy, 1982)—which simply means that it subsidises or adds to the news that the media finds itself. As well as the media release and media conference—both of which are described in detail in later chapters—there are a range of other channels for distributing information or news either to the media or directly to the public. These include:

- talkback radio public responses
- letters to the editor
- media interviews
- speeches
- attendance at public meetings
- emails
- Twitter
- Facebook postings
- YouTube videos
- blogs
- leaks
- phone calls.

As the media and communications environment becomes increasingly cluttered with this activity, it is becoming much more difficult to track the sources of news. Reich (2010, p. 81) refers to the 'elusive and fragmented streams of textual and oral PR input reaching the journalists inside and outside newsrooms', concluding that 'items free of PR input are an exceptionally rare phenomenon'. If this is the case—or even close—we all have a big job ahead of us in media relations!

THE MEDIA AS A MONITORING TOOL

The media provide two critical services to the public relations professional. The first is to *get information out* to a target public—which, as discussed above, is a growth industry. The second is to provide a *monitoring tool* about industry, organisations, events, issues or products, competitors, trends or society as a whole. To achieve this, we use the media for research, forward planning, targeting, analysis and evaluation. They can be used in the following ways as a monitoring tool:

- to gain an understanding of our publics and a perception of our product or service
- to gain a broader understanding of the industry and society within which an organisation operates
- to gain knowledge of how our competitors operate
- to assist in evaluation, research and analysis of opportunities and trends
- to analyse the effectiveness of public relations plans, including sponsorships and community relations, and
- to inform and equip us to act when issues or crises arise.

One part of systematically monitoring the media environment is the identification and management of issues that may affect an organisation, group or individual. In this way, we can use the media as a barometer to give us useful information. Media monitoring thus forms an important part of the public relations field of issue management—itself a separate field of public relations.

ISSUE MANAGEMENT

The term 'issue management' was first coined by corporate American public relations officer Howard Chase in 1976. Chase was interested in how organisations were pressured by outside influences, and the timing of organisational responses to these influences. The original model of issue management (also known as 'issues') consisted of five primary steps:

1. issue identification
2. issue analysis
3. issue change strategy options

4. issue action program, and
5. evaluation of results (Crane, 2004).

A large part of issue management involves planning for an event or series of events—for instance, when the federal government began the national campaign to switch from analogue to digital television, it put in place a massive communication and media campaign beginning in 2007 for a 2010–13 switchover. Changes along the way meant the start date was put back from 2008 to 2009 as the government dealt with technical and timetabling problems. Consumers could locate their area's switchover at a 'My Switchover' panel on the 'Are You Ready for Digital TV?' website or phone a seven-day-a-week hotline for information. Not surprisingly, television provided a logical primary medium through which to inform the viewing public about the changeover, and by the time 2010 came around, saturation publicity had occurred. The government used the media, in all forms, to get its messages out, but it also used all forms of media for incoming information to inform its strategies and adjust these according to the various communities affected—which ultimately made up the whole of Australia. Since issues that are left unaddressed can result in crises if not managed correctly, it is extremely important to ensure smooth and well-informed transitions.

Monitoring and ultimately managing issues—especially on this level—are tasks undertaken at many levels within any organisation (in this case, the federal government). Issues require multiple skills and disciplines working together. Crane (2004) notes that issue management involves the following fields of expertise:

- public relations, lobbying or government relations
- futurism, trend tracking or media monitoring
- strategic or financial planning, and
- law.

So while issue management is clearly far broader than media monitoring, we should be aware that media relations is integral to this mix, and is part of strategic planning within organisations and the maintenance of their well-being.

HACKS AND FLACKS

Traditionally, there has been an uneasy relationship between public relations professionals and journalists. Perhaps ironically, this sometimes adversarial relationship has grown as the role of public relations has expanded and journalists have tended to rely more and more on PR support due to commercial pressures and staff cuts in media organisations. The distinction that is sometimes drawn between the two industries was illustrated in an email to a journalism group, which described the two roles as 'the poacher and the gamekeeper'. Just which was which might be a good topic for discussion! The emailer was a very senior journalism academic who held considerable sway within the academic community. Lamentably, this 'them and us' approach to public relations and journalism continues to be fuelled by some, keen to keep not just distance but to foster mistrust. The division is illustrated in a critique of the relationship by a media commentator who refers to journalism being 'contaminated from outside' (Franklin, in Turner, Bonner and Marshall, 2000, p. 29). It is also shown by others who, in mourning the changes to journalism, argue about how 'the diseases of PR spin, political management of the news cycle and office-bound reporting crippled "quality" journalism even before the business model began to stumble' (Moore, 2010, p. x). However, as Moore also points out, public relations did not cause the end of the old models of journalism—technology did.

Scepticism and cynicism have resulted in tags like 'hack' (journalist) and 'spin doctor' or 'flack' (public relations). History shows that bad journalism and public relations practices are clearly a reality, with each industry playing its part in unethical practices. Realistically, there will always be such practices—this applies to every profession. However, in recent decades codes of ethics and practice have evolved that can guide the working lives of practitioners in both these communications industries: the Australian Journalists Association's (AJA, now part of the Media Entertainment and Arts Alliance, MEAA) Code of Ethics and the Public Relations Institute of Australia's (PRIA) Code of Ethics. These codes govern the practice of professionals in these fields and are available online. Professional ethics must be considered central to the relationship. The need for honesty and transparency underpins the development of what is known as a 'trust bank'—like a savings account, you have to put something in if you ever plan to draw anything out—and it is no different from a reward system in which relationships are built up and positive input is met with positive responses. The idea of building this 'trust bank' and the need for ethics are further analysed in Chapters 4 and 5.

Media relations can bridge the divide between the 'poacher and gamekeeper' or 'hacks and flacks'. Developing these areas—bridging the gap, developing trust banks and working on the relationship—does not mean that either industry should lose its edge or professional distance from the other. If journalists and media relations professionals both accept that the other has a job to do, and that at times it may conflict with their own job, then they can go into the relationship with realistic expectations. And as journalism moves through its crossroads of change, media relations can be a positive part of the transition.

CONCLUSION

The media are currently in a state of widespread change, and so too is the field of media relations. This book will draw on these changes—technological, economic, social and cultural—as it takes the reader through various pathways that are central to the work of the media relations professional. The changed environments, and the need for all sectors to harness them, have made media relations as important as ever to corporations, political and government organisations, small and large not-for-profits and individual causes. Adaptability is, and will remain, one of the key elements of the successful media relations professional. At the same time, some things never change: what is important is the need for managing relationships with the media, sometimes face-to-face as well as online or on the telephone. Media relations is a field that requires special skills, general knowledge, expertise about the media and their practices, and an understanding of global and local current affairs. Rather than be daunted by change, professionals in this industry can ride the wave and help others navigate their way through these exciting times in new and shifting terrain.

WORKING WITH THE MEDIA

There are opportunities and challenges in working in media relations. The following list will be amplified throughout the chapters of this book.

ADVANTAGES

- Raise awareness and get your point of view heard.
- Create impact within your chosen audience.
- Save money by using editorial to gain exposure rather than paying for advertising.
- Gain legitimacy and creditability through editorial.
- Reach targeted audiences, both large and small.
- Build public support and mobilise public opinion.
- Link to news and entertainment media which also use social media to distribute their news.

DISADVANTAGES

- Lose control of your message because of the uncontrolled nature of the media.
- Accuracy can be compromised.
- Stories can be too brief, superficial or lack depth.
- The desire for conflict may mean worthy stories are overlooked.
- Sensationalism can occur, especially if the story is perceived to be bland.
- Stories can be handled with bias because journalists are, after all, human.
- Social media increasingly beat mainstream media when it comes to breaking stories.

2 UNDERSTANDING THE MEDIA ENVIRONMENT

Traditionally, the functions of the media have been to educate, inform, entertain, investigate and make money. Schultz (1994, p. 23) refers to various 'guises' of the modern media: 'a political player, an economic agent, a social agent and a technological innovator'. However, these functions clearly are not all aligned, and can at times bring the media's missions into conflict—for example, their roles of social responsibility and their commercial imperatives. Common themes of the modern news media are seen in the media's increasing need to move within tight budgets and across a variety of media platforms, as well as the trend towards increased entertainment function.

The importance and pervasiveness of the news media, even as they move through changing and challenging times, should not be underestimated. According to Craig (2004, p. 4), the media have become 'the sites where politics and public life are played out'. Amidst the growing climate of social media saturation, the media's uptake of an issue is seen to validate it. If something is 'picked up' by the media, it is seen as more significant, as having importance and being on the public agenda. In this way, the media are used to help position a person, event, issue, organisation or industry within the context of public life. As Deitz puts it:

> It is not just the content of what or who is written about in the media; it is the way journalistic norms shape ideas about what is and isn't news, what

14

is and isn't political, what kind of knowledge counts as expert, and how people should relate to news or should use it. (2010, p. 58)

While this may have been challenged by what is seen as the more democratic media choices available to everybody—Twitter, blogs, Facebook, YouTube and so on—the fact remains that the news media, using both traditional and online communication platforms, have a major part in the establishment of public opinion (this is taken up in the discussion of agenda-setting in the next chapter). Thus the value of the media to media relations lies in tapping into the media's radar and ultimately their agenda.

This chapter aims to provide a broad framework of the media: its ownership, functions, working models, regulations and its role as 'the Fourth Estate'.

THE FOURTH ESTATE

This term was first coined in 1790 by British politician Edmund Burke, who referred to the media as the Fourth Estate because of its relationship with the three existing estates in the British parliament: the Lords Temporal, the Lords Spiritual and the Commons (otherwise known as the nobility, the clergy and the commoners). The reference was about the importance of the media when positioned against the ruling sectors of society. Indeed, Burke was noted to have said 'yonder sits the Fourth Estate and they are more important than them all'—identifying the importance of the media both then and now.

The term is used today to refer to the mass media as a watchdog in liberal democratic societies like Australia, the United Kingdom, the United States and New Zealand. According to Sussman (2004):

The premise of watchdog journalism is that the press is a surrogate for the public, asking probing, penetrating questions at every level, from the town council, to the state house to the White House, as well as in corporate and professional offices, in union halls, on university campuses and in religious organisations that seek to influence governmental actions.

However, the news media's role should not be seen simplistically, nor should it be idealised. Schultz (1998, p. 17) notes that the ideal of the Fourth Estate must be 'juxtaposed with the reality of the news media as an expanding industry operating in global information and capital markets, constantly exploring new technologies and searching for new audiences'. In other words, the ideal must be balanced with the practicalities of the marketplace, and this includes changing platforms of journalism and economic pressures.

In their book *Four Theories of the Press*, Siebert, Peterson and Shramm (1956) divide the news media into four models: the authoritarian, the Soviet communist, the libertarian and the social responsibility. For the purposes of our analysis of democratic media, we will consider the latter two of these. The libertarian role of the media in the eighteenth and nineteenth centuries primarily was to provide a public forum for debate about the issues of the day, to articulate public opinion, to force governments to consider the will of the people, to educate, to channel communication between groups and to champion individuals against abuses of power (Schultz, 1998). But while libertarianism emerged out of the authoritarianism of government-dominated press, its concentration of ownership simply transferred power from government into the hands of rich and powerful media owners (Siebert, Peterson and Shramm, 1956). Under this model: 'The owners and managers of the press determine which persons, which facts, which version of these facts, shall reach the public' (quoted in Siebert, Peterson and Shramm, 1956, p. 5).

The response to the libertarian model was the twentieth century social responsibility model, which saw the media as having the responsibility to ensure that all sides of a story were presented. Siebert, Peterson and Shramm (1956, p. 5) note that this theory should provide 'a reflection of the diversity of society as well as access to various points of view'. However, one of the criticisms of this theory is that it does not take into account the need for the media to balance internal commercial realities with their other obligations to society. That is, it can be difficult to be socially responsible on a tight budget when you are owned by a public company that expects financial returns, and where business decisions can impact on journalism. Many argue that the social responsibility approach has foundered, with a primary criticism of modern media resting in their lack of diversity, concentration of ownership and big-business approach.

Critics of modern media say that, when the news media is subsumed by big business and monopolistic control, they cannot function as an effective watchdog and can no longer offer a full range of perspectives. The principal objection to the high concentration of ownership relates to the lack of diversity of viewpoints that comes from limited ownership (Butler and Rodrick, 2007; McChesney, 2008). This view is supported by research showing that the Australian public is very sceptical about the media. Three-quarters agree that 'media organisations are more interested in making money than in informing society', while 59 per cent 'don't trust journalists to tell the truth' (Roy Morgan Research, 2006). This issue is developed later in the chapter with an analysis of the media environment since the News International scandal of 2011 and also in Chapter 4 in a discussion of media ethics.

MEDIA OWNERSHIP

The foundations of several of the still-existing media empires in Australia were established in the nineteenth century. In 1831, Warwickshire publisher John Fairfax purchased the *Sydney Morning Herald*. Melbourne's media ownership began with David Syme, who established *The Age* in 1854. Other still existing papers were Hobart's *Mercury*, established in 1854, Adelaide's *The Advertiser* (1858), Perth's *The West Australian* (1833) and the *Brisbane Courier* (now the *Courier-Mail*) (1846). The first owners of television were predominantly newspaper owners. Consolidated Press (Packer) had the Nine licence, Fairfax had Seven in Sydney and the Herald and Weekly Times (News Ltd) had Seven in Melbourne (McQueen, 1977).

Concentration levels of ownership have been firmly entrenched for some time. Of the daily metropolitan papers, Murdoch's News Ltd owns seven of the twelve daily metropolitan and national newspapers in the country (the *Daily Telegraph*, the *Herald Sun*, the *Courier-Mail*, *The Advertiser*, the *Mercury*, the *Northern Territory News* and *The Australian*), plus the daily commuter paper *MX* in three capital cities; five are owned by Fairfax and Rural Press (the *Sydney Morning*

Herald, The Age, The Australian Financial Review, The Canberra Times and the online-only *Brisbane Times*) and one by Seven West Media Group (formerly Western Australian Newspaper holdings—*The West Australian*).

What follows is a summary of the holdings by major media companies in Australia and some in New Zealand, outside the daily metropolitans (listed above)—a summary that can be used as a guide but is far from exhaustive. Since media ownership changes, the best way to do an up-to-the-minute check of ownership is through the various organisations' annual reports or websites.

- *News Ltd* owns a total of 120 community newspapers across all states and territories except the Australian Capital Territory and Tasmania, plus the major regional dailies the *Geelong Advertiser,* the *Cairns Post,* the *Gold Coast Bulletin* and the *Townsville Bulletin,* and approximately 30 magazine titles. News Ltd is part-owner of Foxtel and Sky News and, internationally, News Corp (the parent company) owns book publisher HarperCollins, Twentieth Century Fox and Newspoll market research. Despite its portfolio diversity, News Corp is best known for, and arguably chooses to favour, its newspaper holdings due to their historic significance and the culture of newspapers for which it is famous.
- *Nine Entertainment Co.* (previously Publishing and Broadcasting Ltd, run by the Packer empire) owns most metropolitan and regional licences for the Nine Network. It owns Ticketek and is part-owner of Foxtel, Ninemsn, Sky News and a wealth of online properties. In 2012, it sold its ACP magazine holdings to the Bauer Media Group.
- *Fairfax Media* (which merged with Rural Press in 2007) holds a major share of community and regional newspapers in Australia and New Zealand. In Australia, this includes 20 regional dailies and more than 200 community papers—106 in New South Wales alone, nine radio licences and more than a dozen magazines. In New Zealand, it includes more than 50 community newspapers and is the largest publisher of the country's newspapers, magazines and sporting publications.

- *Seven West Media Group* (created after a merger between West Australian Newspapers Holdings Limited (WAN) and Seven Media Group in 2011) with its dominant shareholder Kerry Stokes, own metropolitan licences for Channel 7, Yahoo!7 and a significant stable of magazines under Pacific Magazines.
- *Southern Cross Austereo* (a merger between Southern Cross Media Group and Austereo Group) owns 80 commercial radio services and 21 commercial TV licences.
- *APN News and Media* publishes 20 daily and more than 100 non-daily newspapers across Australia and New Zealand, including the *New Zealand Herald* and regional newspapers across the east coast of Australia. It owns three of the top five national radio networks in New Zealand and radio networks in the south and east of Australia. Its many regional Australian dailies include the *Sunshine Coast Daily, Queensland Times (QT)* and it is part-owner of several billboard advertising companies, including Adshel.
- *WIN Corporation* is Australia's largest regional TV network, with the Adelaide licence for the Nine Network and a 13 per cent stake in the Ten Network. It part-owns radio, cinema, TV production and online companies and properties.

(Simons, 2007; Fairfax Media, 2006; Rosenberg, 2008; relevant corporate websites)

WIRE SERVICES

Many media organisations subscribe to 'news agencies' or 'wire services' for daily and particularly breaking news. News agencies are staffed by journalists and photographers who compile news and current affairs stories and photographs, which can be accessed 24 hours a day by subscriber media organisations. International examples are Associated Press (AP), Agence France-Presse (AFP), the Press Association and Thomson Reuters. Australian Associated Press (AAP), Australia's only news service, began in 1935 and has a long history of researching, writing and supplying news. AAP covers the following news categories: national news; world news; sports news and results; finance and business news; lifestyle news; and racing news. Access to news agencies is simply a matter of paying a subscription fee and linking on to a website. Despite all the attention paid to concentration of ownership and diversity of voices, there has been little attention paid to the ownership of this primary news supplier that is owned by key media organisations: News Ltd and Fairfax both own 45 per cent, Seven West Media Group owns 8 per cent and Rural Press owns 2 per cent (AAP, 2009).

AAP and the other news agencies may well be significantly under-estimated by public relations in terms of their audience reach. For example, one study found that most of the stories in the 'breaking news' sections of two daily online papers were predominantly AAP copy (Johnston and Forde, 2009). A subsequent study, which tracked media releases from four government offices including the Prime Minister's Office, found that most press releases were followed up by AAP and then republished in online newspapers (Forde and Johnston, 2012). Other international studies support the idea that news agencies provide a high percentage of media copy and also utilise media releases (Lewis, Williams and Franklin, 2008). In 2011, AAP launched NZ Newswire when the New Zealand Press Association (NZPA) folded after more than 130 years in operation.

In addition, news agencies also include media release services: AAP's is called 'Medianet for Journalists'. This media release distribution service sends out releases, and AAP news subscribers can also access the database of releases for free. AAP is one of the many media release-distribution services offered in the country. This is discussed in more detail in Chapter 7.

GROWTH IN INDEPENDENT COMMUNITY AND ALTERNATIVE MEDIA

Crikey.com has become a serious news contender in the Australian media industry. It is an independent online news service that publishes each weekday (at lunchtime), both in a limited web edition and as a daily subscription news service, *The Crikey Daily Mail*. Crikey has found its position in the daily news media by focusing on its independent coverage, and it regularly reports on what the other major news organisations are doing. According to its website, a subscription will get the subscriber 'daily email packed with over 25 unique subscriber-only stories [and] the best spin-free, mogul-free journalism in the country' (Crikey, 2011). It also identifies itself as part of the:

> so-called fourth estate that acts as a vital check and balance on the activities of government, the political system and the judiciary . . . In addition, Crikey believes the performance and activities of business, the media, PR and other important sectors are worthy of public scrutiny. (Crikey, 2011)

Currently owned by Private Media Partners, Crikey was established by former News Ltd journalist and political press secretary Stephen Mayne in 2005, and has continued to run news and commentary about politics, media, the environment and business. Crikey is part of a growing tradition of online news services such as salon.com, Slate and Politico, which are well respected and independently owned.

Smaller, independent media outlets have emerged in spite—or possibly because—of the concentration in mainstream media. These are often described as 'alternative', 'niche', 'community' or 'public' forms of media. Print and online formats include the growth in left-wing and other political publications like *Green Left Weekly*, Indigenous (*Koori Mail*) and gay press (*Queensland Pride*), as well as independents like *The Big Issue*, a street magazine distributed by homeless and disadvantaged people that deals with a variety of serious news and features, as well as arts and entertainment. There are also some local papers that have maintained their independence, such as the Byron Bay *Echo*. The relative cheapness of publishing online means many community and alternate newspapers and magazines are web based and can thus reach their target readership more easily in this way.

Community radio stations in Australia now represent a significant part of the broadcast media sector. There are currently 350 fully licensed community broadcasters, with the majority of these located in non-metropolitan areas (Community Broadcasting Foundation, 2012)—that figure represents 76 more than a decade ago. As explained in Chapter 12, these stations represent a unique opportunity for getting messages to smaller, socially and geographically isolated communities. The higher level of engagement that these smaller, independent media organisations have with their audiences indicates that they are particularly responsive to information about local public events, campaigns, and social and political activity that might be supporting particular causes (Forde, 2011). This provides clear opportunities for media relations.

THE CHALLENGE OF MEDIA POLICY AND REGULATION

Debate about media concentration has tended to fall into two categories: cross-media ownership and foreign ownership. But just how much media is too much when it is controlled by a single organisation? And how much overseas ownership should be allowed? Monopolistic ownership, convergence and related issues have given rise to a raft of inquiries and reports.

In 2006, the federal government passed a suite of media reform Bills that dealt with a range of issues on digital reform and media ownership. Setting out changes in the discussion paper 'Meeting the Digital Challenge: Reforming Australia's Media in the Digital Age' (Australian Government, 2006b), the federal government outlined its case for reforming cross-media ownership laws and relaxing foreign media ownership laws. The changes followed years of media proprietors arguing that the internet had blurred the boundaries of the media to such an extent that it was unrealistic and unnecessary to control media ownership of competing media in the one area. Under previous laws, cross-media provisions restricted one organisation from controlling two or more different types of media in the one market. This meant no one organisation could have controlling interests in a radio station *and* a free-to-air TV station, or a free-to-air TV station *and* a newspaper, or a radio station *and* a newspaper in the one catchment area (city or region).

Central to the changed laws was the relaxation of ownership to allow one organisation to own two platforms within the one catchment— that is, two out of radio, newspapers and free-to-air television. Foreign investment in Australian media was also relaxed. Previous laws had restricted foreign companies from controlling more than 15 per cent of a TV company and more than 25 per cent of a newspaper publisher, but these restrictions were eliminated, subject to government approval.

Those opposing change argued that relaxing the cross-media ownership laws would simply provide more of the same news and current affairs because the same players would be in control of different media, including the internet:

> at present, the internet is incapable of ensuring plurality in Australian democracy. Too few Australians access it for their news and, amongst those that do, the overwhelming majority rely on a repackaged form of the mainstream news. (Downie and Macintosh, 2006, p. 12)

This issue, which relates to the political economy of news, is discussed in more detail in Chapter 3.

These issues were revisited in 2011 when the federal government's Australian Media Convergence Committee was established to review problems associated with the changed media environment and 'examine the policy and regulatory frameworks that apply to the converged media and communications landscape in Australia' (Australian Government, 2011a). In summary, it looked at the following areas:

- layering, licensing and regulation
- Australian and local content
- spectrum allocation and management
- media diversity, competition and market structures, and
- community standards.

More than 250 submissions were made to the review committee, including one from the main government communications regulator, the Australian Communications and Media Authority (ACMA), which argued that convergence had systematically broken or significantly strained many of the laws and regulations that form the foundation of current communications and media regulation (ACMA, 2011b).

Berg notes that one of the points the ACMA and others canvassed was how communications technologies traditionally had been regulated separately and distinctly in 'silos'—that is, in isolation from each other. This approach no longer made sense; instead, a 'layers model' was preferred in which 'all infrastructure should be regulated consistently, no matter what technology that infrastructure is made of. All content should be regulated consistently, no matter how it is delivered' (Berg, 2011).

In December 2011, the Convergence Review committee handed down its interim report noting:

> Whilst technology has eroded the traditional divisions between free-to-air (FTA) television and the internet, newspapers and websites, radio and streaming services, our policy and regulation is still based on the industry and service structures of the early 1990s.
>
> Calibrating the policy and regulatory framework for the new environment is vital. The reforms recommended by the Convergence Review will require fundamental changes to communications legislation. (Australian Government, 2011a, p. 4)

The interim report outlined seven key areas where reform was needed for the content and communications industry. Among the recommendations were the removal of the 2006 (outlined above) change to the two-of-three media rule, which it called 'redundant regulations'. Clearly, the government has a major job ahead of it with unprecedented communication and information challenges confronting society. Staying abreast of change in the fast-moving media and communications environment means governments can inevitably only play catch-up as change continues to unravel, and laws and policies are developed or amended to try to keep pace.

CURRENT REGULATORY SYSTEMS

Meanwhile, the Australian media are primarily governed under three main Commonwealth Acts, which limit impact on the ownership and content of the media in Australia (although as the interim report discussed above indicates, changes may occur in the future). They are the *Broadcasting Services Act 1992* (Cth), the *Competition and*

Consumer Act 2010 (Cth) (formerly known as the *Trade Practices Act 1974*) and the *Foreign Acquisitions and Takeovers Act 1975* (Cth). In turn, these are managed by three Commonwealth authorities:

- The Australian Communications and Media Authority (ACMA) administers the *Broadcasting Services Act 1992* and is responsible for the regulation of broadcasting.
- The Australian Consumer and Competition Commission (ACCC) administers the *Competition and Consumer Act 2011* and is responsible for promoting competition and fair trade in the marketplace.
- The Foreign Investment Review Board (FIRB) examines proposals by foreign interests for investment in Australia and makes recommendations to the government. (Communications Law Centre, 2011)

ACMA was created in 2005 when two regulators—the Australian Broadcasting Authority (broadcasters) and the Australian Communications Authority (telecommunications)—merged. ACMA is responsible for the regulation of broadcasting, radiocommunications, telecommunications and online content, as well as for administering a massive 26 Acts and 523 pieces of regulation (ACMA, 2011a).

In addition to external laws, most media organisations are also governed by internal policies, procedures and ethical practices. The Australian Broadcasting Corporation (ABC), for example, may conduct internal audits of news coverage—for instance, in 2003 the Minister for Communications, Senator Richard Alston, called for such an inquiry into the ABC's coverage of the Iraq war.

The Australian print media are considered to be largely self-regulating. Traditionally, this process has been undertaken through non-government organisations such as the Australian Press Council (APC) and the Media Entertainment and Arts Alliance (MEAA). The APC is committed to self-regulation, arguing in its Charter that:

> The press has a responsibility to the public to commit itself to self-regulation which provides a mechanism for dealing with the concerns of members of the public and the maintenance of the ethical standards and journalistic professionalism of the press. (APC, 2011a, Principle 3)

The APC consists of 22 members (publishers, journalists and members of the public). It was established in 1976 and is 'responsible for promoting good standards of media practice, community access to information of public interest, and freedom of expression through the media' (APC, 2011b). It provides an avenue for complaint by any citizen about the printed news media, and has a professional Statement of Principles that outlines ethical and professional media practice. In 2012, a government inquiry suggested major changes to the self-regulation of Australian print media and the role of the APC, discussed further below.

The MEAA was established in 1992, and acts as the trade union and professional association for members within the media and entertainment industry. In addition, it regulates the conduct of its members. Its twelve-point code of ethics for journalists provides a list of guidelines, which can be followed up through a complaints mechanism if a member of the public believes the code has been breached. Breaches can result in censure, fines or expulsion from the MEAA. In effect, self-regulation deals with areas of ethical behaviour, whereas the government enacts legislation and creates regulatory bodies to control ownership, content, timing and acceptable standards. The code is looked at in more detail in Chapter 4.

While largely self-regulating, at times the government has seen fit to investigate the practices of media and the potential for more government input and control is always present. Most recently, the phone hacking scandal by the *News of the World* (owned by News International, the British arm of News Corporation) saw the Australian government establish a review of media and media practices in Australia which ran from September 2011 to February 2012 (Australian Government, 2011c). (The phone hacking scandal that occurred in mid-2011 led to the overnight closure of the 168-year-old *News of the World*.)

The government described the inquiry as intending to examine 'the pressures facing newspapers, online publications and their newsrooms, as well as the operation of the Australian Press Council' (Australian Government, 2011c).

The report, handed down in February 2012, known as the Finkelstein Report (because it was conducted by the Honourable Ray Finkelstein QC), recommended significant changes to the existing frameworks for media regulation. In short, it concluded that current structures were not working—that they were slow, piecemeal, adversarial and that online news was not covered by existing guidelines. Proposed changes included the replacement of the APC with a new statutory body called the News Media Council which would be government funded. It explained:

> The establishment of a council is not about increasing the power of government or about imposing some form of censorship. It is about making the news media more accountable to those covered in the news, and to the public generally. (Finkelstein, 2012, p. 9)

Finkelstein said he did not believe that the 'laws of the land'— notably those of defamation and contempt—had been sufficient to achieve the degree of accountability required of the media. Under the proposed changes, for example, the New Media Council would have the power to require a news media outlet to publish an apology, correction or retraction, or allow a right of reply—responses which had been difficult to obtain under the current structures. He argued that the APC suffered 'serious structural constraints' (2012, p. 9), that it did not have the necessary powers or funds to carry out its designated functions and that media publishers could withdraw their funding or support whenever they chose. Not surprisingly, the recommendations met with mixed responses. It remains to be seen what, if any, of the recommendations of the report will be implemented.

CONCLUSIONS: THE MEDIA PLAYING FIELD

The Australian media environment is a complex sector. Concepts of the Fourth Estate and socially responsibility are positioned against a media climate of constant developments and changes to technology, commercial pressures, altered expectations and blurred global boundaries, with legislation and regulation trying to keep up. A range of self-regulation and government legislation, enforced through regulatory bodies, governs the Australian media environment. The non-government bodies, the APC and the MEAA, have their own policies and procedures in place to self-regulate the print sector but, as we have seen, the future of the APC is under threat and a New Media Authority has been proposed to replace it.

The media sector is characterised by big players and monopoly ownership, yet at the same time alternative media choices not only exist but are growing and thriving, notably in community radio and on the internet. The parallel contraction of some forms of media and growth in others mean it has become harder than ever to define, impose boundaries on and monitor the media. The lines dividing the separate media platforms are now irreversibly blurred. The playing field on which media relations practitioners find themselves may at times be difficult to navigate; however, it is one on which the practitioner must always keep an eye on the ball, remaining up to date, informed and vigilant in this constantly changing environment.

THEORISING MEDIA RELATIONS 3

As with all areas of practice, a theoretical framework helps to position and explain ideas and activities. Because of its practice orientation, media relations generally has been overlooked in a theoretical context. However, the idea of showing how to do media relations without also investigating some of the underlying reasons for why things happen as they do makes us less likely to be reflexive and evaluative in this field of public relations. Because media relations is much more than just writing media releases, holding media conferences, social networking or schmoozing with the media, it is critical that we develop an understanding of the reasons why we make choices and undertake activities. A solid theoretical underpinning is therefore essential for this important field, which cuts across so much public relations activity. A selection of theories and perspectives will be discussed in this chapter to help our understanding of the relationship between the media and media relations. We will also investigate some theories of news and the media that can inform our practice. These theories will provide a series of frameworks that can be applied throughout the rest of the book and within the world of practice.

Common themes throughout this chapter are the importance of sources to the media, how the media construct and frame news as reality and the role of media relations in the production of news.

HOW NEWS IS MANUFACTURED

When Fishman wrote *Manufacturing the News*, he observed that 'news organises our perception of a world outside our firsthand experience' (1980, p. 51). In media relations, through our dealings with the news media, we play a central part in presenting words and images to society to create these perceptions. But we all know that events and issues that occur do not miraculously metamorphose into a news story. In deciding what is news today, a journalist will use their 'nose for news' and their judgement, coupled with processes of selectivity, omission and creation, to transform the issue or event into a news story. Take, for example, a court case. Court cases run every day in Magistrates, District and Supreme Courts all over the country. In themselves, they are simply court cases—a process that is a part of a democratic society. Most court stories are quite unremarkable, uninteresting and of little significance to those beyond the people they affect directly. So at what point does a court case become a news story? The 'nose for news', and the judgement, selection, omission and creation process, will transform certain court cases into news stories. During this process, the journalist will instinctively and automatically use their knowledge of news values to determine the newsworthiness of the court cases.

A list of journalistic news values (discussed in more detail in Chapter 5) includes impact, conflict, timeliness, proximity, prominence, currency, human interest, the unusual or novelty, and money. In categorising stories like this, journalists assign a value to them. These news values in turn 'frame the event, rendering it understandable in the terms of the ideological system' (Drechsel, 1983, p. 14). Court cases will incorporate these news values if they are to become news stories. These form the basis for selection from the plethora of court cases from which the journalist may choose. News values are reinforced at the news organisation level because they help those who are putting the news together to sort where the stories should go in the broadcast lineup or in the online newspaper. From this we see the emergence of news themes, also discussed in Chapter 5, as stories develop into groupings to provide continuity and context within an otherwise haphazard news agenda.

Thus news is constructed or manufactured from real life: news itself simply reflects and recreates life on the screen or page or airwaves. But if we look closely at the news, it becomes apparent that some news just happens and some news is *made* to happen. News may be divided into 'actual' or 'created' varieties. These have been defined over the years as 'routine journalism' and 'manipulated journalism' (Fishman, 1980, p. 15). Or, as some see it, events may not be *real* at all. Daniel Boorstin famously observed more than 50 years ago that news creates a 'synthetic novelty' (1961, p. 11). He noticed how, in the first half of the twentieth century, 'a larger and larger proportion of our experience, of what we read and see and hear has come to consist of pseudo-events' (1961, p. 12). Since he made that observation, we have seen another half-century go by, and the 'pseudo-event' has gained even greater traction within the news media and popular culture—think about the 'theatre' of politics, the rise of reality television or the development of celebrity. Would any of these even exist without the media and the audience for which they are intended? Boorstin further observes that society *wants* to create illusions of reality based on 'extravagant expectations' of life (1961, p. 7).

IMAGES, MEDIATION AND REALITY

Boorstin (1961) discusses how society creates events and people for the purposes of news, impact and image. Television is a major part of the pseudo-event because of the blurring it can produce: audience becomes actor, unreal becomes real, created becomes spontaneous—or so it can seem. Reality television is probably the most profound example of this, discussed further in Chapter 10.

Much has been suggested and written about television and its place in society and modern culture with relation to these ideas of mediating, creating and representing reality. These theories and related discourses can be helpful when we consider working with a medium that is so centrally focused on pictures. Ericson, Baranek and Chan (1987) believe journalists reproduce order and disorder through vision. Because television is based on images and pictures, it is suggested that its power as a medium is pervasive because when we see things on television we perceive these to be reality. In fact, it is only a reality as presented by the journalist (or media worker). As Hartley points out, 'part of the sham actually has nothing to do with the stories as events, but with the presentation of them *as true*' (1992, p. 144)—or, as Carpignano and colleagues note: 'There is no distinction in terms of truth between live pictures and framed events, not because the equation between live and real is ideological but because reality as such is socially constructed' (1993, p. 104).

Questions of truth, reality, fiction and fact are raised through the use of editing, packaging, omission and interpretation. A day or a year can be compacted into a one-hour documentary; a life can be summed up in a two-minute news story. An image can represent something quite different from what it is—or was. We are all aware of how computer software can transform the old to look younger, the blemished to look clearer and the impossible to seem possible, but recreating reality is also part of everyday news practice.

Take, for example, the use of file footage that is used as overlay in the absence of original images on the TV news. In a study of the recycling of news vision on Australian television, Putnis (1994) notes how the use of file tape results in dramatisation, stereotyping and conflict enhancement. He found that in political stories, for example, file tape was used on average in 73.5 per cent of stories. In accident/chance events, it was used in only 17 per cent (1994, p. 77): 'Once it was thought that television news provided a "window to the world" . . . then it was realised that the window had a frame which could manipulate our field and angle of vision . . . the news was a "constructed reality" of images' (1994, p. 1).

The idea of what is real and what is created is the focus of much considered thought and debate. Questions of the real, the constructed and the created are part of postmodern discourse. Postmodern thought considers reality and images of reality as a simulacrum: the two exist as a single concept. This concept of the simulacrum was suggested by French philosopher Jean Baudrillard: 'Baudrillard's idea is that in a world that is full of media(ted) images there is little point in trying to separate what is real from what is represented for they are essentially the same' (Devereux, 2003, p. 105). Baudrillard further argues that the media feed off themselves, drawing ideas from each other with the end result of not knowing what was real in the first place. News increasingly is recycled, 'churned', copied, cut and pasted, and linked. This has become a focus of much media criticism, including the discussion about the political economy of media later in this chapter.

What we can take from Baudrillard, Boorstin, Hartley and Putnis is the need to question images of reality as they are presented to us, and to think about whether mediated images are real or simply based on our experience and perceptions of life. Moreover, we can ask ourselves how our role in media relations might fit in with the creation and production of reality.

NEWS AND SOURCES

While the strongest form of information-gathering for a journalist is usually through first-hand observation, the reality is that practical issues such as time, money and staffing levels require journalists to use sources. Journalists need sources to link up with the corporate, political, social and cultural world around them. This use of sources underpins the role of the media relations professional. At the same time, the internet has seen the evolution of citizen journalists, either working independently of the news media, as bloggers or as semi-independent of the news, contributing to existing news outlets, commenting on existing stories or being part of the media itself—like the famous *Huffington Post*, with its 1800-plus blogger army (Alterman, 2011, p. 7). The internet may have blurred the boundaries of the producer and the consumer—the media and the source—but in the mix of it all, external sources who can verify and clarify remain important to media coverage.

TYPES OF SOURCES

Early studies of how news is constructed identify news sources being central to the process (Tuchman, 1978; Fishman, 1980; Ericson, Baranek and Chan, 1987; Tiffen, 1989). This, in turn, provides a way of viewing the role of media relations in the communications mix. Sources have been called 'relevant knowers' (Fishman, 1980, p. 51). So when a journalist seeks to construct a story based on tip-offs, hints or assumptions, the automatic pathway to verify the story is through sources in positions of authority. Government officials or the bureaucracy are frequently used as sources. These people become conventional or standard news sources for the media. So too are middle and senior management in the corporate and third (non-profit) sectors. Often these people are the most easily accessible, but they also have the knowledge that the media need to clarify or verify their story. For example, Brown (2003) explains a trend of using scientific experts as sources: 'Currently fashionable are geneticists, for scientists, environmental scientists, psychologists, psychiatrists, crime profilers and even criminologists. To the media, never has the mantle of science been sexier' (2003, p. 40). These people have been called 'authorised knowers' (Ericson, Baranek and Chan, 1987, p. 18), 'news shapers' (Soley, 1992, p. 18) and 'primary definers' (Schlesinger and Tumber, 1994, p. 17). The media, in turn, become 'secondary definers' because they are one step removed from the facts.

This theory suggests that the source may be more in control of defining the news than the media, but of course many would argue that this is not the case and in fact the media, in seeking out selected sources, maintain control over their news-gathering. In turn, when the media need expert interpretation, sources can define the parameters of a debate. For media relations, this provides an opportunity to become established as authorised knowers—and thus primary definers or news shapers—in particular areas of knowledge. As the role of commentary and opinion has risen, these authorised knowers now also have to be commentators, more savvy than ever in working with news media, finding what Harris (2011) calls 'fault lines' in a story—which in turn drives the debate.

Fishman (1980) observes that it is necessary to consider more than one version of facts because facts can be ambiguous. A source's version of facts will depend on three things:

- the source's level of competence
- their positioning, and
- their interest.

Clearly, we see a correlation with the role of media relations here because we, as a source or the spokesperson within our organisation, should rate highly in all three categories. We therefore work within this theory to ensure we become the source the media trust and to which they return as their preferred source of information. More than ever before, the multiple voices that are available via different media platforms need to be scrutinised by the media to ensure they can bring authority to their stories.

FRAMING AND AGENDA-SETTING

When we refer to a 'frame of reference' in life, we are talking about a way of viewing or interpreting information. Media framing is not so different. Frames 'largely unspoken and unacknowledged, organise the world both for journalists who report it and, in some important degree, for us who rely on their reports' (Gitlin, in Scheufele, 1999, p. 106). So framing is practised by journalists when they package information as news, and it is also practised by the media relations professional or the expert source who presents information to the media.

Entman identifies the two important elements of 'selection and salience' in framing:

> To frame is to select some aspects of a perceived reality and make them more salient in a communicating text, in such a way as to promote a particular problem definition, causal interpretation, moral evaluation, and/ or treatment recommendation. (1993, p. 52)

From this definition, we can see why framing is important to us in media relations—audiences receive the news in terms of how it is framed or presented. Take, for example, the use of a government report on climate change. We would expect that an online left-wing newspaper like *Green Left Weekly* might write up a story using this information differently from a more conservative newspaper like *The Australian* or the tabloid *Herald Sun*. There would also be differences in how commercial news would cover the story, compared with the ABC news or FM radio news or an SBS documentary. The framing of the story would depend on the intended audience and the style of the journalist writing the story. Scheufele (1999) says there are at least five factors that potentially can influence how a journalist frames an issue:

- social norms and values
- organisational pressures and restraints
- pressures of interest groups
- journalistic routines, and
- ideological or political orientations of journalists.

This list identifies how framing of news is quite complex—this is despite how simple a news story might appear to be when we read, hear or listen to it.

Where framing focuses on *how* an issue or event is covered, agenda-setting focuses on *what* issues or events are covered. For this reason, framing has been described as 'second-level agenda-setting' (McCombs, Shaw and Weaver, 1997). For an organisation or individual, agenda-setting is all about creating public awareness and getting important issues seen, heard, read (and ultimately believed) in the mass media. Agenda-setting theorist Maxwell McCombs (2004) notes:

> The ability to influence the salience of topics on the public agenda has come to be called the agenda-setting role of the news media . . . The public uses these cues from the mass media to organize their own agendas and decide which issues are important . . . in other words the news media set the public agenda. (2004, p. 1)

While we know that other things in life—such as personal experience and peer or interest groups—also influence public opinion, agenda-setting focuses on the mass media's role in the process.

Rogers and Dearing (1988) created a model of agenda-setting that sees the process begin with the gatekeepers of the news—gatekeepers are those people in the newsroom who determine what news is used. First they choose what is important and newsworthy, then they allocate it a place of importance, designated by how prominent the story is. In media relations, it is therefore important to know who are the gatekeepers in a media organisation in order to be aware of who should be targeted with news and information. While the role of the traditional gatekeeper (usually the news editor or producer) has diminished with other media like bloggers and citizen journalists also 'breaking' news, the professionals who hold these roles in newspapers, television and radio nevertheless remain very important. The roles of people in the newsroom are discussed further in Chapter 5.

HELPING TO SET THE AGENDA

So how does the media relations professional feed into the agenda of media gatekeepers who determines the news lineup for the day?

There are two ways in which the media relations professional can fulfil the role of information provider, which ultimately becomes integral to the news agenda. These are:

- *proactively* (without media prompting)
- *reactively* (following a media prompt).

These might also be conceptualised as 'push–pull' approaches to working with the media—a theory used in customer relations. Using the push approach, we would send releases out, make contact with the media to pitch a story, and so on. Using the pull approach, we make our materials and ourselves available to the media to access when they need it. It might seem that using the push approach will more likely get a response, and the pull approach might be too passive. But both approaches have their place. Information is supplied to the media both proactively and reactively, as push and pull, depending on circumstances—being mindful that we don't overdo or mis-target the push approach, or equally under-do our contact with the media. With a big news event, it is almost always best to be proactive and announce a story, but then, the bigger the news event, the more likely the media will be to seek out a response to a story.

RELATIONSHIP MANAGEMENT

Also central to the discussion of sources is a public relations theory based on the idea that public relations is about relationships. This has clear application to our consideration of media relations—which pivots on this relationship with members of the media. Centred on the principle that public relations should offer benefits to both an organisation and its respective publics (and not just the organisation), and that outcomes are more important than outputs (that is, we should measure achievements and not just activity), relationship management suggests that it is important to foster the media in an ongoing and productive way rather than focusing on an approach based simply on using the media as a means to an end. Ledingham (2003, p. 194) suggests a major shift that is occurring in public relations theory 'involves recognition that the appropriate domain of public relations is, in fact, relationships'. He further suggests that this has ramifications for specialised fields such as media relations, which sometimes are viewed as the 'softer' areas of public relations:

> Public relations functions such as special events, public affairs, development and press relations are not—in and of themselves—communication, but practice areas distinct from communication production, such as the preparation of news releases, speeches, videos, annual reports and the like. Within the relational perspective, communication functions as a strategic tool in the building and maintaining of organisation–public relationships. It is the management of these relationships—through both communication and behavioural initiatives—that is the appropriate framework for the study, teaching and practice of public relations. (Ledingham, 2003, pp. 194–5)

Ledingham suggests that specialised fields of public relations—media (or press, as he calls it) relations included—are more than just communication production. The dual focus on communications and behaviour is consistent with the idea that we need to foster relationships with the media as a special and important public—that media relations is much more than just publicity.

LIFEWORLD AND IDEAL SPEECH

These two theories come from critical philosopher Jürgen Habermas, and they offer some ideas about connecting and working effectively with sources. Habermas (1998) refers to a 'lifeworld' that is shared with or known to others. Lifeworlds provide shared understanding because they are all about speaking the same language. When working with the media, the media relations professional can draw from shared understandings that result in strong connections and collaborations.

McCarthy (1981) confirms that the lifeworld must be considered in the context of understanding speech. He refers to a 'double structure' of ordinary language. In it, if speaker and listener are to reach an understanding they must communicate simultaneously on two levels:

- the *capacity* to understand each other, and
- the *desire* to understand each other.

Hence the double structure represents a circle of understanding. In source–media relationships, such a double structure must exist with both a mutual understanding of a subject and a desire to want to learn or impart information about it. If either of these steps breaks down, then the communication will be flawed, and may result in incorrect reportage or misquoting a source. Given this, it follows that media relations practitioners who deal with journalists 'connect' best if they share some common understanding of the lifeworld.

Likewise, the concept of 'ideal speech', which is based on a fair and equitable common ground between parties, can further our understanding of relationships with the media. Ideal speech assumes an equality of access for all those involved in a specific discourse. Because of this, it does have limitations in its practical application because not everyone has equal access to communication channels. Ideal speech is based on listening to the opinions of others and being open to counter-arguments—hence it is sometimes viewed as too utopian to work effectively. But it is suggested that ideal speech can make sense of argumentation (McCarthy, 1981), and that ideal speech really refers to the *potential* for meaningful discourse and outcomes to occur (Holub, 1991). Ideal speech can best describe the *process* of discourse rather than the actual outcome.

Habermas's concept of ideal speech may be compared with Grunig and Hunt's (1984) two-way symmetrical model of public relations. This model argues that 'practitioners use research and dialogue to bring about symbiotic changes in the ideas, attitudes and behaviours of both their organisations and publics' (Grunig, 2001, p. 12). While posited in an organisational context rather than the broader theoretical context of ideal speech, the two have similarities in terms of their win–win approach. Grunig (2001) suggests that the two-way symmetrical model is the normative model that explains how public relations *should be* practised, rather than how it actually *is* practised.

ACHIEVING THE IDEAL?

Thus ideal speech and two-way symmetrical public relations represent the exemplar in the interface between the media and the media relations professional. Many other factors can, of course, impede this exemplar or ideal. Neither public relations nor the media work in a vacuum, so many other factors come into play: time restrictions, deadlines, space limitations, competition, commercial pressures, other media input and organisational expectations can present so many other variables that they appear to render the ideal impotent or useless. Therefore, we should see these principles as underpinning the potential best-case scenario, a point to which we refer back as a goal, while still working within real-world contexts and limitations. The relationship with the media may be viewed on a continuum from the ideal or the exemplar to the practical day-to-day. If we aim for the former while working within the restraints of the latter, we can hope to create working relationships that have a solid base and a sound foundation.

MEDIA AS THE PUBLIC SPHERE

The term 'public sphere' came into common usage after Habermas published *The Structural Transformation of the Public Sphere* (1962, translated in 1989), in which he argued that the public sphere was the 'space' in which individuals could gather to develop public opinion. His 'transformation' referred to how public opinion was being overwhelmed by big organisations and institutions—one of these being the media. In its original state, Habermas defined 'the public sphere' as 'a network for the communication of contents and the expression of attitudes, that is opinions, in which the flows of communication are filtered and synthesised in such a way that they condense into public opinions clustered according to themes' (in Outhwaite, 1994, p. 147). This was a good thing because it enabled citizens to have a voice, but in the 'transformed' state, the media became too dominant and other voices were not heard. This dominance of the media in place of what once incorporated a culture of public forums, open discussion and debate has been criticised because it is not truly representative and cannot provide fair access. As Carpignano and colleagues note:

> The mass media are the public sphere . . . Public life . . . has been transformed by a massive process of commodification of culture and of political culture in particular by a form of communication increasingly based on emotionally charged images rather than rational discourse. (1993, p. 103)

But while Habermas was concerned with the mass media of the 1900s—notably the domination of television—we have now entered an era that has a new public sphere. The internet is said to have 'democratised' the media—to have handed it back to the people, enabling the broader citizenry to be heard (though we must be mindful that many people globally do not have access to the internet or digital technologies, so not everyone can be heard). However, even with its limitations, the internet certainly has shifted the power base and, as the following observation shows, expanded the public sphere beyond the traditional media borders:

> New journalism—by including far more people, ideas, causes and genres—represents a reinvigoration of the Australian public sphere. Digital media's breaching of the border between a new type of amateur commentator, a latter-day revival of the 19th-century . . . 'organic intellectual', that is surely a plus for civic life. The national conversation proves to be broader—and much less earnest—than the agenda editors in both the 'quality' and the 'tabloid' newspapers deign it to be. (Moore, 2010, p. ix)

This expanded public sphere provides opportunities and challenges for the media relations practitioner. Other communication channels have clearly opened up and the media themselves now more fully embrace contribution from the citizenry. Strategic media choices are now more important than ever in the new public sphere.

POLITICAL ECONOMY OF MEDIA

Part of the concern for Habermas was how the media had developed into such powerful institutions at the expense of the individual. This has a fundamental similarity to the theories that underpin the political economy of media. Political economy theory suggests that commercial decisions affect the content the media produce, as well as the way they present that content. Moreover, it links the media to the ways in which political and commercial systems work, and how social power is exercised in society (McChesney, 2008). It also has something to say about the role of sources. Political economy arguments put forward by McChesney (2008) and others focus primarily on the ways in which mainstream news practices fail democracy. This includes an over-reliance on official 'experts' and sources, a lack of context in most news reporting, the prominence of the commercial motivations of media organisations, and the concentration of news ownership, which leads to a lack diversity in news coverage and approach.

While McChesney is positive about the ways in which citizens, activists and scholars have responded to the 'neoliberalism of the 1980s', an era in which profit was seen as more important than the good of society, he does not see the internet as a means of locating diversity: far from it. He says: 'The idea that . . . technology would automatically introduce viable competition has proven to be false . . . in industry after industry— e.g. Amazon and Google—the network effects combine with market economics to point more toward monopoly' (2008, p. 19). So while citizen journalism is being applauded by others, McChesney and other political economy critics argue that it does not solve the fundamental issues of both funding resource allocation and big-business building of the media, or the hyper-commercialism that they argue is derailing quality journalism.

What does this theory suggest for media relations? With democracy at its core, political economy requires vibrant and robust debate as well as transparency in the corporate and government sectors; media relations has a major part to play in these. With journalism at a crossroads of change, media relations practitioners will become increasingly important in facilitating local, national and global conversations within the media.

CONCLUSION

Media relations might appear a simple part of the public relations process, but when we consider some of the theories that contextualise it beyond the basics, we can review it for the multi-faceted and complex process that it really is. It combines the identification and construction of news and other events that feed into the mass media. Important in the mix is the role played by the sources that underpin the articulation of stories, and ultimately the media's framing of reality. These sources provide input into the media agenda through proactive and reactive responses, which filter stories at an early stage in the news cycle. Through shared understandings, transparency and knowledge of each other's roles and functions in society, the media and the media relations industry can work productively and efficiently in professional and mutually beneficial relationships.

4 LAW AND ETHICS IN MEDIA RELATIONS

There are many legal and ethical situations through which communications professionals navigate in their day to day life. This chapter focuses on just a few of the key ones—those that deal with defamation and reputation, privacy, confidentiality, copyright and the fair use of others' work, as well as the ethical and strategic use of social media and other communication channels. The legal frameworks can apply equally to the user or monitor of information, as the supplier of information to the media, or simply to taking part in public conversations. Just as importantly, the chapter also outlines some ethical issues and strategies to consider in working either with the news media or in the broader communications environments and provides an overview of the importance of corporate governance for the media relations practitioner. It also takes a close look at the two codes of ethics that govern the work of public relations and journalists. What might be surprising is that while these two professions represent the work of very different communications industries, they fundamentally have much in common when it comes to ethical practice.

These days, it is easier than ever to send out information quickly and widely—and irretrievably. It is just as simple to access information that is the work of others. In a professional context, we would expect that communications would be strategic, carefully thought through and targeted. But professional and private communications have blurred for many people, and it is our job in public relations, as part of media training, to advise clients about the importance of careful communications practices—whether on blogs, Twitter, Facebook, web pages, emails, posting imagers or undertaking interviews. Think about your own social networking pages: have you used material from another internet site without permission? Have you ever passed on negative or nasty comments about another person? Or linked to a blog that might have included confidential or private details? The internet represents a maze of legal and ethical pitfalls—not all of which will have immediate, or any, effect. Others, though, can have a sting in the tail that could lead to embarrassment or humiliation, a fine, a take-down order, a court-ordered apology or even imprisonment. They might also result in the loss of a sponsor or expulsion from a professional body

Individuals and organisations have more power than ever to publish their own information and opinions. If you are contributing to the online discussion—as part of the news media, as a professional communicator or simply as a private social media user—you should be aware of some of the key fields of communications law, and consider the best ethical practices.

DEMOCRACY AND FREE SPEECH

What do we mean when we talk about having a right to free speech? In democracies such as Australia, this freedom is taken for granted, forming a fundamental building block in democratic life. Some countries have charters or bills of rights that set out specific rights, including the right to free speech; New Zealand, Canada, Britain and most famously the United States have such charters or bills. Australia does not. It relies on Commonwealth and state laws to find a balance of various freedoms. Free speech is balanced by laws that relate to defamation, contempt of court, privacy of information, national security and so on. For example, the law of defamation suggests that all people should use care in saying or publishing things about others that may result in members of the community thinking less of those people. The laws of *sub judice* contempt restrict what may be published about a case before the courts. Laws relating to anti-terrorism restrict the media from reporting matters of national security. Privacy laws restrict the use of private information about a person (but do not extend to personal privacy).

Butler and Rodrick (2007) say free speech is needed for three reasons:

- It enhances our humanity.
- It is the way 'truth' is discovered.
- It enhances the quality of democracy.

Let's take a closer look at these three lofty ideals. To enhance our humanity, free speech must incorporate reason and critical thought. This lies in contrast to the doctrine of authoritarianism, which is conferred upon the individual and society by government or religious authority. So our humanity is developed by the individual being able to question authority, speak out and be heard, even if others do not agree—as in the famous quotation, attributed to the French philosopher Voltaire, 'I disapprove of what you say, but I will defend to the death your right to say it'.

The second point, the discovery of 'truth', is a contentious one since 'truth' itself is open to interpretation. The postmodern approach might argue that claims to truth are relative, and truth cannot truly be discovered. Nevertheless, if we accept Butler and Rodrick's (2007, p. 8) argument that 'In its simplest form, the argument is that even if truth cannot be certainly established, more knowledge will still be better than less knowledge', then we can apply the argument of free speech to the notion of truth. Free speech becomes an opportunity to circulate ideas, with the most 'truthful' winning out or a range of 'truths' presented.

Finally, free speech leads to the workings of a democracy. Citizens can access information about the political process—including politicians, legislation, working documents and so on—in order to make informed choices, develop consensus within communities and question the political process.

One of the most important reasons for free speech to exist in a democracy is to ensure that a range of points of view are placed into the melting pot of discussion and debate. Thus decision-making is preceded by consideration of a representative range of views. It follows that a decision made after consultation and discussion is more likely to mirror the opinions, interests and needs of a range of people than one made without consultation. For example, the open forums of all levels of government allow for unfettered debate. Parliamentary question time and question time at local government level offer plenty of open and frank comment and debate. The news media thrive on this unrestricted forum for exchanging points of view, known for its theatrics and emotional outbursts—and thus supplying colourful news stories.

Freedom of speech—for both the media and individuals—can thus bring a variety of views and perspectives to a topic or issue, and give a voice to a range of people, communities or groups. Where once the media were deemed to be the watchdog, acting on behalf of society, now society—or individuals—can make themselves heard independently of the media. Access to avenues of free speech has never before been so open to the individual. Nevertheless, the news media continue to provide the means to deliver information to wide and mass audiences. They also provide the ability to interpret increasingly complex topics of discussion. Downie and Schudson (2009) note that news reporting undergirds democracy by explaining complicated events, issues and processes clearly and simply. So for many people their knowledge of Wikileaks, climate change, the Global Financial Crisis (GFC) and the wars in Iraq and Afghanistan has been based on, or enhanced by, media explanations of what was going on. In most Western democracies, a strong media sector continues to be seen as a fundamental element, running parallel to the concept of free speech. As McChesney and Pickard aptly point out:

> It is impossible to conceive of effective governance and the rule of law—not to mention individual freedoms, social justice and effective and enlightened solutions to daunting problems—without a credible system of journalism. (2011, p. ix)

Indeed, it is the media's job to pursue free speech, so we should be neither surprised nor offended when they publish. What we hope for and encourage is accuracy, and fair and balanced reporting.

Pearson (2012, p. 168) explains that 'the flip side of free expression is censorship'. Where censorship occurs, material is banned from being published. This is known as 'prior restraint' because of the fact that it is banned *before* publication. This happens less often in democratic countries, which prefer to deal with any issues (or clashes in freedoms) *after* publication. Where there is a tendency not to impose such prior restraints, other laws are intended to balance free expression (Pearson, 2012).

FREE SPEECH AND THE INTERNET

As if finding a balance with regard to free speech isn't complicated enough within individual countries, the fact is we are increasingly publishing and working within a global community and have to consider legal jurisdictions beyond our physical borders. As Pearson (2012) notes, anyone posting material on the internet needs to be mindful that even if they live in a democracy like Australia, the United States, New Zealand or Canada, their words, images or sounds are subject to laws the world over, and this includes countries with different laws:

> Each time you post your latest blog or social media message you may be subject to the laws of more than 600 nations, provinces, states and territories. Of course, you might not have 600 hits, views or retweets, so you might only be reaching some of them. But you can never quite be sure where your words, sounds and images might finish up. (Pearson, 2012, p. xv)

There is no easy answer to this; publishing on the internet can mean you can breach a law in the United States for a blog in Australia, or in New Zealand for a website in Singapore. However, some logical principles can be applied to keep the sensible internet user out of trouble. As Pearson warns: 'Whenever you press that "Send" or "Publish" button on the device of your choice, most countries expect you to refrain from committing a crime, destroying someone's reputation, interfering with justice, insulting minorities, endangering national security, or stealing other people's words and images' (2012, p. xvii). The message is clear: think about your communication, whether it is a single tweet, a regular blog, a press release, an updated website or even an email. There is an old saying: 'Doctors bury their mistakes. Lawyers jail theirs. But journalists publish theirs for all the world to see' (Pearson, 2012, p. 12). These days, the same applies to anyone publishing online. Individual publishers, corporate, political or not-for-profit communicators, and media conglomerates all need to remember some basic guidelines about publishing online.

WORKING LEGALLY AND ETHICALLY

Ethical and legal considerations often overlap but, paradoxically, they can also come into direct conflict. For example, it is good ethical practice to consider the reputations of others; it is also good legal practice under defamation law. It is ethical not to steal the creative work of others; this is also important under copyright law. However, things are not always so clear-cut. For example, while it might be ethical practice for a journalist to offer a news source confidentiality (sometimes certain situations require this), it may break the law if they refuse a judge's order to divulge the name. Likewise, a conflict can occur if a public relations practitioner signs a confidentiality agreement with an employer and then discovers improper activity occurring in the company and is faced with the prospect of acting as a whistleblower. Because such conflicts can arise, it can be a good idea to think through the 'What would I do?' question in a range of situations. Not every scenario is black and white, not every choice is clear. The St James Ethics Centre posts regular conflict scenarios that deal with applied ethics on its website, and these can provide some dilemmas for reflection and discussion.

We will now look at several key areas of law in which public relations practitioners might find themselves working with the media. It is not an exhaustive list; rather, it flags some of the higher-risk zones for the communications professional. It will also highlight some of the ethical issues that you might encounter along the way.

COPYRIGHT

Sometimes in media relations, a media campaign will be inspired by a similar campaign somewhere else in the world, or a past campaign or idea. Be careful when being 'inspired' by the work of others that your work is sufficiently original. Just as importantly, be mindful that once you make your ideas available for others to see, they become easy pickings—even if you've just been chatting about them on Facebook or in a blog. The internet makes it very simple to trace a copied campaign, document or phrase. These are some of the key points you need to know:

- There is no copyright in an idea, only in the expression of an idea. You therefore should be mindful of expressing your own ideas in 'a tangible form' because a great idea on a blog or a tweet can be picked up and developed by others.
- You do not need to identify your copyrighted work with the © symbol. Once your work is expressed, it automatically attracts copyright protection.
- Copyright is based on the idea that work eventually moves into 'the public domain' to be shared and to advance society; however, the creator of the work (or their designee) also receives some benefit—usually in monetary form—as well as appropriate acknowledgement.
- Copyright ownership of most works in Australia, and many other countries, extends to 70 years past the death of the creator.
- A copyright licence can be transferred—for example, Michael Jackson owned the copyright of much of The Beatles' work after buying the rights in 1985.
- Other rights, called 'moral rights', require the creator to be attributed even if a licence is transferred, and the work to be dealt with integrity.
- Copyright materials (in limited amounts) may be used without permission for:
  - news reporting
  - criticism and review
  - parody and satire, and
  - research and study.

USING WORDS AND IMAGES

Just because something is on the internet does not mean anyone can use it without permission. Providing a link to a site where the work is posted, rather than the work itself, is a simple way to ensure you don't over-use a work without acknowledgement. When you do need or want to use work from the internet, check to see whether it says you can use it with acknowledgement. The use of other people's material for commercial purposes, such as a campaign or words or photos on a company website, should be handled very carefully. Just as you would not want another company or individual to use your designs or words, you should not use the work of others without permission, as the following example illustrates:

> When 16-year-old Texan teenager Alison Chang flashed a 'V' sign in a travel snap taken by her church youth counsellor she would never have imagined her image would be posted on a bus stop on the other side of the world, triggering an international legal dispute . . . The multinational conglomerate Virgin Mobile had lifted the picture from the photo-sharing site Flickr as part of a billboard advertising campaign in Australia. It had plastered its advertising slogan 'Dump your pen friend' above Alison's head and had put the caption 'Free text virgin to virgin' right under her image. (Pearson, 2012, p. 1)

MEDIA RELEASES

Working in public relations presents an anomaly in the field of copyright because much of what we write is intended to be copied by others without any acknowledgement. Media releases, for instance, are written with the sole purpose of being used by the news media. We do not expect our name as the author on them—in fact, it is not uncommon for well-written media releases to be published with a journalist's byline on them! Though this may not be entirely ethical, it is not something to which we should take exception. In sending out a media release, we are actually providing an 'implied licence' to the media to use the material. Media releases—or any media relations material—should be readily available online, in a user-friendly format (not PDFs) so they can easily be cut and pasted by the media.

COPYRIGHT AND THE INTERNET

Pearson (2012) points out that Twitter posts may be less prone to copyright infringement because the medium limits the amount of another person's work which can be borrowed and the retweeting function implies that everyone expects work to be recycled by others. Just like the media release, reusage of the words is therefore implied in the distribution of Twitter. On the other hand, newspaper stories are not there for reuse without permission. As noted in Chapter 2, it is not unusual for the media to use other media for their news pages, bulletins or online sites. To some extent, news organisations have even turned a blind eye to this in the past. However, the rise of indiscriminate copying and pasting from internet news sites has presented some significant hurdles for the news media. One way of countering this has been to sue bloggers—who are major users of media stories—for use of online news. Though not widespread, 'copyright trolls' work as online detectives, trolling the internet to find copyright infringements and then securing the copyright of the stories and suing the infringers. As one such company has argued: 'Media companies' assets are very much their copyrights' (Weiss, 2010). As we will see in Chapter 11, online newspapers have begun to use other strategies, which might be a simpler way to control the reuse of their stories.

ALLIED AREAS OF LAW AND ETHICS

Copyright is a form of intellectual property (IP) law. Other areas of IP law include trademarks and patents, passing off and trade practices. A trademark is a registered sign or symbol used to identify a company or its goods and services—McDonald's golden arches, the Coca-Cola 'C', the Apple apple. Trademarks can include 'any letter, word, name, signature, numeral, device, brand, heading, label, ticket, aspect of packaging, shape, colour sound or scent' (*Trade Marks Act 1995*, section 6). Trademarks are established to limit competition from others, to set a company apart as part of their branding. Chocolates and alcohol have been at the centre of many trademark disputes. For example, Kit Kat tried (unsuccessfully) to register the shape of its chocolate biscuit, while Cadbury has (successfully) argued that Darrell

Lea chocolate should not be able to use the same colour purple as it does (Luck in Carrick, 2010).

Companies that decide to take legal action against another organisation for a trademark breach should be mindful of the potential negative publicity that may result. In the following example, Johnson & Johnson received not only negative publicity about its case against the charity American Red Cross, but the judge openly expressed sympathy for the Red Cross:

> In 2004, pharmaceutical company Johnson & Johnson challenged the American Red Cross's use of the Greek red cross symbol against a white background. While the two had amicably shared the symbol since an agreement signed in 1895, Johnson & Johnson sued the Red Cross, claiming the organisation's use of the symbol on products sold in stores was a violation of the arrangement. After four years of litigation, the companies settled out of court in 2008 after a judge ruled 'a Congressional charter gave the Red Cross the right to use the symbol even for business purposes'. (Saul, 2008)

'Passing off' is a field of law that protects your work from being misrepresented by another. It involves the protection of a business name and its goods, as well as the reputation and goodwill of the company against false connections or associations (Pearson and Polden, 2011). Similar protection is offered through the Commonwealth *Competition and Consumer Act 2010* (formerly known as the *Trade Practices Act 1974*) and state fair trading legislation in Australia, both of which prohibit 'misleading or deceptive' conduct. These laws make it clear that work should not only be original, or include permission for use, but must clearly be identified for what it is. So, for example, if you are running an advertorial, such as the one discussed in Chapter 11, it should be marked clearly (also see astroturfing at the end of this chapter). Equally, if you are using a celebrity to endorse your product or company, this endorsement should be formalised in a contract.

Finally, an allied field of which students should all be aware is plagiarism. This is an ethical breach involving the use of the work of another without attribution. There is a fine line between getting an idea from another person and developing it with or without attribution.

Charges of plagiarism in universities—but also the communications industry—can have serious effects. A *60 Minutes* journalist who was said to have plagiarised a story idea ended up suing the TV program for defamation. Software products like *Turnitin* make students more conscious of plagiarism—this level of awareness should be carried through into the professional world and steadfastly maintained.

DEFAMATION

We all need to be mindful of how we express opinions or convey information about other people or organisations. Once something is published—especially in mass or social media—you cannot remove it entirely from the public domain by taking it down from its posting site. For this reason, and to be professional in our approach to what we publish, it is important to understand the law of defamation, which is all about reputations and public perception. Key points you need to know include the following:

- Defamatory matter may include anything that holds another up to ridicule, lowers another in the estimation of others, damages a reputation or causes a person to be shunned by others.
- Anyone can be liable for defamation—not only the news media.
- Defamatory matter can include newspaper reports, emails, pictures, tweets, letters or notes, TV or radio reports, Facebook comments, fiction or non-fiction books, or anything else that can be communicated to a third person.
- A statement can be defamatory if it:
  - includes content that has defamatory meaning
  - can be interpreted to refer to someone in particular (it does not need to be by name)
  - is published to at least one other person (than the defendant and the plaintiff).
- Defences for defamation in Australia include:
  - truth
  - fair report
  - qualified privilege

- honest opinion
- absolute privilege
- triviality
- innocent dissemination.

REPUTATION MANAGEMENT

Reputation management is at the centre of public relations, so it stands to reason that the law of defamation should be one we take very seriously. Defamation has traditionally included libel (written) and slander (spoken) forms, although the term slander has recently been removed from Australian laws so now all defamation is considered libel. Although it will usually exist in a permanent record such as written words or pictures, this need not be the case. For example, an end-of-year stage performance by a group of Year 12 students which conveyed the information that two of the school's teachers were having an affair was taken to court. While no names were used in the skit, it was enough that it implied the two teachers in question (Pearson and Polden, 2011, p. 193).

One of the best-known international defamation cases in public relations terms is known as 'the McLibel case'. *McDonald's Corporation v Steel & Morris* was an English defamation action filed by the McDonald's Corporation against environmental activists Helen Steel and David Morris. At the centre of the case was a pamphlet, *What's Wrong with McDonald's: Everything They Don't Want You to Know*, which was distributed outside British McDonald's restaurants, critical of the company. The negative publicity resulting from the David-vs-Goliath case meant that, while the case was a legal win for McDonald's, it was widely acknowledged as a public relations disaster. Following the court's ruling in 1997, the case was taken to the European Court of Human Rights (ECHR), which in 2005 ruled that Steel and Morris had been denied a fair trial.

Under revised Australian defamation laws enacted in 2006, large companies cannot sue for defamation. Only companies with fewer than ten employees or organisations that are not-for-profit can sue. (There are other ways in which large companies can take action against defamatory material, such as arguing 'injurious falsehood'.) But while you cannot defame big companies, you can defame individuals *within* a company, or groups of people can claim to have been defamed if they are identifiable in defamatory material. For instance, all doctors at a local private hospital may have grounds to sue in response to a story about dodgy medical practices that went on at the hospital, or all bar staff at a named nightclub may have grounds to sue if the club is identified in association with prostitution or illegal drug activity. Because staff at that particular hospital or nightclub can be identified by a small section of the community, and because they may believe their reputations have been impugned, they may be able to argue that they have been defamed.

The truth is that defamation does occur quite regularly, in everyday life and also in the media—a key is to know whether any potentially defamatory material is defensible through one of the defences listed above. It is also important to know that just hurting another person's feelings is not enough to claim a defamation—their reputation must be affected. This said, care should be taken at all times about publicly (and this only means to one third party) expressing hurtful, disparaging or humiliating material about other people because while it may not be defamatory, or it may be defensible, it may still likely be unethical or unprofessional.

DEFAMATION AND THE INTERNET

With the capacity to publish 24/7 on the internet, the news media now work with an urgent imperative to get news up quickly. The 'need for speed' results in journalists rushing to get stories up to beat the competition. For public relations, this means two very important things: first, we are primary suppliers of news and hence have to accommodate this hunger for it; and second, we have to monitor the seemingly endless pool of online material that impacts on or relates to our industry or organisation. In this hurried environment, it is important to still spend time making sure material is not only accurate but that it does not defame another person—even inadvertently. Unintentional defamations are still defamations. We need to be mindful of this as publishers of online material, as suppliers of information to the media and as consumers of the material of others.

Because defamation can be defended by a range of defences (see above) and, as Pearson and Polden (2011, p. 190) point out, defamation is 'not a perfect science', a judge will look at many elements to determine whether a defamation is defensible. As Pearson (2012, p. 16) notes, brief references can sometimes be the most problematic:

> Twitter can leave you more exposed in the area of defamation because there is so little space for you to give context and balance to your criticism of others. Longer, better argued critiques lend themselves to some of the fair comment defences in many countries.

PRIVACY

The flipside of defamation is privacy. It is about keeping certain information private, just as the two teachers in the school skit cited above would most certainly have preferred. Privacy is a highly contentious field in Australia because there is no common law right to it. There is a law that protects privacy—the *Commonwealth Privacy Act 1988*—but in its current form it covers only private information, so does not protect what might be referred to as 'invasions of privacy' into workplaces, homes or life more generally. These are currently protected by a range of other laws—namely trespass, surveillance, defamation, breach of confidence and nuisance. As a signatory to the International Covenant on Civil and Political Rights, Australia does have some responsibility to guard individual privacy, but this does not provide overriding protection.

Currently, then, privacy is governed by codes of conduct that are managed by self-regulatory bodies—principally the Australian Press Council (APC) for the print media and the Australian Communications and Media Authority (ACMA) for television, radio and the internet. In addition, the Media Entertainment and Arts Alliance (MEAA) has a code of ethics that includes a privacy provision, discussed further below. It is interesting to note that the 'Finkelstein Report' discussed in Chapter 2, pointed out that current privacy protections governed by the APC do not extend to online media publications (Finkelstein, 2012).

THE PRIVACY DEBATE

While there has been a decades-long debate about whether Australia should adopt a tort of privacy (a tort is a civil rather than a criminal law), which would certainly impact on media activity, the free speech/free press argument has been a stronger one, and it has so far been resisted (Pearson, 2012). In 2008 and 2009, the Australian Law Reform Commission and the New South Wales Law Reform Commission recommended a statutory right to privacy after defamation laws were amended in favour of the media. Where previously a defence of 'public interest' and 'public benefit' had to be shown by the media (in some jurisdictions), this was removed in the development of unified defamation laws introduced in 2006. The resulting defence of 'truth' alone meant that the media no longer had to argue any public interest or benefit in a story, simply that it was true. The proposal for a privacy tort therefore was suggested to balance out the 'public interest' gap that had been removed. Not surprisingly, this met with opposition from the news media, who see any broad-ranging privacy protection as an impediment to their work.

The *News of the World* scandal in 2011, which saw the 168-year-old British paper closed overnight because of widespread phone hacking activities, placed the whole issue of media reporting and privacy squarely in the international spotlight. As Patching notes:

> *News of the World* journalists, aided by consultant private investigators, used immoral, unethical and illegal methods to hack into the phone messages of celebrities, politicians, and as it turned out, even the phone of a murdered 13-year-old schoolgirl and possibly the voice messages of terrorism victims and fallen soldiers.
>
> The *News of the World* reporters created a false ethical standard—that 'getting the scoop' was always right. To them, the end (getting the much-wanted information) justified the means (the invasion of privacy). (Patching, 2012, pp. 121–2)

In order to determine public opinion about privacy, the Australian Communications and Media Authority (ACMA) conducted a survey of viewers' expectations of privacy of the news and current affairs media in 2011, in preparation for updating its Privacy Guidelines for Broadcasters in December 2012. It found the following:

- Most media users believe it is 'very important' for broadcasters to safeguard a person's privacy in news and current affairs programs.
- Most media users believe that showing extensive footage of a person grieving, using a hidden camera, or revealing information about a person's sexual preferences are 'very intrusive' of personal privacy.
- Most media users believe it is 'very intrusive' to broadcast personal material from online social media sites where access has been restricted to online friends. (ACMA, 2011c)

Potentially there is a gap in public expectations of privacy and media activity. For those who work in public relations, this is a space that should be watched because sometimes there is a great difference between what is in the 'public interest' and what is interesting to the public. These differences can easily put the news media and public relations imperatives at odds with each other. Among the most controversial elements of the new ACMA guidelines is a specific protection of 'seclusion', 'effectively guarding against invasion of a person's privacy—even in a public space' (Christensen, 2011c). The application of this guideline to news stories on asylum-seekers gained considerable media attention in the early part of 2012.

CONFIDENTIALITY AND GOING 'OFF THE RECORD'

Keeping confidences in the media and communications industries is most certainly an ethical consideration. In addition, there is an area of law that covers 'breach of confidence'. This exists where a contract—written, verbal or even 'implied'—has been entered into. These can relate to employee–employer relationships and professional–client relationships, and can also pertain to keeping certain government information secret (Pearson and Polden, 2011). A breach of confidence can include exposing ideas, documents or conversations—usually financial, security or private details such as tax records or business plans. A breach of confidence is determined by looking at three elements:

- The information must have a 'quality of confidence' about it—that is, there must be a secret.
- The circumstance under which the information/material is passed on should be identifiable as a confidential one.
- The information/material must expose something that someone does not want exposed.

In a follow-up, separate case to the McLibel case above (which became known as McLibel 2), Steel and Morris claimed that police had disclosed their confidential information to investigators working for the hamburger chain. They won the court action and the following occurred:

> Scotland Yard agreed to the payout saying it regretted any distress that may have been caused to the pair by the alleged disclosure of their details. As part of the settlement, all police officers in Greater London are being reminded of their responsibility not to disclose information held on the Police National Computer to third parties. (BBC, 2000)

The media relations practitioner must be mindful of this field of law when it comes to providing confidential material to the news media. However, in most of our dealings supplying information will be more straightforward—though it might require a choice of going 'on' or 'off' the record. One of the main reasons for the media seeking 'off the record' information is in exposing corruption, illegal activity or unethical behaviour. The field of investigative journalism is premised on these overriding features of keeping the public informed and prioritising the public interest. These, of course, may be balanced against the right to a reputation by an individual or an organisation, as well as certain expectations of privacy. Thus the role of the source must—like the role of the media—be balanced, and careful consideration should be given to providing leaks or off-the-record comments.

The media relations practitioner should be very clear about where they stand in such communications. Conley and Lamble (2006) discuss a range of on-the-record and off-the-record scenarios. These are:

- *On the record:* Everything said and every document supplied can be used and attributed to the source who provided it.
- *Off the record:* The person supplying the information does not want to be quoted. It may also mean that the source does not want it used in any form. This should be clarified. It might be permissible to quote a 'reliable source' or to verify the information elsewhere. Someone may say that something is 'off the record' because they do not want their name used, but are not opposed to the information being published.
- *On background:* This means that no names of individuals can be quoted. The information can be used, but only generally sourced, with an attribution such as 'a senior National Party figure'.
- *On deep background:* This means that the reporter may use the material but without any kind of attribution. Politicians release 'trial balloons' (a story leaked on purpose to gauge public response) to test public opinion on various issues or in leadership challenges. (Conley and Lamble, 2006)

So how do you know when to provide confidential information, leak a story to a journalist who you trust or release a 'trial balloon' (also called a 'kite-flying' exercise, to see if it will 'fly')? One possibility is to provide information that may be verified elsewhere—in other words, you might 'tip off' a journalist about an issue or story knowing that they can get the facts from another source. However, another school of thought is that you should be prepared to own up to a tip-off and go on the record.

Where media releases and media conferences are overt in nature because they are made widely and publicly available, leaks and tip-offs may be categorised as a 'covert' tactic because they are not publicly available and are more difficult to trace. The fact that media relations workers provide news media leaks and tip-offs is well known (especially in politics), but they can backfire, with devastating results for the media relations practitioner, as the following two examples illustrate.

The now-famous 2012 Australia Day protests at Parliament House in Canberra which saw the Prime Minister Julia Gillard hurried to her car by security guards resulted in a prime ministerial press secretary's resignation: the reason? A tip-off to 'an individual' about the where-abouts of Opposition Leader Tony Abbott who had previously made controversial comments about the Aboriginal tent embassy, resulting in the internationally broadcast scuffle that ensued. The Prime Minister's office provided a statement shortly after Australia Day which said: 'A member of the Prime Minister's media unit did call another individual yesterday and disclosed the presence of the Opposition Leader . . . this action was an error of judgment' (Kenny, 2012). This 'error of judgement' resulted in the subsequent resignation of the press secretary. Within weeks of the Canberra incident, a Western Australian political media advisor also resigned after a simple email was sent to the media: 'His apparent crime was to email a publicly available image of an MP's beachside home to journalists' (Colvin in ABC, 2012). The West Australian Premier Colin Barnett said the emailing of the photo was 'careless, foolish and silly' (ABC, 2012). Because the photo was at the centre of a controversial and sensitive political issue, the very act of passing it on was deemed to have been unprofessional.

The lesson in these two instances lies in the ease of distribution of messages and images and the immediacy and irretrievability of their dissemination—once the genie is out of the bottle it is near impossible to put it back in and the media relations practitioner must be prepared to own it.

FREEDOM OF INFORMATION

Sometimes information can be obtained by using Freedom of Infor-mation (FoI) provisions. Each state, territory and the Commonwealth of Australia have FoI Acts (by various names), which were established to enable access to publicly available information. There are quite a few areas that are exempt from FoI, however, and requests are known to be slow in processing and can be very costly. At their worst, Australia's FoI laws have been described as 'close to completely dysfunctional from a user's perspective' (Lidberg, 2005, p. 31)—indeed, they are also known jokingly as 'freedom from information'. Nevertheless, they are worth knowing about in case an organisation for which you work is ever at the centre of an FoI search. While journalists are the best-known group using this procedure, it is available to anyone who makes an application and pays the fees. You can do an FoI search about yourself for free!

ASTROTURFING

Astroturfing is all about fabricating grassroots support for a campaign or issue. Online, these activities can have a major impact; however, this tactic is not new. Astroturfing existed well before the internet: in radio (notably talkback), newspapers (letters to the editor), newsletters and so on.

Astroturfing is based on the idea that support for an issue can be developed by starting a trend—a fake one, which is usually paid for. A Sydney-based advertising strategist explains how this has played out in contemporary social and political issues:

> Public debate in Australia has been shaped in a profound way by astroturfing. If you look at the debate around the carbon tax, the debate around mining supertax, and the public debate around asylum seekers, the public debates in these major areas of policy are being shaped in meaningful ways by astroturfing. (Prasad, cited in Cohen, 2011)

Since few people openly advocate astroturfing as a tactic, there are many questions around who is involved, the scale of the campaigns and how efficient this tactic may be (Cohen, 2011). While most agree that astroturfing is not ethical practice, one commentator described those who use it in the following terms: 'they're not immoral, they're just amoral' (Prasad, cited in Cohen, 2011). Another (digital marketing) consultant who was hiring people to operate multiple fake identities on the internet placed the following advertisement online:

> The job requires you to have very good search skills and to find conversations online. You'll then take on a supplied persona and join in on the conversation. You'll have to be very clever and adaptive and if you don't know about a subject, then you'll have to learn how to sell yourself as authentic.

In this case, the marketer conceded that the non-disclosure of this activity made it difficult to justify (Emersen, cited in Cohen, 2011). This lack of disclosure *is* clearly at the core of what makes astroturfing unethical. Previously, similar activity has come under close scrutiny— not on the internet but on radio. In the 1990s, talkback radio was at the centre of what became known as the 'Cash for Comment' controversy and a subsequent government inquiry into talk-show hosts receiving money in exchange for favourable comments on air. What became clear in that inquiry was that the distinction between paid and non-paid airtime should be defined clearly, so that there could be no suggestion of impropriety.

Astroturfing also pushes the boundaries of legal acceptability. One legal analyst says that where astroturfing is undertaken around a commercial or trading activity/product, it would be considered misleading and deceptive under the *Competition and Consumer Act* (formerly the *Trade Practices Act*) and hence illegal. However, if it is outside of trade or commerce—such as within the political arena—then it would not be covered by Australian consumer law and would also be outside current Australian legislation that regulates truth or accuracy in political advertising (Hall, cited in Cohen, 2011).

The 'colonising' of social media in this way is undoubtedly widespread. One operator has created what he calls the 'Twitter bomb', which can take control of thousands of Twitter accounts to generate hundreds of thousands of fake messages (Cohen, 2011). What does all this mean for us in media relations? We know that the media follow Twitter, blogs and Facebook in determining public opinion and trends; it therefore follows that using social media within the bounds of legal and ethical activity must be part of our media strategy. As this practice becomes more pervasive and embedded, however, it may be tempting to cross the line—but common practice does not always make for good practice. As the saying goes, 'just because you can, doesn't mean you should'. This is reinforced at the professional level with both the PRIA and the Chartered Institute of Public Relations (CIPR) repudiating the practice of astroturfing as unethical and unacceptable, and as the ethical frameworks below outline, transparency is one of the core elements of ethical practice.

Most organisations now have social media polices and protocols for staff. Professional codes of practice and ethics—like the two discussed below—are increasingly including strategies and procedures for tweeting and using other online information channels, as well as more traditional modes of communication.

CORPORATE GOVERNANCE

The field of corporate governance deals with internal systems within an organisation which ensure that the organisation is run with competence, integrity and consideration of ethical standards and stakeholders. These days it is more important than ever that an organisation's public image reflects its internal practices and policies, because what goes on within an organisation is so often widely communicated outside the organisation. Scrutiny comes from all levels—staff (and former staff members), customers, clients, community members use social networking to talk and message about their likes, dislikes, concerns and so on. In addition, journalists are always after a good story. And, as many of the examples in this book show, many of these communications are connected. If practices within an organisation are not transparent, open and honest, media relations can find itself caught in the middle, as the media come to the person in this role to confirm speculation or rumour of impropriety, ethical or legal breaches, or lapses of judgement.

The role of media relations should not be underestimated in corporate governance. As the link between an organisation and the media, including the financial media, accurate and informed media communications is critical. Where companies have collapsed, and been found to have had poor corporate governance practices, media materials, including media releases, are often part of the problem, incorporating partial truths or total cover-ups.

Among the most famous global corporate governance collapses was the bankruptcy of energy trader Enron Corporation, one of America's largest companies with more than 20 000 employees, operating in 40 countries. Its lack of corporate governance was at the centre of its downfall.

> By utilising deceptive accounting practices, Enron was able to maintain an apparently healthy balance sheet. However the result was a mess of paper shuffling, false reports and insider trading. There were no internal safeguards to protect investors or employees . . . Enron's corporate governance model was too weak to prevent the problems from escalating. (McCoy, 2009, p. 128)

Since Enron, the Global Financial Crisis (GFC) has brought corporate governance into the global spotlight. Financial meltdowns on a massive scale have laid bare the poor governance practices of many organisations and governments. Corporate governance brings together ethical, legal, business and financial practices, all of which will contribute to a corporate culture that the media relations practitioner will be working within and should be contributing towards.

We now turn to an examination of the ethical frameworks of public relations and the news media by examining their codes of ethics.

TWO IMPORTANT CODES OF ETHICS

Trust, relationship-building, professional consideration and a general sense of fairness underpin the codes of ethics of Australian journalists in the MEAA Code of Ethics, and Australian media relations practitioners in the PRIA Code of Ethics. In determining the best ethical practice in media relations, it is worth taking a brief look at both these codes, identifying key points of intersection between the two professions. The MEAA twelve-point code begins with the following introduction:

> Respect for truth and the public's right to information are fundamental principles of journalism. Journalists describe society to itself. They convey information, ideas and opinions, a privileged role. They search, disclose, record, question, entertain, suggest and remember. They inform citizens and animate democracy. They give a practical form to freedom of expression. Many journalists work in private enterprise, but all have these public responsibilities. They scrutinise power, but also exercise it and should be accountable. Accountability engenders trust. Without trust, journalists do not fulfil their public responsibilities. Alliance members engaged in

journalism commit themselves to Honesty, Fairness, Independence, Respect for the rights of others. (MEAA, online)

The PRIA fifteen-point code begins with the introduction:

The Public Relations Institute of Australia is a professional body servicing the interests of its members. In doing so, the Institute is mindful of the responsibility which public relations professionals owe to the community as well as to their clients and employers. PRIA requires members to adhere to the highest standards of ethical practice and professional competence. All members are duty-bound to act responsibly and to be accountable for their actions. (PRIA, online)

The two introductions are very different, but have several key words in common:

- accountable (or accountability)
- responsible (or responsibility), and
- public.

These provide a useful starting point when considering the exchanges and relationships between the two professions, but let's delve deeper into the two codes to locate other commonalities (web addresses for the codes are available in the References section at the end of this book):

- fair (or fairness)
- honest (or honesty), and
- safeguard/respect confidences.

These are common words from the two codes of ethics. So far we have a combination of ethics that is accountable, responsible, public, fair, honest and safeguards confidences. If we dig even further, it becomes apparent that many of the guidance clauses also overlap in meaning, if not words:

PRIA: Members shall not knowingly disseminate false or misleading information and shall take care to avoid doing so inadvertently.

MEAA: Report and interpret honestly, striving for accuracy, fairness and disclosure of all essential facts. Do not suppress relevant available facts, or give distorting emphasis. Do your utmost to give a fair opportunity for reply.

PRIA: No member shall represent conflicting interests nor, without the consent of the parties concerned, represent competing interests.

MEAA: Disclose conflicts of interest that affect, or could be seen to affect, the accuracy, fairness or independence of your journalism. Do not improperly use a journalistic position for personal gain.

PRIA: Members shall be prepared to identify the source of funding of any public communication they initiate or for which they act as a conduit.

MEAA: Do your utmost to ensure disclosure of any direct or indirect payment made for interviews, pictures, information or stories.

These examples show how each profession, in achieving its goals, is based on similar fundamental ethical principles. The core values of the two professions overlap considerably when they are considered alongside each other. This may not be surprising when we remember that both are fields of professional communication. But where practices in the two professions diverge, ethical practice need not do so.

Lelde McCoy (2009) uses Seib and Fitzpatrick's five duties of public relations professionals—to yourself, your client, your employer, your profession and society—in establishing a framework for ethical practice. Your own values will guide your decisions based on right and wrong; your professional responsibilities must also be central, but ultimately society becomes the final component:

> Public relations practitioners must serve the public interest. In doing so, the practitioner needs to ask the question: 'Will my decision benefit society, even if I hurt myself, my client, my employer or my profession?' (2009, p. 113)

In both media and public relations ethics this duty to society and the public interest is ever-present.

CONCLUSION

Working within the law and ethically, while still supplying what the news (and other) media need, plus what our employer or advocacy group are aiming to achieve—all within tight deadlines and with an expectation of originality and flair—calls for a combination of skill, knowledge and dedication (and brilliance!). At times, legal and ethical decisions will be simple and the two areas will align, but sometimes they will be complex and may clash. It will be up to the media relations practitioner and adviser to make informed and professional choices. When in doubt, it will be prudent to check practices with a lawyer— such is the complexity and breadth of communications law.

5 WORKING WITH THE NEWS MEDIA

When working with people who are seeking to gain access to the news media, it is not uncommon to hear comments about 'getting the media to run a story'. Such comments reflect many misperceptions, as well as an ignorance of the way the news media work and how media relations professionals interact with this industry. When dealing with the news media, we need to remind ourselves that the media are first and foremost after news stories—they won't run a story just because we send them one. Sometimes we need to explain this to management.

This chapter provides some background on the nature of what constitutes news and how we can identify this in order to provide what the media need. It explains how media relations materials have become such a crucial part of the news diet, and provides some background on newsrooms, news workers (journalists, editors and producers) and common news practices. In working with the news media, we need to consider key conventions such as embargoes and scoops, and how best to prepare senior management or organisational spokespeople for media interviews. Media training is an important part of media relations, and one that will be needed if your organisation faces a crisis. The crisis situation—including how we can manage our relationship with the media in tough times—is also examined in this chapter.

KNOWING WHAT'S NEWS AND WHAT'S NOT

As we saw in Chapter 3, news doesn't just happen—it is created from the vast amount of daily activity on the planet, chosen by the news makers. In the process of making news, decisions are made at many different turns along the way. Certainly, some stories will become news by anyone's judgement—a bombing, calling an election, a major car crash or handing down a budget; these and stories like them are the breaking news stories discussed below. Even as breaking news, they will be handled and framed differently by different media. But a great many other stories fall into the 'maybe' category. Whether they get a run or not will depend on many things—the most noteworthy of them being the 'news hole' of the day—that is, how much space there is for news, and what other news is competing for that space.

For practical purposes, news may be categorised into 'breaking' or 'routine' varieties. For our purposes here, we can further divide it into three groups:

- routine
- staged, and
- spontaneous.

The role of the media relations practitioner is crucial at all these levels. Take, for example, the communications that emerge out of a natural disaster—a spontaneous news event. Crisis communications are critical not only before a natural disaster in terms of planning and preparation, but also during a natural disaster with regard to communication and following the event. At a time of natural disaster, the media can:

- assist in preparation for a pending disaster (for example, through bulletins of strategies to protect property and life and when to evacuate)
- encourage calm during and after the disaster (for example, by advising about evacuation routes and procedures during a bushfire or flood)
- assist with the mobilisation of a community (for example, to move people from flood or fire-affected areas), and

- mobilise a relief force (for example, to call for volunteers to assist with clearing debris after a flood, fire or earthquake).

Of course, all these messages must be controlled, and it is the role of the media relations manager, along with the social media manager—perhaps within a state or local government department or as part of the police or fire brigade—to manage the message. While natural disasters generally cannot be predicted, crisis communications procedures for dealing with the media should be set in place as part of a crisis-management plan. Later in the chapter, we will look at working with the media in crises.

Routine news will usually require, at some point, the management of information for the media. Routine news comes from police, courts, local government, federal and state parliament, and so on. Generally speaking, these events are part of the workings of society, although it is clear that some of them—such as some political activity—are undertaken specifically for the media's benefit and will require organisation during the process. They may therefore have elements of staged news.

Staged, or overtly managed, news or events always require information management, and generally allow the media relations practitioner time to plan and orchestrate how events will occur. Staged events, such as the visit to Australia and New Zealand by Queen Elizabeth in 2011, was news for weeks before she arrived. Then, after her arrival, dozens more stories were reported. Of course, these three categories of news are not all cocooned in discrete compartments of the media diet. Often media conferences (staged events) will emerge out of a spontaneous event, such as those that followed the Japanese tsunami and nuclear disaster of 2011. Or staged events will merge with routine news—take, for example, Barack Obama's visit to Australia following the APEC meeting in 2011. The challenge to media relations is to react to the needs of the time, with careful advance planning and thought. Media conferences are discussed in detail in Chapter 9.

NEWS VALUES AND GATEKEEPING

Knowing how media workers prioritise news can assist with determining what is news and what is not. Part of a journalist being able to locate a good news story is their capacity to have a 'news instinct' or 'a nose for news'. But what leads them to the story? Can you break down the criteria for news versus not news? The answer is usually yes. News stories generally include a range of criteria or 'news values'. While there is no absolute list of news values, the main ones are:

- impact
- conflict
- timeliness
- proximity
- prominence
- currency
- human interest
- the unusual/novelty
- money.

To this list we could add the 'fair go' and the 'tall poppy' value, because the media often focus on these two extremes of justice and injustice. Moreover in television, news vision is a virtual prerequisite so we should therefore add this to TV news values. The idea of news values was first proposed by Galtung and Ruge in 1965; they suggested twelve news values to explain how media in different countries prioritised news. These days, some scholars say that news values are no longer a valid way to view news; nevertheless, we can find them useful to help us examine the daily news diet and try to determine whether or not a story will make news.

Let's take the news values from a series of breaking stories from one day in the online version of *The Australian* (3 November 2011), a day that led with the following headlines:

'Coalition blasts Julia Gillard's pledge of more aid to IMF to help avert Eurozone crisis': This was a story about the Coalition's response to the Australian prime minister's offer to assist with the financial problems in Europe. News values are conflict, money, impact and currency.

'US port shut down by occupy protesters': Three thousand protesters had shut down the Port of Oakland in the United States as part of the 'Occupy' demonstrations. News values are conflict, impact and currency.

'Klimt landscape fetches US$40 million': A painting by German artist Gustav Klimt sells for almost US$40 million after being returned to the family of the painter. News values are money, human interest and prominence.

'Supporters of Julian Assange have rallied as he faces extradition to Sweden': Members of Assange's legal team consider their options after a British High Court orders his extradition to Sweden. News values are prominence, conflict and underdog.

'Hubby fed wife steroids to keep her home': A court story of a man who secretly gave his wife ground-up steroids to make her fat and keep her at home to do domestic duties. News values are human interest, novelty and conflict.

You'll notice that in all but one of these, conflict is a news value. News often requires an adversarial approach to a story just as bad news is more common than good news. Two politicians battling it out over a policy, a corporate chief arguing with the union, police and court stories that include violence or injury, celebrity breakups—these are all based on conflict and the news media can't get enough of it.

Which stories will run and their prominence is determined by the media organisation's gatekeepers, as discussed in Chapter 3. Gate-keeping is a concept that goes hand in hand with news values. If you visualise a person standing at a gate letting some things in and shutting the gate to keep some things out (in this case, the 'things' are media releases, story ideas, and so on), then you will easily understand the gatekeeper role. Gatekeepers are senior staff in the newsroom—a news editor in a newspaper or producer in television—who decide on the daily news lineup. It is an important part of media relations to know who the gatekeepers are—who makes the decisions about the news agenda, which stories will be chosen, where they will run and how. Influential bloggers and tweeters are also gatekeepers, so we can apply this approach across a range of news media, as discussed in more detail in Chapter 13.

NEWS THEMES

One of the reasons why the media rely on sources is because of the construction of 'news themes'. These allow events and issues to be categorised, sorted and developed into a series of stories. This, in turn, means that media rely on other media as well as different sources, day after day, to perpetuate the theme. The daily cross-referencing between newspapers and broadcast media, and their additional scanning of social media sites, clearly illustrates how news follows themes. As Fishman explains: 'The consequence of news is more news' (1980, p. 11). A 'news cycle' refers to the media reporting on an issue or event and the responses and reactions to it. News themes emerge out of this through follow-up stories. In these days of the 24-hour news cycle—in which news is available on demand around the clock—the opportunity to update and develop news stories is more available than ever.

News themes provide opportunities to make news for your own organisation and turn your competitor's bad luck to your favour. Take, for example, the Qantas crisis in late 2011 when the whole airline fleet was grounded by management following a series of strikes by Qantas staff. The crisis had already developed into a news theme—ongoing over several days with dozens of stories—when Virgin Australia took control of the news agenda. The timing could not have been better for the airline, having recently been re-branded under a uniform 'Virgin Australia' banner to better compete with Qantas. A *Sydney Morning Herald* headline several days after the Qantas grounding read: 'Virgin basks in the glow as brand Qantas crashes and burns', and the story ran like this:

> Virgin Australia's boss, John Borghetti, said today that the grounding of Qantas's fleet for two days showed the need for a 'strong second carrier'. Mr Borghetti, who chose his words carefully at a business lunch in Sydney today, said some of the passengers who had switched to Virgin during the Qantas grounding would 'stick'. He conceded that Qantas's predicament presented an 'opportunity' on which his airline could capitalise . . . 'Virgin Australia reacted very, very quickly and made sure Australia kept moving,' he said. (O'Sullivan, 2011)

Some news themes stay in the media for extended periods of time, and these can provide ample opportunities to comment or supply updates. They show how 'currency'—meaning an ongoing and current issue—is one of the news values that has a great deal of traction. For example, throughout 2010 and 2011 two of the main news themes were asylum seekers and climate change. Another issue that emerged as a news theme was the 'Occupy' rallies around the globe, protesting capitalism.

Where there's a division of opinion, or conflict, news is much more likely to stay high on the news agenda and remain a news theme. Former federal press secretary and communications specialist Lachlan Harris explained how this works at the 2011 Public Relations Institute of Australia annual conference: 'The opinion cycle is not based on facts. The new reality is that it's the debate that keeps the story running.' Harris said the best way to get media coverage was 'to start an argument' and that 'opinion needs debate and argument to continue' (Harris, 2011). Others agree with this trend. UK journalism commentator Ian Jack summed it up like this: 'Comment is cheap but facts are rather expensive' (2006, p. viii). It is no coincidence that these changes have occurred as newsrooms have scaled back their journalist numbers. Cutbacks to journalism staff have occurred in major newspaper groups and broadcast outlets since the rise of the internet and the relative 'free' access to news and information.

ROLES IN THE NEWSROOM

The best way to gain an understanding of newsrooms is to visit one and see it for yourself. In the meantime, we will go through the newsroom and its structure here. Knowing who does what in the newsroom makes it easier for the media relations practitioner to do two things: maximise access to media channels and establish positive working relationships and contact with specific journalists.

THE EDITOR

The editor in a print newsroom or director of news in a broadcast newsroom is the senior editorial role in the hierarchy, and is the link between the newsroom and management.

CHIEF OF STAFF/NEWS EDITOR/DIRECTOR OF NEWS

The chief of staff or news editor is usually responsible for the day-to-day running of a newspaper newsroom, making sure that all stories are covered.

SUB-EDITOR

Known as 'subs', these people are responsible for the story editing, layout, headlines and completion of a newspaper.

PRODUCER

The producer of a TV news program or a radio news/talkback/current affairs program is responsible for the news lineup, preparing interviews, researching backgrounds, and so on.

PHOTO EDITOR (CHIEF PHOTOGRAPHER)

This person is responsible for the allocation of photographers for news stories and selecting photographs from the wire services.

SECTION EDITOR

The role of the section editor is to oversee each section and make sure pages are filled with the latest news or features in that area—for example, sport, arts or travel.

JOURNALIST/REPORTER OR ROUNDSPERSON

Journalists will often have a specialty area known as a 'round' (or 'beat' in the United States), which they cover on a regular basis using established contacts.

If you work in a particular industry, like politics, motoring, sports, fashion or education, you will get to know the journalists who cover these stories. In these cases, you would stay in touch them and often advise them about stories informally. If you don't know the journalists

Figure 5.1 Newsroom hierarchy

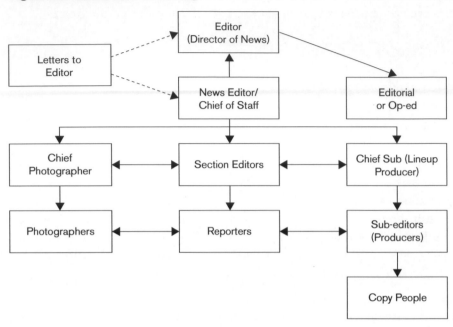

or need to spread your message more broadly, you would be best to approach the news editor in a newspaper or the director of news in television or radio. The titles as expressed above may vary a little, but the most important point to take from this is that you should pitch your story to the right level.

MEDIA LISTS

When sending media releases and other materials out to the media, it is necessary to draw from an up-to-date database of names, usually referred to as a media list. Media lists are composed of the media in specific fields, whether this is a local area, based on a region, city or state, or a list of specialised writers such as those working for a specialist newspaper section, magazine or TV program like politics, sport, motoring, fashion or education. The database that you compile will be unique to your organisation because you will set it up and include names that are most useful to you. For this reason purpose-made media lists are very important to an organisation. They should all include:

- correct name spelling
- correct title
- correct mail/email address
- correct phone numbers, and
- deadlines for the publication.

In compiling a media list, you will probably need to draw from a range of references known generically as 'media guides'. These are professionally collated guides, updated several times a year, that list full details of media in Australia and internationally. Among the best known and most commonly used are *Margaret Gee's Australian Media Guide* and *Media Monitors Media Directory*, both of which list details for all media in separate sections. Provided you can access such guides, you can draw from them to collate your own database, using these to update but also through regular phone calls and web checks. As tiresome as this might seem, it is never wasted time to ensure that your information is up to date. Getting a name wrong or a title incorrect can cause irreparable damage to your reputation. Usually Excel spreadsheets are used when compiling media lists. In addition to your own lists, you will be likely to use a distribution service at times. Distribution services and targeting are discussed in Chapter 7.

DEADLINES

Deadlines have become more difficult to navigate since the advent of the internet. Since newsrooms can now update their online material throughout the day, it might seem that it doesn't matter when you send in your material—but this is not the case.

Most newsrooms still have a morning media conference, when they plan their daily news lineup, whether it's an evening TV news bulletin or a newspaper. The news cycle still exists. It is therefore best to send material to all daily media outlets as soon as you arrive at the office in the morning. If you send releases or statements early enough, the news outlet will have time to follow it up that day (although for morning radio, last thing at night is usually best). You will then need to work to their deadline in providing an interview, photos or some other follow-up.

If you are using social media as well as news media, be aware that news media monitor much of what goes on in social media; so ensure you send your announcement to the news media at the same time that you tweet or blog it. The news media may or may not choose to follow up a story that's already 'out there'.

Deadlines are an extremely important part of the media's daily routine, and these should be respected. Professionals in every industry value their time, but none more so than a person who has to fill a news hole every day with new material. When dealing with magazines or TV or radio programs that are produced in advance, such as lifestyle programs, or the lift-out sections of the weekend papers, you will need to know the special deadlines and requirements of each. Nothing substitutes for personal communication in establishing what might be needed and when it is needed by.

MEDIA CONVENTIONS

There are many conventions and protocols that underpin the way a newsroom is run, how news is gathered and published, and how journalists work with their sources. We saw in Chapter 3 how important sources are to the production of news, but to be considered valuable and reliable, the source must be aware of certain procedures and practices. In many cases, the news source will know media workers personally—especially in smaller or regional locations, or on specialist publications or media programs when it is common to deal with the same journalist regularly. Getting to know journalists personally is a huge advantage in media relations for several reasons:

- You can establish your credibility as a serious professional.
- It allows you to approach a journalist as a 'contact' rather than going through more circuitous channels.

- You can develop what is known as a 'trust bank', which enables you to build credits should you need to deal with a journalist in an emergency or crisis.

DEVELOPING A 'TRUST BANK'

The idea of sourcing stories and citing 'authorised knowers' was discussed in Chapter 3. It can be hugely beneficial to put in some groundwork with the media, as with any other public, to establish a mutually beneficial relationship. In keeping with these ideas is the concept that we must work *with* the media to get a story across.

Veteran public relations academic Al Golin outlined this need for established relationships in his early discussion of the idea of the 'trust bank'. It applies to all publics, including the media:

> We coined the term 'trust bank' to describe programmes designed to demonstrate caring by means of community involvement. Our theory was that 'good works' represent 'deposits' of trust on which consumers would be willing to pay interest in the form of respect and patronage. These same 'deposits,' we believe, would serve us well should 'withdrawals' be needed down the line when tough times or sensitive issues hit. (Golin, 2002)

Golin identifies that there is one central tenet in establishing relationships: 'Trust bank programmes are important, but all the good will in the world can be swept away in an instant when you are revealed to be a liar. Trust is hard to earn and easy to lose!' This idea should be considered in a very real sense when we talk about working with the news media.

SCOOPS AND DUMPS

The idea of the 'exclusive' or scoop story is one that appeals to journalists. For the media relations practitioner, there are some important principles to consider in providing scoops:

- If a journalist comes to you with a story, seeking clarification or comment, it should generally be considered 'their story', even if you see it as providing broader coverage if you were to circulate it to other media.

• If you approach the news media, it is up to you to decide whether to provide your story exclusively to one journalist (or media organisation) or to a range of media organisations.

Certain media outlets or journalists are known to be media leaders, and they can set the general media agenda. If you send out a release on a controversial topic, it can be wise to choose your media carefully, knowing that they will give it fair and thorough coverage. By doing this, the story can be 'broken' with greater control and it will already be in the news by the time the rest of the media gain access to it. Alternatively, if you want to achieve widespread coverage of a story, it may be in your best interest to send it to as many journalists as possible. However, when sending a release to multiple journalists make sure that you have only the intended recipient's name on the release, otherwise journalists will see the release as 'spam' and will be reluctant to run it.

Davis (1999) discusses two approaches to getting news out—particularly bad news. The first is known as the 'document dump'. This is based on a bad news story that is about to break. He argues: 'Better that we put the story out ourselves, with plenty of opportunity to answer questions and to characterize the documents favorably, or at least accurately.' While this advice dates back some time it is especially relevant today when stories are more likely than ever to leak into social media. Breaking your own story provides you with greater control. Document dumps, where vast amounts of material are released at once in the hope that much of it will be buried, are discussed further in Chapter 13 when we look at citizen journalists.

The second approach Davis describes as 'the selective placement of certain stories and hot documents with a particular news organization'. This is known as a 'predicate story'. He describes it like this:

The predicate story ideally must be comprehensive and contain all the facts, good and bad. As such, it will become the foundation block for all other reporters and for all future reporting . . . By its very nature, a predicate story takes time to investigate and time to write, and thus does not lend itself to the competitive pressures and imminent deadlines that are inevitable when there is a general release to all news organizations. That is why it is necessary to select a single reporter or news organization to help generate such a story. (Davis, 1999)

In this case, key media that are identified as media agenda-setters would be approached. A study by Pearson and Brand identified the media agenda-setters as AAP, some newspapers and public radio broadcasters ABC and SBS, while other outlets such as free-to-air television, commercial radio, magazines, the internet and pay TV were seen as less important (Pearson and Brand, 2001, p. 8). Media selection is therefore clearly a strategic move. In reality, the journalists who you feel you can trust to handle stories fairly will likely be the ones you will approach.

NO COMMENT

This response to a media inquiry might seem like a simple way out of a conversation you don't want to have, but nothing could be further from the truth. Journalists love a challenge and they will locate their own version of 'the truth' and fill in the gaps to stories in the absence of the facts. Therefore, the answer of 'no comment' can do much more harm than good, and actually foster rumours. If a journalist seeks a comment from you or your organisation over a contentious issue, there are many more productive things to say:

- 'Leave it with me and I'll get a comment from the CEO.'
- 'I will look into it and get back to you.'
- 'That's all I am allowed to say at the moment because this issue is being investigated; however, I'll let you know as soon as there are more details available.'

All these comments really say very little; however, they all give a response that shows you are on side with the media. But remember that all of these comments should be followed up by the promise they offer—in other words, you should 'get back' to the media who have made the inquiry. Sometimes, a time lag will allow you to better prepare the response rather than offering one unprepared. This is a tactic used by politicians, who will often defer media inquiries through the day to an afternoon media conference in order to consider responses to questions that have been asked earlier and prepare their answers. This enables carefully considered responses that are on the record and available to all media.

EMBARGOES

These should be used sparingly and only when necessary. An embargo means holding a story until a certain understood time. They are used if you want to alert the media to an up-and-coming event or announcement, but do not yet want coverage. The date and time of the embargo should clearly be identified at the top of the media release. Embargoes are useful to both the media relations practitioner and the journalist because they can allow information to be distributed and the journalist to read and understand the information prior to publication of a story. In this way, complex information—such as budget announcements—may be accessed by the media, read and understood before the embargo is lifted.

Similarly, embargoes are used when announcements are made in advance of an event, such as the Archibald Prize or Academy Award winners, to allow the media to have a story ready to publish once the announcement has been made. This means the media can get the story out quickly without breaching the confidence of the organisation making the announcement. The immediacy and pervasiveness of internet news and social media make embargoes more and more challenging, and care must be taken to ensure embargoes are adhered to by all staff members and there are no slip-ups with early publication. Such a slip-up occurred at the Queensland Premier's Literary Awards in 2011 when a media release announced in advance who had *not won* one of the key awards and, in the absence of a clear embargo, details were published online prior to the awards ceremony. The *Sydney Morning Herald* later reported:

Queensland Premier Anna Bligh has apologised after her office 'jumped the gun' by releasing the winners of her literary awards early . . . On Twitter, Ms Bligh said the early media release was issued in error. 'Apologies to all—we accidentally jumped the gun on Literary Awards,' she wrote. (Hurst, 2011)

Social media may have been used for an apology in this instance, but social media also make embargoes very tricky. You need to have very good security within your organisation to ensure news is not leaked.

MEDIA IN A CRISIS

The Queensland premier's response might make it seem that a mistake can be fixed by a Twitter apology, but it is not always so simple. Crisis communications is the field of public relations that requires immediate and strategic responses on behalf of an organisation when a crisis happens. Ideally, crisis communications plans will be compiled and kept up to date *before* a crisis erupts. The Scouts' motto 'be pre-pared' pays off when things go wrong if you have a plan in place and staff have practised crisis responses. For senior management, this might involve media training, discussed below, while for other staff it might involve simple instructions on how to pass media inquiries on to the media/public relations department. Crises come in all shapes and sizes. Examples might include:

- a plane crash
- a bomb threat
- product tampering and extortion threats
- a strike
- a flood, cyclone or other natural disaster
- terrorism
- a leadership challenge
- a company scandal.

It is of utmost importance that media receive information quickly and clearly if you want to keep them as allies in a crisis. This can help with the resolution of the crisis. Register and Larkin (2008) explain a case in which a pet food manufacturer had received an extortion threat where the media agreed to 'hold off' coverage of the story: 'In exchange, we would hold regular press briefings to keep reporters up to date with developments . . . there were no legal sanctions . . . no legal reasons to prevent them' (2008, p. 193). Nevertheless, the media did 'hold off' reporting, the extortionist was captured and the story eventually was run.

Generally, there are three golden rules to remember when working with the media in crisis situations:

1. Tell the truth.
2. Tell it fast.
3. Tell it all.

Sometimes, you can't do all three at once—for example, if there has been injury or death caused by the crisis, relatives of those involved should not hear about the crisis via the media. It is therefore crucial that internal relations runs alongside media relations to inform relatives of the tragedy. Once relatives have been notified, the media should be informed immediately.

The media will usually be looking for specific information, either from the scene of the crisis or from the organisational announcements via media conference, release or statement. They will want answers and they will want them quickly. Among the list of what they will most likely need are:

- details of who, what, where, when, why and how
- a clear, articulate spokesperson
- access to the site and eyewitnesses, and
- a reliable point of contact—available 24/7. (McLean, 2011)

Some crises will make access very difficult, such as a crime site that may be cordoned off, or an underground mine accident; others will be simpler to arrange where access is not an issue. It is important to meet the needs of the media as quickly as possible. If you want to stay in control of the situation, you have to be one step ahead—with a clear head. Social media will spread like wildfire where a crisis is concerned, and the need for speed in internet news means it may be posted first and checked afterwards. So you'll need not only to continue to keep information flowing, but to monitor online media for inaccuracies that will need rectifying.

You should consider all media options to get information out and in. Twitter can be used to provide brief messages and to link back to the organisational website or 'landing page'—where you can ensure that there is comprehensive and regularly updated material available. Online media centres should be easy to navigate, and updated media releases, statements and fact sheets should be posted so they are easily located. One option is to develop a 'dark site' that is ready to activate if and when a crisis occurs. This enables an organisation to build the site in advance and make it unavailable until it is needed. Another tactic is to hold regular press conferences, as described in the pet food example above. This will allow all the media to hear the news at the same time. Chances are the first news will be tweeted from the conference, followed by fuller accounts in radio, television and print.

The shift to multiple media platforms now makes breaking the news extremely competitive, and presents both benefits and challenges for the public relations professional. One positive example is the way in which the Brisbane City Council used social media—in particular Twitter and Facebook—to galvanise the community to action during the 2011 floods. The news media used social media to inform its stories and so the cycle of information benefited the whole community (as discussed in Chapter 13).

Alternatively, the 'United Breaks Guitars' incident in 2009 resulted in a major crisis for United Airlines in the United States, after singer Dave Carroll sought compensation for his broken guitar (apparently broken by baggage handlers). When he did not receive an appropriate response from the airline, he posted his now-famous YouTube musical video, which became a mainstream story across all media and now has more than 11 million views. This showed the power of social media not *in* a crisis, but instead *creating* a crisis for the airline. Since that time, organisations have become much more savvy about the damage that can be done via social media by disgruntled customers. Once an issue goes viral on social media, and the news media pick it up as news—and they usually do—the crisis is compounded. Clearly then, both in crisis situations (the floods) and in dispute or complaint situations (the guitar), social media and traditional media must both be recognised for their impact.

Media conferences, websites, media releases and statements, as well as social media, are all discussed in more detail in later chapters.

MEDIA TRAINING

Part of crisis management is making sure your organisational spokespeople know how to manage media interviews. 'Media training' refers to specialised coaching on the best way to deal with inquiries from the media. It gives senior personnel a greater understanding of how the media works, and equips them with tools that will help turn media encounters into positive results. Where executive training is delivered by an external service provider—and there are many public relations firms and media training agencies staffed by former journalists, media advisers and PR experts—you can expect to pay around $4000 to $5000 per day for small-group full-day training sessions where a TV camera is used to dissect interviews and provide feedback (Sullivan, 2012). For those executives who previously have conducted a media training course, it is recommended that they undertake a refresher course every couple of years.

The purpose of media training is to ensure that those who might come into contact with the media are comfortable working with interviews, equipment and pressure. The training needs to be rigorous to replicate real-life, on-the-spot media interviews. Prior to the training workshops, the training provider will research issues surrounding either the company or the industry, and use these to create a scene for the day. One major mining organisation several years ago hired a well-known journalist to conduct one-on-one interviews—he was so realistic in his training that one member of the senior personnel refused to continue the training session and walked out of the interview.

DEVELOP A CULTURE—THE MEDIA ARE NOT OUT TO GET YOU

It is almost certain that, at some time in your career, you will be required to provide some media training—either formally in workshop environments or informally as the need arises. The need for media training extends beyond the senior executive down the ranks to staff members such as receptionists, front-of-house managers and line staff. Your organisation should have a media relations policy in place where all staff are aware of the need to treat all media inquiries with respect and a calm attitude. All employees of your organisation should be counselled that the media are not out to get you, they are just after a good story. The procedure will go along the lines of:

- We never say 'No Comment'.
- Explain to the media representative that you are not in a position to discuss the matter; however, you will find someone who is. At this point, contact the public relations manager or their nominee immediately.
- If the media team come into your office/shop/warehouse with their camera already filming, don't walk away or put your hand up; instead, calmly ask the journalist and crew to take a seat and tell them that you will find someone to assist them. Politely ask them to turn off their camera while they are waiting.
- It is at this point that the media relations executive will come out to meet the journalist and crew. Introduce yourself and find out their story needs; you should also ask who else they have spoken to and what they said. You will then make a decision as to whether your executives are in a position to do the interview straight away or whether you need to schedule another time for the interview. The latter is extremely likely, depending on the availability of the key executive. Ask the journalist what their deadline is and do your best to organise an interview for this time. In most instances, if the journalist wants the story they will be prepared to wait a reasonable amount of time. However, if they feel that you are trying to cover something up, it is likely that this will be mentioned in the story and possibly reflect badly on your organisation. (Sullivan, 2012)

FIRST PORT OF CALL WHEN THE MEDIA COME CALLING

The above example falls into the category of 'worst case scenario', which will be a distinct possibility if journalists suspect the company has something to hide. Most journalists will telephone first. Whatever way you are confronted by the media, the basic rules remain the same:

- Be as polite and as cooperative as possible.
- Be available. Journalists work shifts, so late evening or early morning availability might be required.
- Don't stand between the journalist and your CEO.
- Know your organisation. Know the key managers. Be up to date and understand policies and attitudes on important issues.
- Be a reliable source of information.
- Don't slant the facts or tell only half of the story.
- Never provide false information or repeat facts or opinions that have come to you second hand. (Sullivan, 2012)

KEY MESSAGES

Once you have established the objective of the interview, you and your senior executives should craft your key messages. These are simple and relevant truths that leave a positive impression as well as being a useful refuge in a stressful or aggressive interview. Your key messages should be concise ideas, points and impressions that you want your target audience to remember.

Your key messages should not be presented to journalists as a dot-pointed list of facts. Remember that the media's goal is to inform *and* entertain. You need to focus on making these points interesting by supporting the key messages with facts, anecdotes and examples. One of the easiest ways to do this naturally is to use the word 'because'; this not only allows you to elaborate on your key messages, it can also be used to tie your messages together.

ANSWERING THE QUESTIONS

All of the journalist's questions should be answered, using the following strategy:

- Communicate your key message.
- Back up with credible evidence.
- Share some examples, facts or analogies.
- If necessary, provide background information that supports the key message as well as answering the question.

Sometimes a journalist will ask questions that cannot easily be answered with your key messages. The best technique is to guide the interview down a middle path where the journalist's questions are answered at the same time as your key messages are communicated. International public relations company Fleishman Hillard suggests that interviews can be summed up as 'A=Q+1'. By this they are recommending answering the question *plus* adding one key message (Fleishman-Hillard, 2001).

Your training should cover how to deflect negative or aggressive questions and bring the topic back to your message. A common media training tactic is the use of 'bridging and blocking', when used with key messages can be summed up by an ABC formula:

- Answer the question.
- Bridge or block as needed.
- Communicate the key message.

Some bridging and blocking examples include:

'You're right, it is serious . . . but we shouldn't forget . . .'
'What's most important is . . .'
'The real issue here is . . .'
'That's an important point because . . .'

Politicians generally are masters of this, but there is a fine line between getting your message across and sounding too rehearsed, too controlled and too scripted. The result can be not getting your message across at all because the interview might be scrapped. So, while staying on message is important, it is also crucial to remember that the media will use what is newsworthy when they are selecting a grab or a few quotes. This will all depend on the context, the topic, the speaker and, of course, the news themes of the day—but remember to choose words that are strong, powerful and precise to get messages across while avoiding personal attacks. The best answer is a complete, brief response that can stand alone—this is what television, in particular, is looking for; ideally 15 seconds for television, which is about 40–45 words. Short, pithy answers also provide a quick 'grab' for radio or quotable-quote for print and online. Answers or statements are most likely to be used if they use the three C's of interviewing:

- Concise—keep your message on target and keep it short.
- Conversational—keep your message clear and easily undertstood.
- Catchy—say your message cleverly.

Some senior managers are born communicators, who work instinctively with the media—those who present as unflustered, in control, never defensive. Others are more likely to freeze, get flustered or defensive, or even aggressive. The latter group are more likely to go off topic, lose their key message—or use it so blatantly to render it unusable by the news media—or lose control of the interview if they are placed under pressure. Consider personality types, voice resonance, general appearance and demeanour, and quick-wittedness when choosing which of your senior personnel would be the best spokespeople. Watch programs like the ABC television's 'Q&A' to see people in action and under pressure so you know what makes a good and poor performance in interviews and public speaking scenarios.

CURLY QUESTIONS

Sometimes questions are phrased—often deliberately—in a way that makes them difficult to answer with a positive message. Following is a series of such questions which have been framed around a scenario in which a spokesperson for the Greatest-Ever Music (GEM) concerts is being interviewed prior to the launch of this year's big event. Using these question types, develop another scenario and practise your own media training exercise, conducting videoed interviews which can then be analysed for performance.

IRRELEVANCE

A question that has no bearing on your agenda . . . perhaps not even on your area of expertise or the stated focus of the interview.

Solution: Block the questions and bridge to a relevant point.

Reporter: Concerns over the safety of outdoor concerts have been under focus in recent weeks after the disaster with 'Big Band' in England. Can you comment on how you think that was handled?

GEM: Safety is paramount in our planning. We are proud of our track record on safety and, as always, we will be using the best facilities available to ensure the concert goes without incident—this will include trained security guards, barricades, bag inspections and we will be working with local police both inside and outside the venue.

SPECULATION

The reporter asks you to predict the future or address a hypothetical situation.

Solution: Don't play this game unless the answer is a positive message for you. Block the question and bridge to a relevant point.

Reporter: What if any of the bands don't adhere to the regulations and bring drugs into the venue?

GEM: We have no reason to think that will happen. We have briefings with all the band managers in advance of the concert and we have clear guidelines for everyone—including the bands.

A OR B DILEMMA

Reporter asks you to choose between two or more options or scenarios.

Solution: Same as above. Don't choose unless it benefits you. As always, make a positive out of a negative. Block the question and bridge to a relevant point.

Reporter: Noise levels are always an issue. Will local residents just have to cop it sweet or do you have an alternative option for dealing with the noise?

GEM: We take noise regulations very seriously. Many of the locals will attend the concert—our research shows that local residents either love walking to the event to take part or are happy to enjoy a 'free' concert at home.

ABSENT PARTY PLOY

The reporter attempts to create controversy by getting you to lock horns with an adversary.

Solution: Most often this is unproductive, can distract from your major points and make you seem petty. Even if it is appropriate for you to question the goals or tactics of an adversary, do not appear mean-spirited.

Reporter: The Silver City Council has always opposed the concert on various grounds—they say your event is a bad influence on the community's youth. What's your response?

GEM: We work with all the interested parties to ensure the event presents the least possible disruption and best outcomes for the whole community. We'll be doing that in Silver City as always and we've invited the Mayor and her family as out special guests.

LOADED PREFACE

The question begins with a premise that is negative or incorrect.

Solution: Correct the inaccuracy, or else you will be tacitly agreeing with it. However, state your correction in a positive way, without repeating the falsehood or slur.

Reporter: Given GEM lost money last year, how many more years is the event viable?

GEM: Actually, we broke even last year and made a profit in the previous two years. Ticket sales are on track to put us back into a really positive financial position and we've also introduced new merchandise which we believe will be a great hit this year.

MACHINE GUN QUESTIONING

This is an issue of pacing, rather than actual wording. The reporter asks a series of rapid-fire questions, perhaps not waiting for you to finish your responses.

Solution: Set your own pace, taking sufficient time to think. As an equal participant in the interview, you can answer questions as slowly as you wish, regardless of the reporter's pace.

Source: Adapted from Fleishman-Hillard Media Training Manual, <www.appa-net.org/eweb/Resources/National_Branding/AFORCE_ MediaTrainingManual.pdf>.

Also be mindful that at times journalists will take a media interview into a totally different direction than planned. The Commonwealth Games bid case study in the next chapter illustrates this. In such instances it is crucial that the media relations practitioner has anticipated questions that may come from 'left field' and briefed the interviewee so he or she is not taken completely by surprise. This is where issues management and anticipating the media agenda will be of great importance to the media relations professional.

CONCLUSION

Working with the news media can be a hugely rewarding job; however, the media relations professional needs to be knowledgeable and informed about media practices to achieve the best outcomes in this relationship. There are many key issues that must be remembered, such as knowing how to identify news values and news themes, and making the most of these, knowing who to approach with a news story and how to apply deadlines. Certain conventions and protocols, such as working with embargoes and dealing with crises, will require careful attention by not only media relations staff but all others in the organisation. It is likely that you will need to either undertake media training of key staff, or be able to facilitate this with a specialist trainer. This will ensure your key senior management are able to manage media interviews and get their key points across as effectively as possible.

6 MEDIA RELATIONS CAMPAIGNS

In their simplest form, media relations campaigns consist of a series of media-oriented tactics aimed at achieving set goals and objectives. The media are always a primary stakeholder, and generally the goals and objectives include the publishing or broadcasting of your key messages in order to reach targeted publics or stakeholder groups. Such messages can be as broad as providing information on health and safety in crisis situations, motivating commuters to use public transport rather than driving, change or reinforce perspectives of a holiday destination, engage public support in a nationwide police search for a missing child or altering the perceptions of a political candidate. Media relations campaigns encompass many of the tactics outlined in other chapters of this book. Among the most popular tactics are the staging of media conferences, writing and distributing media releases and kits (this also includes social media releases), developing dedicated media centres on organisational websites, and the use of photography and videography. Careful selection, targeting and ultimate placement of these tactics, coupled with the ability to deliver information when the media need it, is what will set the good media relations practitioner apart.

Media campaigns are often part of an overall public relations campaign or program, and they will just as often be used in conjunction with other forms of communication such as social marketing or advertising, sponsorship or events. Smith (2002, p. 10) defines public relations campaigns as 'systematic sets of public relations activities each with a specific and finite purpose, sustained over a length of time and dealing with objectives associated with a specific issue'. Media relations needs to fall within this definition—with specific purposes and clear objectives in mind. Sometimes direct approaches to the media are the best way to achieve this; at other times, a social networking conversation will alert the media to an issue, or the media will seek information from your website or you directly. A strategic approach can garner positive publicity, deflect negative coverage or in some way inform, educate or motivate behaviour via the best media channels. But to be most effective, you need to have a plan. You can use a range of approaches to work through your planning and execution of media campaigns.

PROCESS MODELS

One of the more traditional approaches to developing campaigns is known as the RACE model (Marston, 1963), which calls for:

R   Research
A   Action
C   Communication
E   Evaluation.

This is a tried and true formula, which suggests four distinct stages. As the field of public relations developed and matured, the ROPE model evolved, with the setting of objectives as an early part of the campaign (Hendrix, 1998):

R   Research
O   Objectives
P   Performance
E   Evaluation.

Others have developed this model, with Kelly (2001) suggesting that 'stewardship' should be added to makes ROPES. Stewardship includes 'reciprocity, responsibility, reporting and relationship nurturing' (2001, p. 279). Kelly argues that adding stewardship 'ensures that the public relationship process is continuous; it does not stop and then start with entirely different and unknown publics' (2001, p. 281). She says this makes the public relations process truly cyclical. In effect, this element is all about looking after the publics that are already engaged with an organisation, such as donors who provide funds, investors who own shares, or members of the media with whom a relationship already exists. As such, we would see stewardship as central to effective media relations—indeed, it underpins this entire book.

More recently, Stacks (2011) developed ERASE as a mnemonic; this provides a circular approach to developing campaigns. This is valuable in public relations, as evaluation feeds back into the process and informs either the ongoing existing campaign or the next one. This formula is based on:

E   Evaluation
R   Research
A   Action
S   Strategy
E   Evaluation.

Essentially, though, Stacks notes that most approaches follow a four-step model, which:

1. defines the problem
2. states the campaign's objectives
3. creates a campaign that meets the objectives, and
4. evaluates the campaign. (Stacks, 2011)

Whichever model you use, or even if you prefer to combine existing ones to come up with your own acronym, the key to the success of your media relations campaign lies in a structured and systematic approach to planning and execution while keeping in focus your key publics or stakeholders. All campaigns need to begin with research.

RESEARCH

The theorists agree that the first—and often the most overlooked—stage in media relations is research. This needs to be done at various levels. This first part of the research involves what is known as environmental scanning or monitoring. This will include collecting information obtained from your client as well as from other resources such as existing media clippings/coverage, annual reports, organisational collateral such as brochures, and searches for similar campaigns that may assist your planning process. You may also need to conduct internal interviews or use email or social networking to research the organisation or issue. This will lead to an examination of the organisation and/or the issue, which will build into a solid understanding of its strengths and weaknesses as well as opportunities and threats (your SWOT analysis).

The next phase of research involves analysing the organisation's publics. Who do you want to reach in your media relations campaign? Can you prioritise the stakeholders or publics in a logical way—passive and active/primary and secondary? Which media will be the best channels to reach these publics? Media workers—journalists, publishers, editors and so on—represent a key public in themselves, so in any media relations campaign various publics will need to be considered.

The final areas of research in a media campaign are:

- gaining an understanding of the available media, and
- determining which will suit you best by exploring the style of stories covered, the topics covered by specific journalists, as well as analysing historical coverage received in these publications/programs in terms of key messages and tone.

In media relations, knowledge of the news and entertainment media is essential. No research is wasted so you should always take the opportunity to thoroughly investigate the media you aim to target. This book should assist you in this process.

Much of the research will be undertaken using informal means, often accessing secondary sources. This means that your research will use existing data that are already available from various sources. In addition, interviews are an example of formal research—they are a qualitative form of research. A survey taken within an organisation or within an online community, or a content analysis or audit of news stories, are examples of quantitative formal research. For example, in the 'It's Not OK' campaign, below, audits of media coverage were conducted as part of the ongoing research and evaluation.

Research can thus be as simple as conducting some internet searches or as complex as carrying out in-depth analysis of previous media coverage, and compiling and distributing an online questionnaire. The choices you make should be informed by your objectives, the time you have to undertake your research and your budget.

OBJECTIVES

The next stage in the campaign process is to set your goals and objectives, which will inform your strategy. Goals (the overall aims) and objectives (the series of outputs and outcomes in achieving the goals) can be summed up using a SMART approach:

S   Specific
M   Measurable
A   Achievable
R   Relevant
T   Time-bound.

The point here is to determine clearly and precisely what it is you want to achieve. Meyer (2003) explains the five-step process:

1. *Specific:* refers to the need to be clear and unambiguous, explaining exactly what is expected, why, who is involved and so on.
2. *Measurable:* refers to the need to measure progress of objectives as you move towards your goal. Only measurement of objectives can show progress.
3. *Attainable:* refers to the objectives and goal being realistic and achievable. Objectives need to work in a step-by-step way to reach the goal.
4. *Relevant:* refers to identification of those objectives and goals that are most appropriate for the organisation and/or issue.

5. *Time-bound:* refers to the need to commit to target dates and work towards these. There may be various dates within the one campaign for evaluative purposes.

This phase is crucial because without clear objectives it is difficult to determine a strategy. The objectives (and over-arching goal) are what you want to achieve; the strategy is the thinking or approach you use to achieve this. A strategy requires the practitioner to think competitively and to gain some advantage by taking some specific actions (Stanton, 2007). For example, in the Best Job in the World campaign discussed at the end of this chapter the primary goal was to (re)establish the Great Barrier Reef as a preferred international holiday destination. The strategy was to start a global social networking buzz using a unique social media competition. The objectives and tactics emerged out of these, as you will read in the case study.

ACTION

This phase is based on the need to formulate a plan to move forward and achieve the objectives, often called an 'action plan' which then leads to the communication phase, next. This may involve:

- developing an organisational narrative
- planning a media conference
- preparing media releases
- setting up media interviews
- developing a social networking profile
- briefing senior executives about an interview
- preparing a Q&A for senior executives
- holding regular meetings with journalists
- determining who will be your spokesperson (especially in a crisis)
- determining your main message
- updating media training
- being quick to offer an authoritative comment or develop an existing story.

COMMUNICATION AND PERFORMANCE

This is the tactical implementation part of the model. Here you decide which media relations tactics should be employed for the campaign and which media you will target to achieve your objectives. Will you use controlled media such as advertorial features or will you rely on uncontrolled media initiatives such as media release distribution, story pitching, media conferences and one-on-one interviews with targeted media organisations? All of these tactics are discussed in various chapters throughout this book.

You will also outline how and when the story will be revealed to the target media. Options include breaking the story to one media outlet (as an exclusive or scoop) or releasing the news to all media at the same time via a media conference. At this time, you need to consider who your key spokespeople will be. You should know the talents of your internal executives because of previous media training. You may also look further than your own organisation to find talent for a media story, and consider other stakeholders who can assist in the positive placement of key messages such as those who have strong Twitter or blog followings. Your communication activities should be illustrated in a timeline or on a Gantt chart (or both) to ensure a SMART approach to your object-ives. These will be useful as concrete points of reference for your client, others in your department and senior management briefings.

In addition to your spokesperson, consider other resources you may need to implement in your campaign. This may include photographers, videographers, editing and production, as well as your professional services, all of which should be covered comprehensively in your campaign budget.

EVALUATION

This phase determines how well you reached your goals and objectives. Before you begin your campaign, you need to define how you are going to monitor the campaign, how you are going to measure the success of each of the tactics and how each tactic contributed to achieving the campaign's goals and objectives. Evaluation is undertaken at the end of a campaign, but it may also be undertaken at measured intervals throughout a campaign. Usually, this is called monitoring, for example in the 'It's Not OK' campaign following, monitoring media outputs led to a decision that police, judges and mayors should be added to the list for media training.

Evaluation of media coverage in major campaigns increasingly is undertaken by commercial organisations such as the Newscentre division of Australian Associated Press (AAP), which monitors thousands of newspapers, magazines and broadcast hours of Australian and international news. Alternatively, smaller or not-for-profit organisations will often simply monitor media coverage to see where the media stand on an issue (and they often *will* take a position on an issue, despite general claims of objectivity). Sometimes media will 'get on board' in a major way, as illustrated in the case study within the 'It's Not OK' campaign, below. At other times, the media may attempt to divert the key messages of a campaign, as illustrated in the Commonwealth Games Bid example, below.

The idea of using models or guides such as RACE, ROPE, ROPES or ERASE is to make sure all the boxes are ticked as you work through a media campaign. Such campaigns are all around us; we just need to take the time to notice. Government and political organisations, the corporate and the third sectors all use the media to get their messages across. Public relations practitioners in-house and in consultancies utilise the pervasive and diverse media sector that, over a period of time, can present challenges but also achieve sustained or continued results. As the previous chapter pointed out, getting to know the media can help; keeping focused on news values, news angles and news themes is a must; and knowing the range of media available—including all forms of news and entertainment media—will provide the best outcomes for media relations campaigns. Below we examine a selection of campaigns that integrated many forms of media to successfully achieve their goals and objectives.

'IT'S NOT OK' CAMPAIGN—MEDIA ADVOCACY STRATEGY

In 2006, the New Zealand Government allocated funding for a long-term campaign to change attitudes and behaviour towards family violence—the 'It's Not OK' campaign. The campaign used TV advertising, printed resources, a community action fund and media advocacy to address high rates of family violence and high tolerance in the community for all types of violence in family relationships. Historically, the media had minimised family violence crimes in terms of size and placement of stories, number of stories and quality of spokespeople. Stories often sympathised with perpetrators and offered excuses for their crimes.

GOAL

The media advocacy project aimed to change the way the New Zealand news media reports family violence.

STRATEGY

The media advocacy strategy was to work with all the audiences who could influence the quality and quantity of news stories across print and broadcast media.

COMMUNICATION TACTICS

1. Developing spokespeople

News stories are shaped by the sources reporters go to. In New Zealand in 2006, the number and quality of spokespeople on family violence was poor. Community organisations working to prevent family violence rarely engaged with the media out of fear, lack of skills and ignorance of the contribution they could make.

A media training workshop was delivered free of charge to community organisations in the family violence sector. A media manual was produced giving step-by-step practical information on the importance of being part of news stories and how to go about it in a safe way. The full day workshop demystified the news media and showed participants how to get into the news media on their own terms. The workshop was delivered all over New Zealand. Participants were put on a database so that story ideas could be shared and they could be alerted to news opportunities. Follow-up support was offered for writing press releases, identifying story ideas, contacting news outlets, preparing for interviews and developing media strategies.

2. Training for reporters

At the other end of the news story, a seminar was developed for reporters, made available to journalism schools and newspaper newsrooms. The 90-minute seminar gave basic information on family violence—what it is, who is affected, latest statistics, the law and the dynamics of abusive relationships. The seminar alerted reporters to common myths and stereotypes and illustrated best practice for reporting family violence incidents, using New Zealand examples of good and bad stories. Guidelines for reporters were distributed to seminar participants and have remained a popular download from the campaign website.

RESEARCH AND EVALUATION

A media audit was commissioned by the campaign in 2007. A three-month historical sample showed that before the media advocacy project started:

- news stories about family violence were shorter and fewer than stories about non-domestic violence crimes
- 40 per cent contained a myth
- stories were reactive, and
- community spokespeople were rarely used.

Three subsequent samples showed that the media advocacy strategy was working. In the second half of 2007 there were:

- twice as many stories
- 16 per cent of family violence stories were on the front page or the lead item in a broadcast bulletin
- experts were used more often as sources, with
- a 15 per cent increase in stories in local media.

By 2008 these changes had been sustained:

- 90 per cent of stories had a family violence prevention message
- there were fewer myths

- the language used by reporters condemned family violence, and
- judges were speaking out about the issue.

A CASE STUDY

In 2008, a provincial daily newspaper the *Wanganui Chronicle* ran a two-week campaign on family violence. The year before, media training had been delivered to local family violence prevention organisations. Subsequent media activity brought the topic to the attention of editorial staff at the *Chronicle*. They requested the campaign's seminar for journalists.

The editor and reporters were astounded to discover how much they did not know about family violence and how myths could creep into their stories. At least one page and up to four pages were dedicated to family violence every day for two weeks, generating unprecedented public interest.

PHASE TWO: MEDIA TRAINING FOR POLICE, JUDGES AND MAYORS

The audits showed where more work was needed and led to new partnerships, in particular with police, judges and mayors.

The media audit had shown than much of what police said would be used in news stories, even just a simple phrase like 'family violence is not OK'. Police engagement with the media tends to be reactive and factual, so the idea of being proactive and using prevention messages was new to them. The media training workshop was delivered to police districts across New Zealand. A 'media tips' sheet was produced for Police Family Violence Coordinators to use, followed by a media handbook to assist detectives to speak out when they are working on family violence crimes.

The media audit also showed that any comment made by a judge about family violence was included in news stories, usually in the headline. Audit results were shared with chief justices along with a file of clippings showing the prominence given to judges' comments about family violence. Judges were encouraged to use their high media profile to talk about the seriousness of family violence in New Zealand and call on communities to take ownership of the problem.

Finally, it was determined that city mayors could use their public profile to take leadership on preventing family violence in their community. The campaign produced media guidelines for mayors with key messages, suggested media opportunities, useful statistics and examples of successful media engagement by mayors.

OUTCOMES

The media advocacy project was successful because the campaign worked *with* the media not against them. Reporters and editors were given sound reasons for reporting family violence differently.

The strategy was mutually beneficial for all involved, showing that:

- community spokespeople can get their message out,
- reporters can get better stories,
- other sectors can get positive media exposure,
- the general public is better informed, and
- victims and perpetrators are able to ask for help.

The changes achieved by this project have been sustained. In New Zealand, family violence stories continue to be given prominence by print and broadcast media. Family violence is treated as unacceptable and a serious problem. Stories are no longer sympathetic to perpetrators, they contain statistics and details of how to get help. Expert spokespeople are quoted. More and more newspapers are deciding to run campaigns and support local efforts to reduce and prevent family violence.

Source: Courtesy of 'It's not OK' campaign, Wellington, New Zealand, 2011.

COMMONWEALTH GAMES BID: WORKING TOWARDS 2018

On 12 November 2011, the Gold Coast won the rights to host the 2018 Commonwealth Games. The announcement followed a ten-month communication campaign during which the Gold Coast had competed with the Sri Lankan town of Hambantota for the event. The final vote was 43 to 27 in favour of the Gold Coast.

BACKGROUND

The official communications campaign for the Commonwealth Games bid was launched in February 2011. In the short period of time before the November 2011 announcement, the communications and media team needed to develop a campaign that would engage and excite the media at all levels—from local to national and international. Commonwealth Games Federation delegates come from all over the world, so it was important to reach them; however, it was also important to get the local community on board, so the campaign called for a multi-channel approach. Considerable research was required to locate the best and most effective communication and media channels to reach the various groups and individuals who would impact on, and determine, the Games bid outcome. The campaign worked through three phases:

1. *Inform:* get the message out, explain the benefits of the Games, build energy.
2. *Engage:* develop strategies to bring the community into the bid and excite the delegates.
3. *Inspire:* move to a final level of showing the best the Gold Coast and Australia had to offer.

While the local media were known to the campaign's media team, the campaign also required developing relationships with international media, identifying what stories they needed, their style of writing, their primary readerships and so on.

The delegations from Asia, Europe, Oceania, the Americas and the Caribbean visited the Gold Coast for three-day periods during July to October 2011 to judge the destination for their final vote.

GOAL

To win 36 of the 71 votes of the Commonwealth Games Federation delegates and be awarded the 2018 Commonwealth Games on the Gold Coast.

OBJECTIVES

- Win local support for the event so that by the time the delegates visited Australia during July to October there would be a local buzz and excitement about hosting the event.
- Show the delegates the support for the Games and the Gold Coast in the best possible light.

STRATEGY

- Run an extensive communications and media campaign, achieving significant coverage at the local, national and global levels.
- Use social and traditional media to work through three phases: inform, engage and inspire.
- Establish a Business and Community Consultative Committee and an Athletes Advisory Committee to inform and engage their networks and provide additional spokespersons.
- Find an ambassador for the Games who would become the 'face' of the 2018 Games bid.
- Gain supporters and endorsements to back the bid.

TACTICS

- Regular media releases and fact sheets to media at all levels.
- Media conferences for key announcements.
- Development of a Facebook page from Day 1.
- Twitter feed—used to reinforce all news feeds and particularly to leverage support from the London Olympics and Glasgow 2014 Commonwealth Games.
- Celebrity endorsements.
- The 'face' of the bid was 'Eve', an 11-year-old local school girl who is a swimmer, gymnast and runner; she will be 18 in 2018.
- Development of a DVD showcasing the Gold Coast, which was presented to delegates.
- 'Adopt a Commonwealth Country' campaign in local schools—75 schools took part, directly involving 18 000 children (and every parent and teacher involved with the schools).

- Regular radio interviews on the Gold Coast and across Southeast Queensland.
- Specialised media stories to online sports publications and online games magazines *Inside the Games* and *Sportcal*, targeted at the high-end readership of delegates and athletes.
- Regular presentations and guest speaking engagements at local chamber of commerce, business and tourism networking functions, universities and colleges.

MEDIA OUTPUTS

- Some 12 000 media articles across all media over the ten-month period.
- Some 36 000 Facebook fans, including support from Olympic and world-class athletes.

OBSTACLES AND CHALLENGES

A media conference held just prior to the arrival of the first delegation to the Gold Coast occurred just after a Gold Coast policeman had been shot and killed. In addition, there had been considerable coverage of local crime in the Gold Coast media at that time. It became clear at the conference that the media may choose to focus on this as an issue when the delegates arrived. While media were needed to support the event and continue covering the bid campaign, their potential to undermine the bid was also a real possibility. In effect, they had to be provided with access, while at the same time controlling it. It was determined that, due to the limited time on the Gold Coast of each delegation (three days per group), access would only be offered in small groups (no one-on-one interviews), with selected delegates and the media manager of the bid on hand. This achieved the aim of providing access within a controlled environment.

An additional challenge occurred due to demands for travel away from the Gold Coast by the bid's chairman and CEO. This meant they were often not available for interviews or immediate comment for the media, and there was often no readily available spokesperson. In addition, media releases needed to be cleared at the top level, and this slowed down the process when senior executives were away. While this did not present a major issue, it nevertheless required a great deal of planning and organisation, and at times the media manager was required to source other suitable spokespersons from the business community or Athletes Advisory Committee.

OUTCOME

The Gold Coast won the bid by an overwhelming majority, and the communications and media team has now moved to the next phase of preparation for the event in 2018.

Source: Courtesy of Tamara Morris, Commonwealth Games bid marketing and communications manager, 2012.

AN INTERNATIONAL MEDIA CAMPAIGN: TOURISM QUEENSLAND'S 'BEST JOB IN THE WORLD'

In January 2009, Tourism Queensland launched its first global consumer campaign and its most high-profile and successful campaign to date, the 'Best Job in the World'. The campaign was the second phase of the Islands of the Great Barrier Reef program, and was Tourism Queensland's major international campaign for that year. The campaign was driven by digital and media relations initiatives in a quest to find candidates for the Best Job in the World, attracting more than 34 000 applications from over 200 countries. Britain's *Sunday Times* commented: 'Not since Willy Wonka and the golden tickets hidden in chocolate bars, has something come along like this.'

Tourism Queensland's CEO Anthony Hayes wrote the following report of the campaign:

> It seems almost incongruous that the most recognisable natural wonder of the world, the planet's largest reef, and earth's only identifiable object from space, would need any more publicity.

But by 2007, the mounting dilemma facing the team at Tourism Queensland was this: while the Great Barrier Reef was undoubtedly the leading lady, her supporting cast, some 600 islands and associated experiences, had somehow become the understudies.

The challenge was to convey to the rest of the world, in an already saturated global travel market, that surrounding this vibrant living organism was tangible product and a new tourism story for Australia.

Think Queensland; think Great Barrier Reef. Think Australia; think Reef, Rock and Opera House.

The mission was to make the international stage think again.

Hence the Islands of the Great Barrier Reef campaign was born and 'the best job in the world' campaign conceived.

What nobody imagined was just how big 'the best job in the world' would become, not only catapulting Queensland into the international spotlight for its creative marketing, both inside and outside the tourism spectrum, but scripting an entirely new business model for savvy organisations across the globe.

Stage one of the three-pronged campaign began 12 months out from the 2009 launch and involved working with Tourism Queensland's 13 international offices and Queensland's regional tourism organisations to establish the 'story' of the Islands of the Great Barrier Reef; an international holiday destination to rival other island paradises such as the Greek Islands or the Caribbean.

For the campaign to work, we needed to convince the Queensland tourism industry to include this new 'destination' into their brochures; that there was something to sell. Australia is a remote destination, so to introduce a new message was hard work.

By the end of 2008 the groundwork was laid, the tourism regions and operators along the 2300 kilometres of the Great Barrier Reef had come on board under the 'Islands of the Great Barrier Reef' banner, we had agreement from our international travel partners to start including Islands of the Great Barrier Reef product into their packages and marketing collateral had been produced. Now all we needed was an idea or a 'hook' to sell the Islands of the Great Barrier Reef to the world.

Stage two was the big idea itself. Brisbane-based creative agency SapientNitro was given a brief to devise a campaign to promote the Islands of the Great Barrier Reef. While several ideas were floated we realised that 'The Best Job in the World' was The One; a dream job offering one candidate something priceless, the role of Caretaker of the Islands of the Great Barrier Reef with six months to explore the Islands of the Great Barrier Reef while based in a luxury house on Hamilton Island for a pay cheque of AUD$150 000.

While the caretaker's duties, cleaning the pool, feeding the fish and collecting the mail, were tongue-in-cheek, for the campaign to work, it needed to be a real job.

We were pushing it uphill as it was the worst possible travel time following the global financial crisis and swine flu, but the promotional timing could not have been more perfect. People had just come back from Christmas, it was cold and miserable in the Northern Hemisphere and many people were facing an uncertain financial future as the global financial crisis took hold.

Then on a cold January morning they opened up the newspaper or turned on the television and were hit by a ray of Queensland sunshine; an advertisement for 'the best job in the world' with the initial criteria of 'anyone can apply'. The application process simply asked people from around the world to submit a one-minute video of themselves telling Tourism Queensland why they deserved the best job in the world.

In order to get the global publicity machine rolling, Tourism Queensland also invited select journalists and bloggers from around the globe to a secret announcement on Hamilton Island, in the Whitsundays, where the story would unfold. Many had flown from a cold Northern Hemisphere winter into what was a far cry from where they had come; a balmy tropical climate, a media conference held on the balcony of a luxury villa overlooking the Whitsunday Passage and interviews with a Tourism Queensland Chief Executive Officer dressed in shorts and bare feet.

We knew we had a great idea but the day we launched a virtual media tidal wave hit us. With more than 200 000 website hits in 24 hours, we exceeded our key performance indicators almost overnight and the interest just kept growing. At one stage we had around 100 people of our entire head office of 120 people working on 'the best job in the world' to some degree.

This was the ultimate example of having a strong project management approach. It touched every part of the organisation, from the receptionists receiving 2000 emails and telephone calls to our IT department; we went from having a simple hosting solution of one web server to a solution which included 11 servers and would have been able to host major news network websites.

During the six-week application time-frame, 34684 people from almost 200 countries uploaded their video applications onto www.islandreefjob.com and YouTube, providing an independent promotion for the Great Barrier Reef and Queensland viewed by more than 8.6 million people.

The campaign was not without its challenges and controversies; some of which threatened to discredit the entire project. Among them:

- The 'fake video'; a promotional video we used of a girl getting a tattoo which we should have marked as a 'sample' on the website. In a social media world where transparency is king, the so-called 'fake' video threatened to discredit the legitimacy of the campaign.
- Website overload; in the first day we received 200000 hits which crashed our server.
- A 30000 cap on applications which we lifted in the last 24 hours.
- An application from an alleged Russian porn star.
- A man purporting to be Osama Bin Laden applying for the role.
- The premature leaking of the successful candidate's name around 30 minutes before the announcement.

One of the most crucial things of which we were aware of on a daily basis was the tight rope we were walking. There were a number of things that we did not anticipate, including errors we made. The most important thing we learned was to admit our mistakes and quickly fix them. This is the golden rule of working in the world of social media. If something goes wrong and you try and cover it up and bluff your way through it, people smell it a mile away and your credibility is gone.

Some of the other challenges we faced included picking the final 50 applicants who were given one month to gain attention for themselves and the Islands of the Great Barrier Reef campaign through media interviews, stunts and social networking while not excluding any market and maintaining interests in our key markets.

This group was then narrowed down to a final 16, which included two Australians. The final event was held over three days in the Whitsundays where the 16 applicants, along with more than 60 media from around the world, converged on Hamilton Island for the final selection process. During this time, we set up a major media centre on the island; no small challenge for a remote island location more than 1000 kilometres from a capital city.

We attracted coverage through BBC, CNN, *Good Morning America*, Canada TV, Sky News London, *The Times* in London and *The Sunday Times*, plus a contingent of domestic media. We had a huge challenge for those three days but we had things planned for all contingencies. We had a lot of overlay footage; the pretty pictures even though the weather went against us at one point.

We were also very good at packaging footage in a way that media wanted. News journalists at the launch said it was better organised than a G20 Summit or an Olympics.

Our team ignored the temptation to acquiesce to requests from at least 50 production houses from around the world to film a reality television show based on the concept and, instead, asked companies to tender for the job of following the successful candidate and selling the story. Australian-based Beyond Productions made a six-part series which they sold to National Geographic. This series was aired around the globe. Additionally we employed our own television production team to run the media centre, organise the live-cross points and produce a daily video news release that was distributed globally through Thomson Reuters news wire service.

Tourism Queensland also appointed its own stills photographer and enabled free, easy downloadable photos to be used by media. We knew this was a real job, we knew it was a news story and if we were to sell ourselves to a reality television type show, we would lose our credibility. We had to make sure we kept it real.

On 6 May 2009, Ben Southall, a 34-year-old British charity events organiser, was announced as the successful candidate for 'the best job in the world'. In the first 24 hours of his announcement as the successful candidate, Ben undertook more than 100 media interviews and featured in news stories around the globe.

Two months later on 1 July 2009, Ben started his role as the Caretaker for the Islands of the Great Barrier Reef. During his stint he visited almost 100 Queensland destinations, fielded more than 450 media interviews and posted more than 60 blogs of 75 000 words, 2000 photographs, 47 video diaries and more than 1000 tweets.

Dealing with the very public feedback of who we finally picked was also a challenge. You pick a Brit then the argument is: 'well Brits spend more money than any other market so you were always going to pick them'. Pick a New Zealander: 'well more New Zealanders come to Australia than any other market so you were always going to pick a Kiwi'. Pick a Chinese person: 'well China is your fastest growing market'. Pick the American: 'well you are just pandering to the market'. With social media, you have no way of controlling the message. The best you can do is monitor comments, correct inaccuracies fix major problems and believe that the network will moderate itself; that the disgruntled complainers and detractors will be overridden by your supporters. The key is to be open and transparent, to be flexible and adaptable in addressing issues, make changes where necessary and seize new opportunities that may not have been part of the original brief when they arise.

For example, after the selection process concluded, we realised that while we had one Island Caretaker, we also had 15 talented, energetic and passionate people who had become global ambassadors for Queensland. We made the call to appoint some of these individuals as Queensland Tourism Ambassadors in their home countries to perform a range of promotional roles over the next 12 months.

We also had to convince other parts of Queensland that they stood to benefit from a campaign focused around the Islands of the Great Barrier Reef. Our message here was that 'the best job in the world' elevated global awareness of Queensland to new levels, which would have flow-on effects to other parts of the state. Since Ben Southall finished his stint as Caretaker of the Islands of the Great Barrier Reef on 31 December 2009, we have re-employed him as a Queensland Tourism Ambassador, taking his experiences to the world.

The estimated publicity value of the campaign topped AUD$430 million and penetrated almost every country on earth. Not bad for an investment of around AUD$4 million over the three-year life of the campaign.

Source: Courtesy of Anthony Hayes, Tourism Queensland, 2011.

CONCLUSION

This chapter has provided some tried and tested models for developing media campaigns and walked the reader through several case studies from a range of fields to show these models in action and illustrate key activities. Each of these campaigns had highly successful outcomes— but none of them occurred without careful and thorough research, planning and implementation. Media relations is most effective when it is carried out in this systematic and focused way. Developing such campaigns requires the media relations practitioner to start with research and address the key questions: What are the goal and key objectives? And how can we go about achieving these? Only then will the practitioner be ready to implement a set of strategically selected tactics to achieve their goal.

7 MEDIA RELEASES

A primary tool of the media relations professional, and the most commonly used uncontrolled tactic, is the media release. Lamentably, it is also often poorly researched, written and checked before it is sent out. The massive volume of media releases emerging from government, politics, industry and third sector has resulted in the news media being swamped by these items. Additionally, it has become an easy option to simply 'send out a media release' to placate demanding clients or employers, who see media coverage of their issues, events or products as their right. The challenge for the media relations practitioner is to be both selective about which media releases they write and to write them well.

As one of the items most associated with the technical function of the public relations practitioner, media releases are often written by junior practitioners. Chances are that university graduates will have to hit the ground running in readiness to prepare and write media releases, so it is essential that students learn the skills needed and understand the importance of getting the media release right. The demand for strong writing skills is more acute than ever, so do not under-estimate the value of the perfectly honed media release. Media alerts, the younger sibling of the release, are a targeted and shorter media tool, used for brief announcements or to invite media to an event. Online and social media releases (SMR) can include embedded material, audio and video links and keywords to maximise search engine searches. Video news releases (VNR) provide packaged news for television. Each of these is examined in this chapter.

NEWS BY ANY OTHER NAME

For the most part, media releases supply news. But just what is news? One of the great clichés about journalism is that when a dog bites a man it's not news, but when a man bites a dog it is news. Planes fly every day without crashing, so that's not news; however, it is news when they crash. The prime minister being well is not news, but it is news if the prime minister is hospitalised. News has been defined as 'anything you can find out today that you didn't know before' (in Conley and Lamble, 2006, p. 79). In addition, news must have the 'so what?' factor. Generally speaking, news is new: it is not what has already been reported unless there has been a new development or it offers a new angle on an old story.

News may be divided into 'soft' and 'hard' news. Soft news generally refers to human-interest, quirky or offbeat stories, often without an urgent timeframe—like an animal rescue or a story about a 'quiet achiever' or 'Aussie battler'. Hard news is said to have an 'edge'—that is, it has a sharper angle and is usually more urgent, such as a federal election being announced, a major accident or an international conflict.

News may further be divided into sections: news—usually up front in the newspaper or in the TV or radio bulletin—and features— usually later in the newspaper, maybe in their own 'Features' section, or in longer formats in broadcast media. In addition, columns and commentary are a major part of the news collection—more so now than ever. The 'news hole' incorporates all that part of a newspaper or program that is not filled by advertising or service pages/sections (like weather and comics). In newspapers, it is made up of soft and hard news, features, columns, sports, social coverage and any other reported items. Sometimes the distinctions are blurred—you can find feature stories within news pages, news stories can be written with a column approach, hard news can be written as a 'next day' feature and soft news written as a column. Media relations feeds into all these, so it is important to be familiar with all types, sections and formats that provide potential opportunities.

MEDIA RELEASES

As outlined in Chapter 1, the news media have become increasingly dependent on media relations materials. The best known of these is the media release, also known as the news or press release. No one can guarantee the use of a media release—a lot will depend on the news hole of the day—but you can maximise your chances of having a media release used if you make sure you fulfil three simple functions:

- Make sure it contains information or news that will interest the media and its audience (content).
- Make sure its style adheres to news format (style).
- Make sure it reaches the correct gatekeeper at the correct time (targeting).

Essentially, the functions are all about content, style and targeting.

CONTENT

A media release that misses the mark or makes no real news point will not be used, and the media relations practitioner must be prepared to answer the inevitable question: 'Why didn't we get a run?'

Writing media releases is often more difficult than writing news. Journalists have to seek out and write news, using their news sense to sift through material and write stories they perceive to be newsworthy. On the other hand, the media relations practitioner not only has to identify the newsworthiness, but must also get a message across. Very often, this message will have a promotional element, so the release has to serve two purposes: to get the message across and to make it newsworthy. Be prepared to advise your client or your superior if you believe material should not be sent out in a media release. If you make a habit of sending out media releases that have little or no news value and are ultimately time wasters, you will place your credibility on the line. And your credibility is crucial to your role as a media relations practitioner.

Bivins (2011, p. 86) notes that editors take only 30 seconds to peruse most media releases; therefore, the release must be effective. The first three criteria on which a media release will be judged are:

- who you are
- the headline, and
- the lead.

You might add to this who your organisation is, as this can alert the media to previous experiences—both good and bad. The content of your release must be driven by something newsworthy and must have an angle to it. The announcement of a new product or service might be new, but is it newsworthy? For example, banks introduce new accounts and packages all the time (not news), but what makes news about banks is when they reduce or increase interest rates, announce their quarterly profit/loss statement, appoint a new CEO, merge with another bank, lay off staff or announce the closure of regional branches. These are the stock standard bank news stories. But how else might a bank get into the news? Behind-the-scenes stories can make soft news or features—for example, if the bank employees support a developing world enterprise, or if a manager is the youngest ever appointed to the role. If you determine that either of these stories would make a good news story, you'd then need to identify which media would be most likely to use it. You will best be able to do this by first determining the nature of the story—is it a local story, a human-interest story, a quirky or novelty story or one that has widespread impact? Look to your news values to be guided here. Then you will need to consider the purpose of the release: What do you want to achieve with your release? Who do you want to read it? Be realistic and honest with all these questions before you write or distribute your release.

Proximity is a news value that can often provide guidance with soft news stories—a local story will be of interest to local media. Take a look at the Eagle Boys release later in the chapter—it focused on a quirky angle and was targeted at local media.

The only way you will know which media to target will be through reading, listening to and viewing a range of media. Knowing what's in the news will help to determine what will make the next story a news story. As discussed in Chapter 5, if a story has also started trending, or a theme has emerged, you can jump on the 'bandwagon' and present a new angle or develop the next phase of a story. How might you do this? Following up on a current theme about your industry or sector can work. Here are some examples:

- If an airline is grounded, then the hotel industry comes up with a new story angle.
- If a Fisheries Department releases figures about reduced stock numbers, it might be timely for an animal wildlife NGO to come up with a response.
- If a plane crashes after a bird strike, the makers of aviation safety products might send out a media release about the latest technology.

Every one of these scenarios is based on an actual media relations response from an organisation that was quick to act on a real-life situation.

Alternatively, locating a local angle in a national or international story can make news—for example, a celebrated soldier returns home from an international war zone. Or a local story can go national—see the story of the toddler later in the chapter which ran in the local paper and then was followed up by a national magazine. If you are not monitoring current events, new legislation, political manoeuvrings, social trends, the weather, and just about everything else that is going on in your own backyard and beyond, then you will most likely miss an opportunity for a story somewhere in your career.

STYLE

This function focuses on the release looking the part: conforming to journalistic formats while indicating clearly that it is a media release. Releases are usually presented using the following guidelines:

- identification that it is a media release
- where it came from on the front page (usually letterhead)
- a clear date
- a short, catchy headline that should conform to journalistic style and be written in the active voice
- an indication of whether the release is to be embargoed, and if so until when
- one sentence per paragraph
- white space for the journalist's annotations (in hard-copy versions); this includes wide margins, space beneath the header, 1.5 line spacing or double spaces between paragraphs)
- if it goes over the page, page 1 marked '1 of 2' (two pages maximum)
- the public relations practitioner's name, an after-hours number, mobile number, email address, Twitter hashtag
- information about whether photo opportunities or good clear stock photos are available, and
- information about whether an interview is available.

This is a reasonably standard checklist, but styles will vary from one organisation to another. The best way to find out about style is to become familiar with the releases used by your own organisation.

You will be able to practise writing in news style if you read newspaper stories. Usually, simple and short is best; given that newsreaders—especially online newsreaders—are skimmers, it is important to make your point quickly and clearly. Because journalists are going to be the people who will read your release, you need to replicate news style as closely as possible. Some points of style are consistent across the media:

- *Dates:* use December 25, 2012 or 25 December 2012, not 25th December 2012.
- *Numbers:* spell out one to nine, use digits for 10 and above.
- *Capitalisation:* use sparingly;
- *Punctuation:* use sparingly and correctly.
- *Titles:* always check. Sometimes titles and honorifics are combined—for example, Prime Minister Julia Gillard then becomes Ms Gillard in later mentions.

THE INVERTED PYRAMID AND BEYOND

The traditional format for news writing is called the 'inverted pyramid', which can be pictured as an upside-down pyramid. In this style, the most important information is used at the top of the story—ideally in the first few paragraphs—with information written in descending order of importance. The reason this style is used is that the newsworthiness of the story can be identified early on and the story can be cut from the bottom without losing the most important information or the thread of the story. One theory has this style dating back to 1860 and the American Civil War, when reporters began using the inverted pyramid because they had to send their stories over the telegraph. The story goes that there was such a volume of news being sent this way that it was imperative for the most important items to be carried in the first few paragraphs to ensure they arrived at their destination. If the story was cut during transmission, the inverted pyramid ensured that the most important news would still arrive. This notion has been debunked by various commentators, including Marcus Errico—who studied American newspapers between 1860 and 1910—and instead found that the inverted pyramid grew out of 'new social trends' of the late 1800s (1996, p. 6). This is the most likely, but less romantic, story of the inverted pyramid and the summary lead. Either way, it has become the most popular of news styles and is often associated with a more objective, unambiguous, succinct and clear approach to news writing.

Unfortunately the temptation in writing in the inverted pyramid style is to cram so much into the first two or three paragraphs that the story becomes unbearably boring, dull or unreadable. The lead (also called the 'intro') should usually be no more than 25 to 30 words, but more importantly it must be interesting and provide a hook to get the reader to keep reading. Following the lead is a transitional sentence which links in the body of the release, which will be made up of facts, names and quotes.

Early in the body of the release (or sometimes in the lead), you must introduce a spokesperson, a source of authority to whom information will be attributed. This person will usually be introduced by the third paragraph—it is their title and name that will provide the authority to the story. Usually this person will be a senior executive—maybe the CEO or managing director, or perhaps a fundraising manager or member of parliament. Once introduced, you will attribute quotes to this person. It is simplest to introduce the source first, along with an indirect quote, and then lead into a direct quote in the following sentence. This will make it clear who is speaking when the direct quote begins. It will work like this:

> The book's author Jane Johnston said *Media Relations: Issues and Strategies* was fun to write.
> 'I had a great time visiting newsrooms and PR consultancies to talk to people in the industry about the latest approaches in media relations,' Dr Johnston said.

Public relations tourism specialist Susan Sullivan says the quotation marks should 'hug the quote' (Sullivan, 2012). This is a good way to remember the way to present direct quotations.

As a general rule in newswriting, there will be a ratio of one direct quote to two indirect quotes, and this can be used as a guide in writing media releases; more importantly, however, the quotes must be strong. You may or may not include more than one voice of authority or spokesperson in a release, but be careful not to overdo this as too many voices can make a release difficult to follow. There is no real conclusion to the story, because an inverted pyramid story simply runs out of news. The conclusion does not need to be a summary or repeat of what has already been said. Media releases may conclude with a call to action, and this will often translate into a news story. This is simply a call to the reader to respond, act or do something explained in the release.

While the inverted pyramid remains the most popular newspaper style of writing, it is not the only style. More narrative structures are also sometimes appropriate in news, and often the preferred choice for features (discussed in more detail in Chapter 10). A close look at many daily newspapers—especially broadsheets—provides examples of this. While there are many more examples of the inverted pyramid, there is also a growing tendency to incorporate conversational and narrative approaches to news. Possibly because of the merging of news and features, the rise of the column or commentary as a popular news form, and the demand for news to be more interesting and entertaining amidst the sea of other media, news has seen a loosening up of style, so that leads have changed from a staunch adherence to the inverted pyramid style. Also, social media releases (discussed below) tend to use a more conversational and sometimes narrative approach. Here are examples of the two styles used on the front page of *The Weekend Australian* on 5–6 November 2011:

Inverted pyramid

The Reserve Bank has sharply reduced its forecasts for Australia's growth and inflation in a dramatic revision of its thinking three months ago, and warned that Europe may pitch into deep recession, dragging the rest of the world economy down with it.

Narrative

Memo to those with cash to spare: if you're rich and have ever wondered what it's like to be poor, buy a Queensland resort island.

These two examples, focusing on the news value of money, represent the way in which both approaches can be effective, especially balanced against each other on a page. You'll also note that the first lead summarises the story—you don't really need to read on to understand it. The second lead gives you a taste of the story, but you have little to work with; such is the idea of the narrative lead, it doesn't immediately give the whole story away. It also ran underneath a photograph, which told the story through a picture.

While narrative writing does form an alternative to the inverted pyramid, generally the summary lead and inverted pyramid provide the best choice for media releases going to most mainstream media. Narrative writing and a more conversational approach can be adopted in social media releases and blogs, discussed later in the chapter and elsewhere in the book.

WRITING THE 'WHAT' LEAD

Media releases follow the style of news stories and strive to answer the six basic news questions: who, what, when, where, why and how (the 5Ws and the H). The most likely outcome is that 'the who, what, where and when' will be covered in the first two or three paragraphs, and 'the why and how' will be covered later in the release. This is simply because the why and the how are usually more complicated than the other Ws (unless, of course, the purpose of a story is to explain why or how a previous event occurred). It is a worthwhile exercise to list the 5Ws and the H quickly on your computer, tablet or a scrap of paper before beginning the process of writing. This will clarify the basic content in your mind. Often, leads that begin with the 'what' factor will be more succinct, newsworthy and written in the active voice than leads that begin with the 'who', 'where' or 'when' factors. Take, for example, the following lead options:

The what lead
A suicide car bomber killed 28 people at an Iraqi army recruitment centre in Baghdad yesterday. (16 words)

The who lead
Twenty-eight people were killed yesterday by a suicide car bomber at an Iraqi army recruitment centre in Baghdad. (18 words)

The when lead
Yesterday, 28 people were killed by a suicide car bomber at an Iraqi army recruitment centre in Baghdad. (18 words)

The where lead
In Baghdad yesterday, 28 people were killed by a suicide car bomber at an Iraqi army recruitment centre. (18 words)

In these examples, the what lead is tighter, shorter, reads more easily and there is less punctuation in the sentence—all important factors in news style. The who, where and when leads are also passive, and in news style the active voice is stronger (although the 'who lead' is an alternate choice because it begins with the number of people killed). Choosing the what lead also helps to ensure you do not 'back into' it—that is, put the news at the end of the lead rather than at the beginning of it. The what lead will not always be the best, but clarifying the 5Ws and the H before you begin writing will always help you work out the best approach.

TARGETING

Placement of a media release depends on delivering the story:

- to the right gatekeeper
- through the right channels, and
- at the right time.

Just who is the appropriate gatekeeper depends on what the story is about and where the release is pitched. A blogger can be their own gatekeeper, but if you are pitching to the wider media you may need to consult a media directory or media website to make sure the release goes to all the right people and that you don't exclude important names. As mentioned previously, *Margaret Gee's Australian Media Guide* and the *Media Monitors Media Directory* are commonly used media guides, either online or in hard copy. These guides are a standard tool of the media relations professional. Updated quarterly, they provide the most thorough and comprehensive list of media, with names and contact details. Some releases will go to just one media outlet, some to a hundred. This will depend on what your story is about. You might make a personalised pitch to a journalist who you know has a strong following in a certain area, suggesting an interview or perhaps a photo idea.

Alternatively, you might send your release to all major media because it is generic in nature. For national distribution, you can use a commercial distributor or wire service such as AAP or Prodocom. Media release distribution services often work on a fee-per-use basis, allowing you to choose whether you want the release to go geographically—by state or territory—or by topic area—such as travel and tourism. Obviously you need to know the costs of using such distribution channels, and clients have to be willing to pay this. However, it can balance out if you spend less time picking through the dozens of media available. Another benefit is the greater capacity that commercial distribution channels can have for sending photographs or video footage in a news package, as this can place excessive pressure on your own internet server.

Even if you regularly use distribution services, it is important to keep your own databases up to date. Chapter 5 noted how mailing lists are compiled for different release purposes. For example, separate mailing lists would be used for education, fashion, tourism or finance stories, or for local, national or international distribution. These lists need to be updated regularly and it is a good idea for someone else in the office to be familiar with your lists to cover your down-times.

Different media have different lead times. Always give them plenty of notice of staged or managed events, such as media conferences, launches or openings. The following serves as a guide to lead times for routine and breaking news:

- Magazines usually need several weeks' notice, but this may be less for news rather than feature pieces. Breaking news is not usually covered in magazines.
- TV news and current affairs need a few days' notice for routine news, but can be arranged the same day (preferably in the morning to enable them to compile vision after lunch), or closer to bulletins for breaking stories.
- Daily newspapers need a few days' notice for routine news. If you are sending a routine release, send it well in advance. Breaking news can stretch limits until late in the day.
- Sunday papers are compiled between Tuesday and Saturday, with the routine stories covered early in the week and the front pages and breaking news written on Saturday.
- Radio has the shortest lead time, and traditionally could be accessed up to minutes before a bulletin for breaking news; however, many radio news bulletins are compiled in 'hubs' (central newsrooms), which may be geographically removed from the station. Aim for last thing at night for morning news (which begins around 4am) or first thing in the morning. Make sure you know whether or not the news is collated locally.

- Internet news sites (for online versions of newspapers or broadcast) often break stories, which are then followed up in more depth. The deadline for internet news is therefore as soon as possible.

Each of these mediums is discussed in more detail later in the book, in Chapters 11, 12 and 13.

Media releases generally are distributed via email, ideally within the body of the email or with a short summary in the body if an attachment if required. Mail and fax have fallen into disuse, but some organisations continue to send releases via these means.

The internet provides a range of options that have enhanced the simple media release, in both distribution and style. Standard media releases are still sent out to the intended media, but they are also placed on the internet news or media centre (as explained in the next chapter) and should be provided in printer-friendly versions. This is a logical use of a release that has been written to announce news— that is, it both announces the news and serves as a future reference. For example, a journalist might want to check what Queensland Premier Anna Bligh said about the 2011 Brisbane flood clean-up for a follow-up story one year on. A simple check of Ms Bligh's media release archives will provide what is needed. Of course, a researcher or journalist will also be able to check the premier's website for interview transcripts, speeches, Twitter feeds and so on to locate relevant information. It is important to make sure releases are kept in a logical order and are easily locatable on your website. A really good example of keeping media materials in order is the media link on the Australian Medical Association's (AMA) website, discussed later in the chapter, which provides briefs, links and keywords. It is clear and easy to navigate, and that ticks two of the most important boxes. Online media sites will be discussed in more detail in the next chapter. It is important to provide the option for journalists (and others) to receive your releases via RSS (Really Simply Syndication) feeds. This is now standard practice for news distribution, and is discussed in Chapter 13. Finally, release summaries can be sent via Twitter with a link back to the website or landing page and placed on organisational Facebook pages. This allows an organisation to keep its followers up to date even if the news media do not pick up on the story. Social media releases are discussed later in the chapter and in Chapter 13.

MEDIA RELEASES THAT FAIL

Whatever format you are using, it is important to make your media release clear and to the point. Poorly written releases are easily deleted. An excellent exercise for media relations students is to find badly written media releases and identify why they failed. In your analysis, you will probably find some or all of the following:

- buried leads
- wordy leads
- no clear spokesperson
- waffly or self-serving quotes
- missing or obscure elements of the who, what, where and when
- long paragraphs, often made up of several sentences.

Poorly written leads and headlines are central to problems with releases, and if these miss the target then generally the whole release will be lost. (As noted earlier in the chapter, the lead and the headline are two of the criteria on which you will be judged.) The following release is a good illustration of how *not* to begin the process.

Water schemes to create 150 000 jobs
Canberra, October 17: LONG-TIME proponent of North Queensland's controversial Bradfield Scheme, Federal MP for Kennedy Bob Katter outlined to Parliament the minimal cost effect that the Scheme would have on government coffers through its savings in unemployment benefits as well as curtailing the massive costs of drought.

This lead is a massive 49 words long and leads with the 'who' rather than the 'what'. The headline, which is written clearly and succinctly, is not borne out until late in the release. It indicates how many jobs would be created by the water catchment scheme, but this figure of 150 000 jobs does not appear again until the second page of the release, in the fifteenth paragraph, just before the end. A headline should provide a clear indication of the release and be reflected in the content. Perhaps you could rewrite this, using the 'what' lead and making it shorter.

MEDIA RELEASES THAT WORK

If a media release translates into a news or feature story with a focus on the main message in the targeted media outlet, then the media relations practitioner has achieved their goal. If a release is run verbatim or close to verbatim, the practitioner has not only pitched the right content but in the right style. Since media releases are written and posted online every day, the best way to access and analyse up-to-date examples is to look online. Here are some ideas:

- Go to your university or college website—usually these are clearly written and you get the benefit of learning about what's going on as well!
- Some of the organisations used throughout this book provide excellent releases on their websites—the Australian Medical Association (AMA) is one.
- The City of Sydney, City of Melbourne, City of Perth, Wellington City Council—to name a few—provide links to clear and concise releases on their home pages. Auckland Council includes localised news stories for each of the city's wards.
- You could look up your own city or town and see if you think the releases tick the boxes.
- Major sporting codes and bodies all include regular releases and news updates on their websites.

The following release was sent to a variety of print and broadcast media. It focused on a quirky, novelty angle and achieved local and national coverage.

EAGLE BOYS PIZZA MEDIA RELEASE

2 August 2011

EAGLE SUIT FLIES THE COUP

Eagle Boys Nambour store owners Tracy and Craig Simpson are on a mission to have their prized pink Eagle Boys Eagle suit returned to its home after it went missing from the store last Saturday night (23 July).

Eagle Boys Nambour staff noticed the suit had disappeared Tuesday evening (26 July) when they went to dress for a routine stint as 'The Eagle'. Surprisingly, the Eagle suit's head and body went missing, but the suit's feet and stockings were left in-store.

Police are currently investigating the incident, but as yet have no leads.

The distinctive pink Eagle suit is part of the franchise's core marketing and branding strategy, and costs on average $2,000 to replace.

Craig said he was unsure if the suit was insured so hoped eagled-eyed locals might be able to assist.

"It certainly stands out so we're hoping the local community will get on board and offer any information they can in a bid to locate the suit and ensure it's returned to its home here at Eagle Boys Nambour," Craig said.

At Shop 4, 14 Arundell Avenue, Eagle Boys Nambour has utilised the services of 'The Eagle' suit for the past two years and is sad to see it's now flown the coup.

"We're shocked and annoyed that someone has even contemplated stealing it as we don't think it would be of use to anyone but us here at the store," Craig said.

"Not only has the Eagle suit helped to market and position Eagle Boys Nambour over the years, but it's also grown to become a much-loved part of the store's character and livelihood.

"The staff love it and enjoy dressing up in it—they miss it and just want it returned."

Tracy and Craig are offering a meal deal with the works as a reward for the person kind enough to return the Eagle suit to its nest and rightful home at Eagle Boys Nambour. They'll receive two large Traditional pizzas complete with a 1.25L drink, garlic bread, potato skins, chicken dippers, chicken wings, a trio of dips, and a dessert option.

"We're keen to see the suit returned so it can once again take up its rightful place promoting the store and bringing the 'Eagle spirit' to hungry Nambour locals," Craig said.

Anyone with more information regarding the whereabouts of the Eagle suit should report their information to the store or police, or simply return the suit anonymously to the store.

ENDS. For more information, images and interviews: [contact details here].

Source: Media release and analysis courtesy of Brumfield, Bird and Sandford, 2011.

MEDIA RELEASE: EAGLE SUIT FLIES THE COUP

The primary purpose of this media release was to generate awareness within the local Sunshine Coast area in a bid to track down Eagle Boys Nambour's missing Eagle suit. At the same time, it was also an opportunity to profile the store among its target publics. The release focused on the unusual circumstances in which the suit went missing, but also acknowledged that it was a quirky story. A call to action was included to encourage anyone with information to come forward.

The release was distributed to approximately 40 local journalists in print, online radio and television. As well as receiving the intended local coverage sought, the release also achieved national exposure. It achieved three local print runs, four local TV runs, as well as a number of syndicated TV and radio broadcast mentions. The missing Eagle suit's plight also received a mention on the Nine Network's *Today Show*.

The curious circumstances in which the suit went missing provided a meaty news hook for local media. The missing suit (of which only the feet and stockings remained) was a quirky angle that provided for

Eagle Boys' red alert

WHAT has the world come to when a pizza mascot is stolen?

We couldn't believe it when reporter Matt Johnston came across the story about the Eagle Boys pink eagle costume being stolen from the Nambour store.

Police issued a call for the thief to return the suit and the store owner was even nice enough to offer a free meal to the person who returns the $2000 costume.

Let's hope this is one eagle that hasn't flown the coop for good.

Source: Photo and story courtesy of the *Caloundra Journal*.

excellent and unusual vision. The release provided enough detail about the story to whet journalists' appetites, with many following up the store owner for additional quotes, vision and photos to individualise their stories. In addition, the release and the subsequent news stories carried the added endorsement of the Queensland Police Service.

SUPERFISH SWIM SCHOOL

Tip-off: 'Coast toddler's fall a lesson for all'

Sometimes a good story will not come from a media release but from a 'tip-off' from a media relations practitioner who knows a good story when he or she hears one, and knows where to 'place' the story in local or specialist media. When Gold Coast media man Wayne Hickson took a call from a client who runs Superfish Swim School, explaining how the school had been contacted by the parents of a toddler who had fallen into their swimming pool and saved himself, Wayne saw a great good-news story. Wayne explains how he went straight into news mode: 'It had all the hallmarks of a great story . . . happy ending, coming up to summer, cute toddler makes for a great pic.' The *Gold Coast Bulletin* ran the story on Page 1 and 3, and it was subsequently picked up by Channel 9 news with a national magazine also keen to follow it up.

Source: Photo and story courtesy of the *Gold Coast Bulletin*

These stories, and the following media alert, show that the media relations practitioners who either wrote the release or phoned through the story:

- knew what the media could use
- developed strong story angles, and
- knew the best media to whom to pitch their story.

If media releases, alerts or story tip-offs are carefully thought through and well-constructed, everybody wins: the client achieves media coverage, the news media get a good story and the media relations practitioner's work is complete.

MEDIA ALERTS

If the purpose of your announcement is to notify the media of an event, a media alert rather than a media release should be used. The media alert is a briefer version of a release that usually has a 'call to action' for the news media to attend or respond in some way. This is a brief document of one page, utilising point form, which uses the following formula:

- *Headline:* what the event is and when it is.
- *What:* what is happening.
- *Who:* who is holding the event.
- *Why:* why this event is being held.
- *Who:* who should attend the event.
- *When:* date, time or range of date and time.
- *Where:* where it will take place, where they can park.
- *Media contact:* name, phone, email, website, etc.

A media alert is a hybrid of an invitation and a release. Because its purpose is usually to advise the media of an event that you want them to attend, you need to be careful that you include sufficient information to get them along but do not tell the whole story. Sometimes an alert will be sent to advise the media about a pending announcement or an address by a keynote speaker or panel, who will be discussing an important issue like law reform, climate change, disability services or a policy development. An alert may also be circulated to the media to get them to attend a media conference, discussed in Chapter 9.

The following media alert from the Australian Medical Association (AMA) has a sense of urgency about it, calling the media to action as it foreshadows an announcement from the AMA about health reform and the Council of Australian Governments (COAG). The alert includes the words 'Door Stop', referring to an interview which is held as a person leaves or enters a building.

MEDIA RELEASE   MEDIA RELEASE   MEDIA RELEASE

Australian Medical Association Limited
ABN 37 008 426 793

42 Macquarie Street, Barton ACT 2600: PO Box 6090, Kingston ACT 2604
Telephone: (02) 6270 5400 Facsimile (02) 6270 5499
Website : http://www.ama.com.au/

AMA

MEDIA ALERT – DOORSTOP

COAG AND HEALTH REFORM

AMA President, Dr Andrew Pesce, will be available to comment on the Prime Minister's COAG health deal at 2.30pm today, Friday 11 February, at Westmead Private Hospital in Sydney.

Dr Pesce Doorstop:

Time: 2.30pm

Date: Friday 11 February 2011

Address: Main entrance
             Westmead Private Hospital
             Cnr Mons and Darcy Roads
             WESTMEAD

---

11 February 2011

CONTACT: John Flannery   02 6270 5477 / 0419 494 761
             Geraldine Kurukchi   02 6270 5467 / 0427 209 753

Source: Media alert and analysis courtesy of John Flannery from the Australian Medical Association, 2012.

MEDIA ALERT: COAG AND HEALTH REFORM

This was a big event. Since Julia Gillard took over from Kevin Rudd as Prime Minister, people were watching closely to see what would happen with Kevin Rudd's 'big picture' health reform agenda. The AMA response to the COAG Agreement would influence overall reaction to the Agreement.

This Alert had to be put out 'on the run' because nobody knew what time the Prime Minister would make her announcement. The AMA had to make sure it had enough time to receive the details, go over them, and develop a response message before facing the media.

The Alert went to national media, the federal press gallery, medical press, targeted Sydney television, radio, newspaper, online and wire services, and the NSW Parliament press gallery. The alert was posted on the AMA website and 'tweeted' on Twitter. In addition, phone calls were made to key contacts. Once the media alert went out, Dr Pesce provided news grabs to radio ahead of the doorstop.

All the TV networks, including SKY News, turned up, along with ABC radio and the commercial AM and FM stations, online services, *Australian Associated Press*, the *Sydney Morning Herald*, *The Australian*, the *Daily Telegraph*, and the medical press—*Australian Doctor* and *Medical Observer*.

Dr Pesce featured on the evening news and in the next day's papers, sparking another cycle with the morning radio in various states. Online coverage was extensive.

SOCIAL MEDIA RELEASES

Social media releases (SMRs) are the logical online extension of the traditional media release. They can combine the text of the traditional release with embedded video, audio and images, as well as useful links and tags to assist with online targeting. Because they are written for the web they tend to be more conversational than the standard media release, provide short snippets of news and may use bullet points. They are also formatted quite differently because of the multi-levels the web provides.

There are free access sites that show how to create SMRs. One highly recommended on many blogs is <www.prxbuilder.com/x2>, which is a web wizard that walks you through the production of an SMR, including main content, links and embedded materials. Increasingly, there are companies that will build specialised web materials, like SMRs. Alternatively, you can usually find a simple template on the web on which to base yours. Conversation Marketing's Ian Lurie has a fun SMR template about the Trojan Horse and the sacking of Troy which is easily located (see Lurie, 2007), or you might find your own online.

The key elements to have in a release are:

- headline
- key points
- a lead paragraph
- related photos—linked
- related video—linked
- related stories—linked (your own and maybe others)
- quotes, and
- tags.

One of the key points of the SMR is its 'findability' due to its tags. Social media expert Brian Solis suggests creating the SMR as a blog or its own landing site, in addition to the traditional media release. That way, traditional search engines like Google and Yahoo News will locate the media release, while blog-specific engines like Technorati, Blogpulse, Google Blog Search and Google Alerts will find the blog (Solis, 2008).

Solis's main distinction between SMRs and traditional media releases is that SMRs are shared in social media communities rather than simply being available on the web. The following box provides a Q&A that covers some of the issues associated with the development of SMRs.

THE VALUE OF SOCIAL MEDIA RELEASES

Question: Should we include sentences or is it supposed to be bullets?

Answer: In order for these releases to show up in search engines, the truth is that an intro paragraph or two are necessary to help them index properly. Simply relying on bullets won't get you anywhere, even if they're sent directly to your contacts.

Question: Are we designing SMRs for 'the wire' or the 'web'?

Answer: That parlays into the next point. SMRs should be designed for the web, while a traditional release (say a compatriot release) is designed for the wire [wire services]. Social Media Releases play to the strengths of the web and also social media, a feature that wire services have yet to conquer.

Question: Are SMRs created for journalists and bloggers and is that what they want?

Answer: I've created SMRs with a private URL and shared with reporters and bloggers before the news was official (basically under embargo). They loved it and the ratio for pitching and publishing was almost 100 per cent. But all I'm doing is creating, positioning and packaging information in a way that's relevant to them. The SMR in this case becomes a wrapper for presenting information in a palatable and digestible way.

Question: Can they, and should they, bypass influencers to reach people directly?

Answer: SMRs are for more than just reporters and bloggers; they're about people. When created properly, they can get discovered by the very people you want to reach and thus bypass traditional influencers. I'm not saying that you should bank on this as a strategy, only think about it when you're creating your press release strategy. You can write for both influencers and customers using a variety of traditional and social media releases.

Source: Adapted from Solis (2008).

VIDEO NEWS RELEASES

The video news release (VNR) is a television version of the media release, complete with visuals, scripted audio and talent, or interview grabs. Development of VNRs is a specialised field because they need to be strong in news content as well as production quality. Because of this, they usually require a team of specialists for their production. This might mean you need to outsource to a specialist company if you do not have the technical skills to do it yourself. Some public relations and production companies specialise in VNRs (and the audio version, ANRs). For example, Medialink Productions have been producing them since 1995. They promote their VNRs as often being about 'the latest technological breakthrough, a new medical procedure or the release of a new product' (Medialink Productions, 2012).

Where VNRs are being produced, developers should be mindful to:

- provide a news angle
- have a third-party endorsement, and
- produce them in a news style, format and length.

As finished versions, VNRs are not widely used in Australia, probably due to a resistance from the media and the cost involved in their production. What is more common is the supply of materials for TV news services to use in the creation of their own news stories—for example, vision and interviews may be supplied. There is further discussion of VNRs, as well as web and audio streaming, in Chapter 12.

THE ABC OF MEDIA STYLE

Often the news media will select and use parts of media releases and discard other parts. The most common parts chosen will often be quotes—if you have provided strong quotes in the first place. This can reduce the journalist's workload because they don't have to make a call to get the quotes. If strong quotes are used by the media, they can end up being copied and pasted from one story to another on the web, but self-serving or boring quotes will never get used. The section of media releases most commonly discarded is the lead, partly because journalists like to write these themselves, putting their 'stamp' on a story, and partly because they will write it in the best style for the publication. A challenge when writing a media release is therefore to write great leads, spend time honing and tweaking them, write them with punch and impact, include something special in them and keep them under 30 words. Try to make your lead so strong that the journalist who is given your release to work from simply cannot do a better job!

A simple rule for all media releases is to use the ABC style:

- accuracy
- brevity, and
- clarity.

If you use this as a guide and keep checking your ABCs, you'll have a much better chance of seeing your media releases in print.

CONCLUSION

Media releases must work at two levels: they must get a key message out for your client organisation and provide news for the media. While there are things in the news cycle that are out of our control, there are simple guidelines that can maximise the chances of getting your story used in part, or in total. Use journalistic style and make your approach interesting and catchy, whether using the inverted pyramid or a narrative approach. Make sure you include relevant and important '5Ws and the H' and strong quotes from someone in a position of authority. Consider using 'the what lead' in inverted pyramid writing and, as far as possible, use the ABC rule of accuracy, brevity and clarity. There are many dos and don'ts associated with writing and sending media releases. The box provides a checklist for you.

MEDIA RELEASE CHECKLIST

WHAT TO DO

- Do focus on the 5Ws and the H.
- Do use letterhead, date and indicate it is a media release.
- Do write a catchy headline—using an active verb if possible.
- Do leave margins to allow annotations.
- Do include contact information, including after-hours contacts.
- Do make sure you have adhered to journalistic style.
- Do make sure your story is newsworthy and appropriate to your media outlet.
- Do make sure you use a credible authority as your source.
- Do use strong quotes.
- Do include photo opportunities or strong photographs.
- Do get your story to the right person at the right time.
- Do use specific information rather than generalities.
- Do provide background material at the end (or separately—see next chapter).
- Do use important dates and times at the top.
- Do know the difference between routine and breaking news.
- Do use 'today' or 'tomorrow' for immediacy.
- Do send your release to a roundsperson or news editor by name.
- *Do eddit you're releas klosly and chek speling bfor sendin.*

WHAT NOT TO DO

- Do not use excessive titles or long names in the lead.
- Do not use excessive adjectives.
- Do not write a lead of more than 30 words—and aim for 25 or less.
- Do not pad out your release—keep it short.
- Do not expect that your release will run verbatim.
- Do not make statements that you cannot back up.
- Do not use self-serving quotes.
- Do not assume others' knowledge of your organisation.
- Do not use acronyms in the first instance—spell out initially.
- Do not include poor-quality photographs.
- Do not nag the media to run your story.

MEDIA KITS, GUIDES AND ONLINE MEDIA CENTRES 8

The main currency we have with the media is the ability to supply information when they need it, in formats that are easily accessible and understood. Sometimes it will be enough to send out a media release alone, update a website, or phone through a story idea. At other times, we need to provide more detailed, specific or background information, which can be compiled in a variety of formats including a hard-copy folder (the traditional media kit), online as a media kit or as part of a media guide. The collection of media-oriented materials can then be made available in an online media centre. The main difference between media guides and kits is that guides usually are developed and used for reference purposes, often explaining the procedures of how to go about reporting on an event or issue, whereas kits provide stories and background materials for the news media to use in writing the news. Media kits are made up of independently developed items that are collected in a folder, either hard copy or online. There is great diversity in these items, but the most important thing is that they supply relevant and up-to-date material, including contact details for follow-up purposes.

This chapter will look at the content and purpose of media kits, media guides and media centres, and provide a range of examples to illustrate each of these.

DESIGN AND STYLE

All media kits and guides should be presented with close attention to detail, and this includes the most up-to-date statistics and facts about the organisation, issue or event. While content will vary, presentation is important, and each item should be uniform in style. There are two elements of consistency that should be adhered to when developing and collating media kits and guides. First, they must be consistent in format—that is, font, margins, capitalisation and so on. Second, they must be consistent in the branding of the organisation they represent—logos, titles and so on. While their content will vary with the industry, event, organisation, product or person they represent, their presentation must have a sense of uniformity and continuity about it. Continuity is a key element in designing and developing media kits. Key phrases and slogans, together with consistency in letterhead, typeface, presentation and style, should mean the media kit is presented as a cohesive whole. In addition, it is essential that these form part of the overall organisational collateral and remain consistent with other key communications, such as TV and newspaper advertising, direct mail and billboard advertising, to ensure the message is clear and focused. You may need to work with a graphic or web designer in developing your kit or guide. With or without such assistance, it is worthwhile understanding some basics of good design.

Presentation of media kits and other printed materials should include attention to the following design principles:

- *Space:* Use space to ensure there is room for the media to annotate and make their own notes. Remember, white space is a good thing because it makes text easier to read. Too much information and content on a page can make it feel cluttered.
- *Emphasis:* This can be achieved by using style options of font size or type—bold, underlining, colour and so on. It can also be achieved by selectively repeating the same words or images.
- *Sequence:* The order of items within a media kit can make all the difference. The most important media release should be placed first, and sequence may be indicated in a table of contents for guides and more complex kits.

- *Continuity:* This principle should underpin how every word, image and space is presented in the kit. Margins, fonts, paper choice, stylistic approaches to writing dates, names, capitalisation and numbers should be consistent for the kit to have a cohesive effect.
- *Balance:* This principle is about how the words and images are placed on a page so they are appealing to the eye. Use of larger font sizes at the top of the page for headlines and other key words, bold for certain words and 12 point font for body copy should combine to provide balance on the page.
- *Proportion:* Wording and images should all work together to provide pages that are in proportion, will be easy to read and follow, and are easy on the eye.

Choice of folder, paper and other items will present a message in itself. In deciding materials, ask yourself what message you want the media kit or guide to send. A sleek and glossy paper works well for a five-star hotel or European car, but would not work well for an environmental or activist group, which would be served better by using recycled and earthy images and materials. The image on the front cover should make a statement—for example, when the Brisbane agricultural show, the 'Ekka', decided to go with a focus-on-families approach, the media kit's front cover featured a close-up photograph of a horse's head and a little blonde girl in a riding habit. Without words, it conveyed that the event was about families, children and beautiful animals.

One of the traps into which some publicists fall when compiling media kits is to cram CDs, t-shirts, pens, mouse pads, stickers and other gimmicky items into elaborate folders. While gimmicks can sometimes work—for example, one media kit used by a Sydney nursery to announce a newly developed citrus plant was accompanied by a small sample of the plant when it was sent to specialist journalists—they should be right on target and appropriate rather than providing clutter.

Because media guides need to provide a comprehensive range of information, they will usually require a table of contents, and may also benefit from clearly marked spacers between sections. CDs became a popular way of dealing with large volumes of copy for a while; however, compared to online options they are now seen to be cumbersome. The move to online has brought with it more positives than negatives, but hard copy gives the media something tangible that they can write on and use independently, so it is likely that both options will remain popular for some time to come.

MEDIA KITS

In general, media kits include a mix of the following items: media releases, fact sheet, backgrounder, feature article, biography or profile, newsletter, brochure, map, calendar of events, list of key personnel, annual report, list of Q&As, key newspaper clippings, business card/ contacts, media pass/application. In hard-copy kits, other items— such as branded pens, keyrings, drink coasters, notepads, caps or even t-shirts—can be included. Not all of these items will be prepared specifically for the media—some will come from the marketing department. There is a wealth of information that may be used in a media kit, but careful selection will ensure it does not become too busy, complicated or weighty. While some references in this chapter refer specifically to hard-copy materials—such as the paper choices discussed above—most information applies equally to online media kits.

MEDIA RELEASES

As noted earlier in this chapter, and in Chapter 7, the media release is the key item to include in a media kit. There may be only one release announcing a major event or issue, or there may be several releases. If there are several, it might be appropriate to include a table of contents in the kit. In the Ekka kit mentioned earlier, a table of contents listed a dozen media releases, all focusing on different aspects of the event. That way, the same kit could be distributed to the media at the launch and there was plenty of material to generate initial news coverage as well as ongoing ideas through the week-long event. Online releases are usually archived, so it is important to link internally to these and make them easily accessible.

BACKGROUNDERS

Backgrounders and fact sheets can provide information that goes beyond the news release or the feature article. Media always need background to write in-depth news, features and assist with research for radio and TV current affairs and feature programs.

Backgrounders provide the background to an issue, event or organisation. Unlike the media release, which lists the information in order of importance, a backgrounder is usually a factual account, which may be written in a chronological or narrative fashion. By providing the background, news angles can be used in media releases—thus they are not 'clogged up' by background information. Backgrounders are particularly useful for providing historical information about an organisation or event, to explain a complicated state of events such as a business merger or a company collapse, or to assist in the overview and understanding of an issue or following a crisis. For example, after the death from a box jellyfish sting of a tourist in Queensland's Whitsunday Islands, a backgrounder was provided to the media on the box jellyfish. Backgrounders are used by the media, but are also useful for other publics and individuals, such as company executives and employers.

Characteristics of a backgrounder include:

- It will take you beyond the news release.
- It must be researched thoroughly and updated regularly.
- It may be written in a chronological or narrative fashion.
- It will refer to specifics and facts, naming new laws, changes in government, company policy, books, articles and reports that played a role in the development of an issue.
- It often accompanies a media release.

FACT SHEETS

Fact sheets are similar to the backgrounder, as both items provide background information. Essentially, the fact sheet is an easy reference guide that lists key attributes of an organisation, issue or event. A hotel's fact sheet, for instance, may record key personnel, facilities, historical detail, conference capabilities, room numbers and configurations, other hotels in the same chain and so on. A fact sheet for an event such as a carnival day might utilise the who, what, where, when, why and how of the event using sub-headings, listing the times for the event, the venue, who will be appearing, whether the event is linked to a charity and so on. Fact sheets are usually used when lists, statistics and figures are involved, often utilising bullet points so they are easy to read and information can be located quickly. A fact sheet should be uncluttered and a quick reference guide.

Characteristics of a fact sheet include:

- It uses facts and figures.
- It is used as an easy reference guide, so shouldn't be too long.
- It should be set out to read easily—using white space.
- It may use bullet point form.
- It is often a 'standard' company document, which must be updated regularly.

See Mt Buller's fact sheet and the Mindframe fact sheets later in this chapter for examples.

PROFILES OR BIOS

Profiles or bios give a comprehensive background to an individual or organisation. They include elements of the backgrounder, but may vary in focus. It is likely that these will include the most up-to-date information first—for instance, in profiling an actor appearing in a theatrical production, the actor's most recent achievements would be listed before earlier credits or training. If, however, an Oscar nomination were the key feature to the profile, this would almost certainly be listed first. Company profiles are often written for the benefit of consumers and shareholders; however, these may also be utilised in a media kit if they include information the media may find useful. Characteristics of a profile or bio include the following:

- It is usually written in paragraph style, often in reverse chronological order, with the most recent information first.
- If about a person, it will include a photo/headshot.
- If about a person, it will list major achievements, career information, awards, what they're doing now.

CALENDAR OF EVENTS

A calendar of events can be useful when providing the media with a list of dates and events that are planned to take place over a period of time. Usually compiled well in advance of the dates, it allows the media and other publics to plan their attendance at an event, or allows the media to include details in news and feature coverage. Sometimes a grid-style chart or table is used to allow a time-event reference to be identified easily. Alternatively, events may be listed month by month (see the Mt Buller press kit online—website reference is on p. 156). Placing a variety of material together in this way provides a simple, quick and easy reference for events that occur over a period of time. For instance when the Winter Racing Carnival began in Brisbane, the calendar of events included not only racing but three other categories of activities and events—sport, culture and social—to encourage a 'total holiday' calendar rather than simply focusing on race days. This calendar of events was used in brochures, magazine lift-outs and media kits.

Characteristics of the calendar of events include the following:

- It is presented as an easy-to-read guide.
- It provides dates in advance of a series of events.
- It may 'package' together different events to broaden the overall appeal.

NEWSLETTERS

The newsletter is one of the most commonly used communication tools for reaching a group or public, but is not usually prepared specifically for the media. Nevertheless, newsletters can provide an excellent reference for the news media, and stories and topics in newsletters may attract media attention. They are generally a written communication distributed among a group of like-minded people for the purpose of conveying news or information items. Newsletters can be made available or distributed through various mediums such as direct mail or letterbox drop, on websites or email. Bivins (2011) identifies two types of newsletter—vertical and horizontal:

- *Vertical* newsletters are distributed within an organisation, and intended to be read by the full hierarchy of people within that organisation, from the most junior to the most senior. The most common example of this type is the company newsletter, intended for employees through to senior management.
- *Horizontal* newsletters are distributed to more narrowly defined groups, such as special-interest groups, lobby groups or progress associations, where there is not the same upward or downward hierarchy that there is in many organisations.

In addition to standard newsletters, some organisations compile teaser newsletters for the media with snippets of information for them to follow up. This can be a purposeful information item that provides more information than a calendar of events, but less than a media release.

Characteristics of a newsletter are as follows:

- It will increase awareness within its target group.
- It will reinforce aims and messages used in other organisational items.
- It can perform a community service.
- It can expand membership of a group.
- It can serve as an advertising vehicle for local or specialised organisations.
- It can provide feedback opportunities from the reader.

FEATURE STORIES

Generally, feature stories refer to the behind-the-scenes or in-depth stories to which the news media will allocate more time or space than to a news story. A feature story may be written up in a media release format but, alternatively, it may be presented to the media as a feature idea—either in a media kit or on its own.

Feature stories are written in a very specific style and should not be put together in a hurry because they require more depth than most news stories or media releases. For this reason, they may be written by a media relations practitioner who is practised in the writing style, but will more likely be supplied by the media relations practitioner as a feature idea to a media outlet or may emerge out of a media release. By supplying a feature idea, rather than the finished feature, a media relations practitioner may enhance their chances of having the work published simply by making a timely suggestion about what would make a good feature. Features allow the media to develop a story beyond the short format that a news story provides and can expand a news theme; they can also provide an avenue into magazines. Features are discussed in more depth in Chapter 11.

Characteristics of the feature story include the following:

- It is longer than news.
- It is more in-depth than news.
- It often follows up on a person, or explores an issue behind a news story.
- It provides an avenue for 'soft news'.
- It uses more description than news.
- It is more creative—this keeps the reader reading.

PHOTOGRAPHS

Photographs can be the centrepiece of a story—and without photographs some good stories can be overlooked. There are generally two ways to work with photographs: either provide them yourself or suggest an idea as a photo opportunity in a media alert or media release. If you choose the former, you can either take them yourself or pay a professional photographer to do so. Either way, you need to make sure you know what the requirements of the newspaper, magazine or online publication are. Following are pros and cons of both options (as well as a few dos and don'ts):

PROVIDING PHOTO IDEAS

- Newspapers and magazines still employ photographers to take professional shots, and they choose to frame them to suit their particular print publication.
- Photographers can be quite proprietorial about taking their own photos (though journalists are increasingly taking their own).
- You get the benefit of a professional photographer to take the shot—but you need to supply 'talent' to make a photo work.
- You can plan what photographers will need in advance of a shoot.

TAKING THE PHOTOS YOURSELF

- Photos can be supplied if the media cannot physically access an event or venue—in out-of-the-way locations, such as in rural or regional areas, or if they are short-staffed.
- Trade publications and community newspapers often don't have the staff to go to a location and take photographs.
- Photos should be sent as a high-resolution JPEG files.
- Make sure you caption them—the photos must be clearly identified and described. One option is to simply list 'photograph captions' numerically on a page and make sure these match up to your list of digital images; alternatively, embed captions using Photoshop or a similar program.
- You can also make the photos available on your website because you own the copyright.

Further discussion of photography, including the need for professionalism in this area and copyright issues, is included in Chapter 11.

OTHER ITEMS

A raft of other items may also be included in media kits—although, as noted earlier, care should be taken when choosing these so as not to over-burden the media with clutter. Ask yourself what suits the event, organisation or issue, and select carefully. The following range of items might be included:

- *Business card:* The inclusion of a business card is essential in a media kit. By distributing a media kit, you are saying to the journalist: 'Call me to confirm or elaborate on any information in here.' It is vital that the journalist knows how and where to contact the practitioner who distributed the kit, both during and after office hours.
- *Frequently asked questions (FAQs):* These (and answers to them) can often work well in a media kit. Not only can they prompt the media into your line of questions, but they can answer questions by distance and thus expedite a story's development.
- *Media passes:* These may be required by journalists, photographers and camera people at major events. Such passes will allow the media access to an event that may otherwise have limited access to the public or media in general. Passes should clearly identify the event, the dates of entry and the person or organisation to whom they have been distributed.
- *Maps:* These may be required in cases where directions are required. Maps should be clearly illustrated and laid out.
- *Brochures and annual reports:* These all-important items may be included in the media kit. The annual report will provide vital information to financial journalists, and practitioners working in financial relations will find this tool a crucial one.
- *Posters:* These usually carry the same message as a brochure or media release, but in a highly visual form. These are valuable for public communication, but the media may also find them useful for reference purposes.
- *Corporate products:* Mouse pads, t-shirts, key rings, caps, chocolates or even wine and water with corporate labels can offer an effective way to get a message across for a continued period of time. Catchy slogans and clear pictures work well for these items, which do not lend themselves to clutter or complicated words.
- *News clippings:* Clippings of previous stories—especially relating to an ongoing issue or event—can add credibility and depth to a

media kit. Obviously these would be used only as support material, as clippings are about old news; however, they may serve as valuable background material and make the journalist's job easier.

ONLINE MEDIA KITS

Online media kits will usually include many of the same items as printed ones; however, going online provides some options that print kits do not. This includes creating a larger media kit with embedded links (often to an archive of press releases) and the capacity to update regularly. Once online, there is less cost involved and it is possible to let the journalist cut and paste into their stories as required. Any online document can also provide the option of feedback from media and others who access your site.

Many organisations are now using online media kits to support their print editions. In some industries—for instance, tourism, where media interest is seasonal and global—this provides the opportunity for easy updating and global access and distribution. For instance, the Mt Buller ski resort in Victoria has included an online media kit for several years—for both its winter and summer seasons. Interestingly, this kit does not include any media releases. Rather, its content is more generic in nature and only requires updating annually. Media releases can thus be produced and targeted to specific media as events occur. The kit is easily accessed online through the Mt Buller website: <www.mtbuller.com.au/uploads/file/armb_winter_media_kit_2011.pdf>.

The 32-page kit includes pages that cover what's new, a Mt Buller fact sheet (see below), a calendar of events, winter and summer activities, accommodation details, a page about media visits and other background information. The kit is housed under the media link on Mt Buller's website, along with a photo gallery (and the separate summer media kit). The media kit is in PDF form, which means it is intended as a reference document, not for copying and pasting. If you want the media to be able to cut and paste from your materials, you will need to provide the kit in a user-friendly format that is accessible to the journalist.

Source: Images with permission and courtesy of Mt Buller.

Part of the purpose of media kits is to make complex information easy and accessible. If you work for an engineering company, in the finance sector or a government department, it will be your job to communicate clearly and in easy to understand terms. The media in all sectors expect material to be readily available for them on organisational websites. A good example is the Australian Tax Office's media kits, which are simple information and explanation sites on topics such as capital gains, rental properties and tax scams. The site simply says: 'These media kits contain accurate information on specific tax issues and are for the use of journalists.' These would be useful for finance, property and investment writers as well as journalists researching financial security (Australian Government, 2011f).

MEDIA CENTRES

In Mt Buller's case, the media kit is available on the website's media centre. Most larger organisations (government, corporate and not-for-profits) have adopted this concept, which has various names including 'press centres', 'press rooms', 'online newsrooms' or just 'media' or 'news'.

Media centres enable journalists and other media workers to access material quickly, at any time of the day. As well as media releases and kits, they are likely to include speeches, interview transcripts, audio and video items, photographs, RSS feed options and links to their Twitter, Facebook, LinkedIn and other social media sites. They may or may not have a 'post a comment' option, but should have phone and email points of contact for members of the the public relations team.

A really good example is the Australian Media Association's (AMA) media materials site at <http://ama.com.au/media>. Here's how it is set up:

- *Media:* Links to a chronological list of all media releases and alerts.
- *Speeches:* Set up in much the same way as media.
- *Transcripts:* Set up in the much the same way as media.
- *Video:* Identified as AMA video news, links to a chronological list of TV coverage as well as promotional videos. All stories are identified

by program, date and doctor, linking to the YouTube clip of the story.

- *Audio:* Set up in much the same way as media, with links to the radio story.
- *Photo gallery:* Set up with a single thumbnail per event, indicating how many photos are available and a single link to these.

Development of online media centres and newsrooms can be done inhouse or outsourced to a specialist organisations such as Wieck Australasia Online Newsrooms. These are discussed in more detail in Chapter 13.

BENEFITS OF ONLINE MEDIA KITS AND CENTRES

- *Expand print information:* Because the internet is a much more flexible platform than print, you can include more information about your organisation, group or event because you don't have as many space limitations.
- *Organise:* Take advantage of the expanded format options on the internet. Create a table of contents by category with live links to that category. Keep it clear and easy to navigate.
- *Better strike rate:* Online kits and media centres can be set up to include embedded material on your websites or links to others, plus keyword tags that maximise the chance of being found in an online search.
- *Provide contact information:* Create a link that connects directly to the appropriate email, mailing address or phone numbers. Have different contact links for different departments or individuals if required.
- *Specialist profiles:* Can provide the opportunity to showcase your executives (who will love seeing their profiles linked to the kit or centre) and assist the journalist or blogger who is looking for an expert in the field.
- *Size doesn't matter:* The size of your organisation is irrelevant to the calibre of your media site or kit. You can have a great, cutting-edge site without having the big premises to go with it.

> - *Easily updated:* Once established, online news centres can be updated easily, which saves paper along the way. Make sure your media kit information is accurate, consistent, fresh and up to date.

MEDIA GUIDES

Media guides can include many of the same materials as the kit—background information, fact sheets, calendars of events, maps and so on. The main difference with a guide is that it is intended as a reference for the media in covering an event or issue, rather than as a source of news. For event-based guides, the format is usually bound and presented in a booklet, rather than in the media kit folder. These should not be confused with directories like *Margaret Gee's Media Guide*, which are developed specifically to provide information *about* the media to the public relations industry.

Among the best-known media guides are those used in sport. When the Rugby World Cup was held in New Zealand in 2011, it featured a media guide for each of the 20 participating teams from around the world as well as the 180-page *Official Media Guide* produced by the host nation (see next page). This included, among other items, a list of media rules, news access regulations, details of onsite media centres and the in-house news service, as well as details of how to gain media accreditation for the event. Media accreditation is an important part of the media relations practitioner's role in major events because access for journalists, bloggers, photographers and videographers needs to be carefully managed and controlled. Media guides can provide information about how to apply for accreditation, details of media centres, access points for photographers and TV crews, no-go zones, what will be supplied for accredited media including identification (passes/colour-coded vests, etc.) and security.

Media guides are available for just about all codes of sport—Google 'media guide' and you will find them for Hockey Australia, Swimming Australia, the PGA Tour, Australian Water Polo and all major baseball and football clubs, to name just a few. Once developed, they need regular updating but are seen as a solid investment in the media

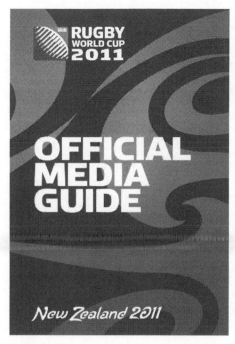

Source: Image used with permission of Rugby World Cup Limited. TM ©
Rugby World Cup Limited 1986–2012. All rights reserved.

management of a sporting or other organisation or event because they
chronicle player lists, records, history and contact details.

Media guides may also be developed for other events or to explain
or background important social, cultural, medical or political issues.
For example, the Australian Federation of AIDS Organisations
(AFAO) publishes online *Reporting HIV in Australia: Information for
Journalists*, which was published first as the *HIV/AIDS Media Guide*
in 1995 and is now in its fourth edition (September 2011). It includes
important information for the media such as the role of the media in
reporting HIV/AIDS, a language guide, key links, facts about HIV,
AIDS in Australia and, internationally, treatment, testing, transmission
and legal regulations. It is available at <www.afao.org.au/__data/
assets/pdf_file/0016/6505/Media_Guide_2011.pdf>.

Likewise, the Mindframe National Media Initiative has developed
a vast array of media materials for reporting on suicide and mental
health. *Reporting Suicide and Mental Illness: A Resource for Media*

www.mindframe-media.info

mental illness

For culturally and linguistically diverse media

facts & statistics

General statistics

▶ Almost 20% of Australians, or one in five people, will experience a mental illness in any 12-month period.

▶ Mental illnesses are the third leading cause of disability burden in Australia, resulting in an estimated 27% of the total life years affected by disability.

▶ About 4% of Australians will experience a major depressive illness and 14% will be affected by an anxiety disorder in any 12-month period.

▶ About 3% of Australians are affected by a psychotic illness such as schizophrenia and bipolar mood disorder where there is a loss of contact with reality during episodes of illness.

▶ 18-24 year olds reported the highest prevalence of mental disorder in a national survey.

▶ Women are more likely than men to report anxiety disorders and affective disorders while men are more than twice as likely as women to report substance abuse disorders.

▶ Many violent people have no history of mental illness and most people with mental illness (90%) have no history of violence.

Statistics for Australians from Culturally and Linguistically Diverse Backgrounds

▶ Cultural background affects how people experience a mental illness and how they understand and interpret symptoms.

▶ In 2001 the prevalence of mental or behavioural problems among people born overseas (9.8%) was the same as for those born in Australia, and rates for those who spoke English at home (11%) were similar to those who spoke a language other than English.

▶ Refugees and asylum seekers are at a high risk of mental health problems as a direct result of the refugee experience and displacement.

▶ Migrant communities do not access mental health services as often as the mainstream population and the hospitalisation rate for those who speak a language other than English is markedly lower than that of the general population.

issues to consider when reporting

Language and Stereotypes

▶ Most media are conscious about using appropriate language. However Australian research shows that terms such as 'lunatic', 'schizo', 'crazies', 'maniac', and 'psycho', are still used by the media. This language stigmatises mental illness and can perpetuate discrimination. This also applies to similar words in languages other than English.

▶ The term mental illness covers a wide range of symptoms, conditions, and effects. Be careful not to imply that all mental illnesses are the same.

▶ Remember people with a mental illness are not inherently violent, unable to work, weak, or unable to get well. Most people with mental illness are able to recover with treatment and support.

▶ Referring to someone with a mental illness as a victim, suffering with or afflicted by a mental illness is outdated. A person is not 'a schizophrenic' - they are currently experiencing or being treated for schizophrenia.

▶ Terms used in the mental health sector may not translate easily into other languages. Check with an interpreter whether terms need further explanation.

Privacy

▶ Media guidelines stress the right to privacy. Does the fact that the person has a mental illness really enhance the story? Are your sources appropriate? What is the possible impact of disclosure on the person's life, especially in small communities?

Interviewing

▶ Interviewing a person with a past or current mental illness requires sensitivity and discretion. Follow media codes of conduct on appropriate interviewing.

Context

▶ A story may be improved by obtaining the views of health and other experts from the particular community group concerned. There are always opportunities to provide positive messages that promote help-seeking behaviour.

Include contacts for support services

▶ Include phone numbers and contact details for medical and support services. This provides immediate support for those who may have been distressed by your story.

For more comprehensive facts and statistics and references see the resource book *Reporting Suicide and Mental Illness,* Commonwealth of Australia, 2010, or associated website at www.mindframe-media.info

Source: Used with permission Mindframe National Media Initiative.

Professionals is a downloadable guide (now in its sixth edition, 2011) covering statistics, facts, the impact of media reporting and other important issues for the media. It is available at <www.mindframemedia. info/site/index.cfm?display=84375>.

Guides such as these, which deal with major social issues, have been developed by communications professionals to assist the media with reporting of these complex issues. As the Mindframe site explains:

> The resource was developed with the assistance of media professionals, suicide and mental health experts and consumer organisations to inform appropriate reporting of suicide and mental illness, to minimise harm and copycat behaviour, and reduce the stigma and discrimination experienced by people with mental illness. (Mindframe, 2011)

In addition to its media guides, Mindframe has developed a series of fact sheets called 'Quick reference guides' for the media, such as the one on the previous page. The organisation has also developed a series of useful tools for public relations education and professional development.

CONCLUSION

Media kits, media guides and online media centres are tactical items that provide a great deal of information to journalists and other media workers. They can be used at media conferences, events or famils, or made available on an organisation's website. They can be developed in hard copy and/or available online. While a kit is a collection of items such as media releases, fact sheets, bios and photographs, it should be considered as a single unit insofar as it must have a cohesive presentation and a consistent message or theme. Guides usually are presented as booklet, online or in bound form. Their presentation and attention to detail, including regular updating, are very important. Consistency and clear presentation can be achieved by careful use of space, emphasis, sequencing, continuity, balance and proportion in both the content and the look of a media kit—which must, above all else, reflect the organisation, event or issue it is representing.

9 MEDIA CONFERENCES, 'FAMILS' AND EVENTS

This chapter looks at three important media tactics: media conferences, familiarisations (commonly known as 'famils') and events. The media conference—also called a press conference or news conference—is an important tool for getting important messages out to a specific group of media simultaneously. Media 'famils' (also sometimes called educationals) often have elements in common with a media conference; they are used when a single journalist or group of media are given special access to a venue, usually with a view to writing about it. Sometimes the two will be part of the same event—for example, a media conference may be called to announce the opening of a new hospital. (In this case, the media may attend the opening and be shown through the facility.) The famil is more about journalists seeing and learning something at first hand, while the media conference is held primarily to disseminate a message or provide a focus on an issue, event or organisation. Events (which can be called special events if they really are!) are occurrences outside the normal course of activity or business of an organisation. They are consciously planned and executed in order to achieve particular goals and objectives, such as fundraising, generating publicity and community engagement.

While these three topics are examined separately in this chapter, they often overlap. The case study on Hamilton Island Race Week at the end of the chapter shows how special events can also include media conferences and famils.

MEDIA CONFERENCES

While leaks and behind-the-scenes stories can place an issue on the media agenda, the media conference has a quality of fairness and democratic access to it because generally it will be open to any interested media. One of the aims of the media conference is its simultaneous dissemination of news. However, getting the media's attention for a media conference can be tricky. You must always have your radar tuned for competing events or big news that might clash with your conference. Once the media are in attendance at a media conference, they may begin tweeting your news straight away—especially if the conference is called to announce breaking news or provide comment on an ongoing controversial issue. Be prepared for this summary approach to your news and start monitoring your coverage straight away.

WHY CALL A MEDIA CONFERENCE?

The ability to disseminate information quickly and widely via email, organisational websites, Facebook pages, blogs, Twitter and SMS means organisations can often avoid calling the media together to make an announcement. However, there are still many reasons for holding a media conference, and they should give the news media something bigger, better or extra than a media release or announcement can offer. A truncated version of a conference, and one which is often used in politics, is the 'door stop' interview, set up to make an announcement 'on the run'. An example of this is illustrated in the AMA media alert in Chapter 7.

Some examples of why you might hold a media conference include the following.

Sponsorship tie-in
A media conference provides a great opportunity to associate your key sponsor/s with your event, individual or organisation. The conference

provides the opportunity to have sponsor logos or products in full view to be captured in photographs and vision. The sponsorship tie-in will often be organised in conjunction with a marketing department.

Celebrity exposure

If you need to showcase a celebrity, then a media conference provides the opportunity to get all the media in one place for interviews. Often celebrities will have limited time to spend, so it is important to maximise their exposure in a limited timeframe.

Timing is critical: Make a deadline

When a hard news story is about to break, a media conference may be the best course of action. When you want to get news to the widest possible audience all at once, then a media conference will provide this opportunity.

To clear the air, diffuse an issue or in a crisis

Media conferences are used widely to set the record straight. Rumour is often the outcome of unanswered questions, and this can be extremely damaging. A media conference can provide the opportunity to give the same message to all media at the same time.

The community consultation approach

Sometimes a meeting or conference will be called to enable community engagement. This can be a more difficult style of media conference to keep under control, especially if it is in a community hall or an open space that will accommodate large numbers of people and more so if it is about an emotional or contentious issue. Likewise, community groups can call a gathering and invite the media and the council or government representatives to attend.

Foster relationships with your media contacts

Media conferences provide an opportunity to meet with media contacts on a face-to-face basis. Thus holding a media conference has the value-added bonus of talking, discussing and explaining issues at first hand. You can use the time to consolidate professional relationships and get to know new media.

Visual appeal and stunts

Sometimes you can incorporate stunts that will provide strong vision and quirky storylines for the media. In some cases, the conference itself then becomes part of the story.

HOW TO CALL A MEDIA CONFERENCE

Usually a media conference is called by sending out a media alert or advisory. As noted in Chapter 7, this is a cross between a media release and an invitation. One of the best ways to set out a media alert is to provide a brief sentence or two announcing your conference and then list:

- who—for example, music celebrity
- what—for example, to announce a new product
- where—for example, XYZ music studio
- when—for example, Tuesday at 11.00 a.m.
- why—for example, to announce details of the new CD.

In this instance, there would be strong visuals for all media, with the musician/s available for photos and interviews only at the conference. Media alerts therefore should provide enough information to make the media want to attend, but not so much information that they have no reason to do so.

WHO TO HAVE AT THE MEDIA CONFERENCE

Part of the planning process for a media conference is the consideration of who will attend. The media will expect a person or people in a position of authority to be available to quote, so there would be no point staging a media conference without appropriate spokespeople. You will recall in Chapter 3 the discussion about 'authorised knowers'. In the case of a media conference, you will need to have such people in place. If you are a corporate organisation, then usually it will be appropriate to have a CEO or senior manager in attendance; a political media conference will call for the relevant MP or councillor; a community or activist group might use a senior spokesperson within the organisation or call in a specialist to provide an added element of authority.

When choosing which media to invite, you will refer to your media lists, as discussed in Chapter 5. It is important to look after all media and not play favourites—after all, the fundamental role of the conference is to announce something simultaneously to all media. This will usually mean considering local, daily, specialist and trade media. If an organisation has not previously attended one of your conferences, still send them an invitation each time. Many organisations simply do not have the staff to attend media conferences, and may need to access material from a website or have material emailed to them after the conference is over.

WHERE TO HOLD THE MEDIA CONFERENCE

The scope for the location of a media conference is huge, but it will likely be determined by the type of organisation and the nature of the news being announced. Media conferences held in boardrooms or venues such as conference centres can provide the best access to services, parking and familiarity to the media. This is important, as the media usually don't want to embark on navigational adventures in finding an off-the-map venue. The down-side of predictable venues is that they can be dull, lack atmosphere and may not provide a creative environment for the media; however, they do allow for greater control of noise and interruptions. You need to use your news judgement about the best venue.

More and more, media conferences are being held at on-site locations to provide a sense of atmosphere. Where possible, hold your media conference in an environment that reflects the content of the conference. Hold a media conference about a new theatrical production at the theatre, or about the birth of a zoo animal at the animal's zoo enclosure. Some news announcements lend themselves to outdoor venues. For example, police public relations personnel often make media announcements about criminal activity at a crime scene to ensure that pictures of the scene are used. This can make for stronger vision for television and photographers, who in turn assist police with getting images out and generally strengthen the news value of the story.

Such media conferences virtually self-select the venue—that is, there will be a logical location in which to hold them. So when planning a media conference for the forthcoming annual 'Schoolies' event, what better place to hold it than at a school? When the 'Schoolies' Safety Response' organisers (made up of police, ambulance, liquor licensing authorities and the department of communities) visited Southport High School on the Gold Coast in November 2011 to talk to Grade 12 students, they invited the media along. The media (and parents) were able to see, at first hand, how the management of Schoolies was being put in place, and the event achieved its aim of strong, positive media coverage by print and television. (A point to remember here: any event in a state school must be cleared with the state Department of Education and adhere to strict protocols.)

WHEN TO HAVE THE MEDIA CONFERENCE

There is no set time at which to hold a media conference. There are, however, some general guidelines. Determining whether news is 'breaking news' or 'routine news' will give a fair indication of whether or not to hold an urgent media conference. Breaking news can be staged at pretty much any time, and the media will attend. In Chapter 5, we considered news within the following three categories:

- *Routine news:* This occurs every day, but of course will vary in its newsworthiness from day to day. Types of news include that relating to courts, council and parliament.
- *Staged news:* This is often event-based and becomes news because it is created. It includes events such as agricultural shows, university open days and rock concerts.
- *Spontaneous news:* This is the unplanned part of life, including the breaking news of the day. It includes accidents, floods, cyclones and terrorism.

Timing should be considered in order to optimise media attendance. Weekends tend to be quiet news days because there are fewer staff on the job; however, there are far fewer routine news events with which to compete because bodies like courts and councils do not work on these days. Weekdays can vary, but as a general rule Friday is the busiest day so the best news day to avoid if at all possible—especially with staged or routine events. Early in the week—Monday to Wednesday—is often best for a planned media conference, usually quite early in the day, before midday.

The timing of the media conference is important because of the timeframes within which the news media work. The popularity of morning news and chat programs has given rise to live media conferences during the 7.00–8.30 a.m. time period. For example, in March 2012 when police arrested 'Australia's most wanted man' Malcolm John Naden, a nine-minute media conference was shown live on all morning news programs. The conference can be viewed at <http://www.youtube.com/watch?v=aBnb0O9-t08>, showing strong police branding of the event and an indication of the media that attended. During other major events, such as floods in Brisbane and Wagga Wagga in recent years, media conferences were aired live during the morning viewing time-slot.

Television evening news usually goes to air between 5.00 and 7.00 p.m., so it is essential to give the TV journalists the opportunity to cover your media conference and then get back to the office, write their script, edit their vision and finalise the story. Daily newspapers work to a later schedule, with their first print edition often being finalised around 9.00 or 10.00 p.m. Their online editions are updated throughout the day. Similarly, organisations such as ABC Online will post news on their online editions before their radio and TV news.

A media conference early in the day will give newspaper staff the chance to judge the importance of the story and position it accordingly. Most newsrooms hold an editorial conference at least once a day, sometimes twice, to determine their news line-up.

Radio will often update a strong news story several times in the one day, so if your story can gain traction early, it can experience good exposure through the day. A trend in radio is to have news compiled in an office quite separate from the radio station—sometimes even in another state—called a news 'hub'. Radio tends to run on very small staffing levels and so often will not attend media conferences; radio journalists are also more likely to do phone interviews or access audio from your website.

Obviously timing should be considered alongside a raft of other issues. It is important to know what else is going on in the community so you don't clash with another media conference. Some things can't be avoided, but remember that breaking or spontaneous news will always win out on the news agenda.

WHAT TO HAVE AT THE MEDIA CONFERENCE

The floor plan

The set-up of a media conference will, of course, depend on the venue. If you are preparing a conference in a building—say, a company headquarters or a conference or hotel meeting room—you can work to a standard style. A simple floor plan is shown in Figure 9.1.

Figure 9.1 Press conference floor plan

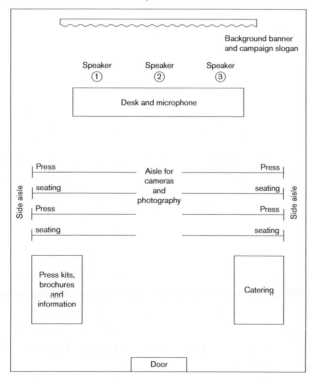

The media materials

The media will expect a range of items to be available at the conference. At the very least, journalists will expect a media release. This will announce and support what the conference is all about. It will assist with the accuracy of key points and provide background to the conference. Some conferences—especially those that can be arranged with plenty of time—will offer a full media kit. This should be available at the door on arrival and also on your website. That way, the media can peruse the documents before the start of the conference and be better informed when the conference begins. You should also make sure these materials are placed on the media link of your website.

The media will need to access people—yourself, the media relations manager (or whatever your title is), senior personnel or speakers. When possible, make sure key personnel are available for one-on-one interviews after the conference. This will allow the media the opportunity to ask specific questions, take individualised photos and so on. In crisis conferences, your senior staff may not be available after the conference or you may determine that they should not stay on for personalised interviews. Ideally, the media will have got what they wanted from the open media conference which will have allowed for questions from the media.

BACKGROUND BRIEFINGS

Before any media conference or interview situation, the media manager will need to provide the spokesperson with a background brief. This will require you to research the current situation or issue and prepare the spokesperson. You may need to write the speech or address they will be delivering, and it is important that you anticipate what the media will want to know and prepare your spokesperson with all the information they need. One general rule of thumb in advising your spokesperson is to remember the three Cs of interviewing:

1. *Concise:* Keep your message on target and keep it short
2. *Conversational:* Keep your message clear and easily understood.
3. *Catchy:* Put your message cleverly.

As well as suggesting likely questions and best responses (Q&As)—including questions you really want to avoid—you also need to have a working knowledge of the media so you can background your spokesperson on who they are likely to encounter in the interview or media conference (including any journalists who may be antagonistic). Any relevant issues that are currently on the media agenda—whether they are relevant to your main message or not—must be identified before the media meet with your spokesperson.

Golfer Greg Norman was clearly prepared when he fronted a press conference prior to the Australian Open in 2011 and was asked to comment on a current issue. A previous story that had gained a lot of media coverage had arisen from a 'racist' comment made about Tiger Woods by former caddie Steve Williams. Instead of trying to deflect questions about the issue, Norman went in prepared and gave a clear, carefully articulated response. Not only did he support Williams and defend his comments ('We have all made stupid comments'), but he ensured Woods' capacity to rise above it and focus on the game ('He is a consummate professional'). Norman's response represented wins for everybody as he 'hosed down' the media excitement about the story—so the event, the game and the individuals involved all came out in a positive light. Outcomes are not always so positive, however.

MEDIA CONFERENCES AND YOUTUBE

Where once the outcomes of a media conference might have made the evening TV news, hourly radio bulletin or daily paper, and they were never seen again, now YouTube has them available to view over and over again. This can be great if the event went well and your spokesman got the message across clearly and concisely, as illustrated in the Australian Open and police media conferences, above. However, the reality is that the YouTube videos people love to watch are those that went terribly wrong so it is unfortunate if your spokesperson makes an error, loses their temper, doesn't know the answer or makes themselves look foolish, ignorant or unprofessional in any other way. This, of course, is not just an issue for media conferences—YouTube represents a public record of a diverse range of events that are available for the world to view. It is therefore all the more important to make sure your spokesperson is media trained and on message if you do stage a media conference. It also means that you need to make sure you choose the *best* spokesperson—someone who can hold their own with the media.

Media conferences usually are staged and controlled, as discussed above. However, journalists may also seek out an interview in a less official environment (possibly a 'door stop') in order to get a comment, particularly for television or radio, which needs vision and/or audio, in a hurry. Such a scenario occurred in February 2011 following a comment made by federal opposition leader Tony Abbott. When a Channel 7 journalist approached him for a follow-up comment, Mr Abbott was quite literally caught speechless and the subsequent 'gotcha' moment—now with more than 28 000 views of the Sky/Channel 7 news story—is on permanent record as he struggles to find words amidst an excruciatingly pregnant pause. As Harris notes, the media environment is 'rougher and tougher' than ever before (Harris, 2011). Bloopers, of course, are not confined to politicians: sportspeople, on-air journalists, musicians all have their place in the stellar lineup of YouTube gaffes. This popular social media form is discussed in more detail in Chapter 13.

MEDIA 'FAMILS'

If a media conference gets a message out, it has done its job. Famils are not so likely to achieve an immediate media response. They tend to provide background or contextual information for a journalist to use in a story requiring description and background. Their importance relates to how they represent a place, often supplying a mood or a context for a story. Famils enable journalists to observe something or somewhere at first hand.

The Meetings Industry Association of Australia (MIAA) suggests that famils are the equivalent of product samples of manufacturers, and are important because you cannot touch or see a tourism or conference site unless you experience it in some form (MIAA, 2001). Famils will almost certainly be planned where a destination is the focus of the news. Look at websites for major destinations and you will find discussion about the value of famils. For example, Tourism Western Australia (2012) says:

> A familiarisation (famil) brings key trade and media from within Australia and around the world to Western Australia to experience first-hand, the products and experiences available. Media report on the state's varied holiday and touring attractions while trade groups (wholesalers, inbound operators and retail travel agents) are educated about the products available for sale to their clients.

When planning a media famil, the following guidelines may be useful, especially in the field of tourism and travel:

- Ensure the invitee is bone fide.
- Invite the media well in advance, and indicate what is included.
- Prepare a draft itinerary.
- Avoid inviting competitors at the same time.
- Media representatives are not travel agents, and their itineraries should reflect this.
- Consider costings—air travel is expensive; accommodation is usually single.
- Don't over-plan the itinerary—free time is not wasted time.
- Allow time for photography.
- Protect media from overly enthusiastic management.
- Be prepared to send media kits home for media. (Sullivan, 2012)

After a tourism famil, take the time to follow up with the journalist. Sometimes a debriefing may be useful to ensure the journalist has all the details they need and you can confirm facts, prices, place names and so on. Never ask to see a story or series of articles before they are published. This is not usual practice for the news and travel media, and will put them offside. Remember, freelance journalists and staff journalists have limited control over when their work is chosen for publication and how it is sub-edited (Sullivan, 2012).

Famils can also be highly useful to showcase an organisation, fixed object or piece of equipment that is not portable—for example, where your client is a boat builder or site engineer. In such cases, it is not just preferable to get the media into your premises, but by far the best way to showcase your new product or development. Similarly, if you are showing a new landmark building, the media will gain a greater understanding of its features if they take a tour through the building. A famil can be of huge benefit if an organisation requires controlled access by the media. Factories, mining sites and just about any industry that requires workplace safety controls will usually result in you inviting the media on tour in a controlled, supervised way.

In many news rounds, a tour of a location or facility can be important. Famils can provide an in-depth understanding of an organisation, industry or place. In any number of journalism rounds, this will occur—whether a journalist is reporting on a mine cave-in, watching an artist in their own art space or wandering around a zoological park observing animal behaviours, there is the opportunity for greater depth and understanding if a journalist has been there and experienced it at first hand.

SPECIAL EVENTS

Special events provide unique opportunities to gain publicity for an organisation or event and, likewise, provide the media with a diverse range of news angles and stories. Special events are run over a limited time period—usually a day, or a series of days—so the media have a limited window of opportunity in which to cover them during the actual event. However, special events also present opportunities in the lead-up to the event to 'drip feed' stories to the media in order to maximise news coverage before and after the event. This can provide a challenge for the media manager to identify ongoing new angles, so it is a good idea to have all staff or group members alert to stories in their department or team.

Media relations tactics for special events should present the media with as many angles as possible. Some events allow coverage in different sections of the same media outlet. For example the Emirates Melbourne Cup is covered every year in sporting, social and general news sections. In the lead up to the event it is not uncommon to see two or three approaches covered in the same publication.

Organised special events can be broadly divided into five categories:

- public events—such as Australia Day celebrations, New Year's Eve celebrations, and parades
- corporate events—such as product launches, conferences, gala dinners, fashion parades and cocktail parties
- sporting events—such as major mass participation events or elite sporting events like the Olympic Games; sporting events coupled with entertainment like grand finals, as well as opening/closing ceremonies and so on
- private events—such as weddings and parties, including those of celebrities
- festivals—such as cultural events like writers or music festivals. (Sullivan 2012)

NEWS VALUES IN SPECIAL EVENTS

- *Impact* refers to the number of people who will be affected by an event. For example, a mass participation event such as a fun run or triathlon with many thousands of competitors, or an event such as a 'welcome home' parade for the Australian Olympic team which closes the city centre for a period of time would both have broad impact.
- *Conflict* is an obvious news value for sporting events, with the opportunity to present rivals clashing head to head. Conflict can be overt or implied—so the adversarial nature of major games, particularly at grand final time, sees this news value as important (sometimes on and off the sporting field).
- *Timeliness* is about getting event news as it happens. Media are more likely to report an event if they have immediate access to information and imagery while an event is in progress, and shortly after the conclusion of the event. Many news outlets will use their online versions to cover events with a series of stories about the event's progress or a summary displayed in an online picture gallery.

- *Proximity* is important when defining your target media. Local media may be interested in covering an art gallery opening featuring a local artist or a story about 1000 people from a local community participating in a fun run or walk for charity, while national media are going to be more focused on football grand finals and major events like the Australian Open tennis championships or Mercedes Benz Fashion Week.

- *Prominence* refers to people of note participating in or attending your event. This may include professional or elite athletes as well as celebrity guests. The case study at the end of the chapter shows how Hamilton Island leveraged the 'prominence' media value in the promotion of Audi Hamilton Island Race Week.

- *Currency* is about how relevant your event is to the current news of the day or news themes. For example, a local fashion designer might launch their new range to coincide with Mercedes Benz Fashion Week in order to provide a local angle to an event of national significance. Event organisers and publicists should also think about the relevance of their event to current public interest.

- *Human interest* is a simple news value to fulfil in the promotion of special events. This is where you present your target media with an in-depth look into some of the competitors or participants. This can provide the basis for a variety of feature coverage.

- *Underdog* as news value is quite evident in some special events. In sporting events, there is always an underdog, a participant who has overcome specific hurdles to win, an unlikely hero. The media are quick to criticise a team, player or umpire who fails to play fair.

- *Unusual events*, whether they are on a local or national scale, have the potential to garner national media exposure, especially if the story is coupled with good-quality pictures and/or vision. The annual Henley-on-Todd regatta in Alice Springs is an unusual event that attracts international media attention as it is a parody of the British Henley-on-Thames rowing regatta—except that it is held on a dry riverbed 1500 kilometres away from the nearest water mass!

Source: Photo courtesy of Henley-on-Todd regatta.

MEDIA FACILITIES

It is important to know the different media's needs for covering special events. Since the opportunities for coverage of the event are limited—that is, if you miss out at the time you will not get a re-run—it is crucial to make sure all necessary equipment and facilities are in place and in working order. Remember, the media provide the opportunity to take your event beyond the audience who see it first-hand, and this wider audience can often be crucial to your sponsors and the event's future. For this reason, media relations is of prime importance in both the lead up to, and during, the event.

If it is a fashion show, ensure that journalists have front-row seats and that there is a two- or three-level platform at the end of the runway for cameras to have access to clear spots. Designate areas for specific media outlets to ensure your platform is large enough and that your key media have the best vantage spots. For sporting events, such as sailing, ocean swims and paddling events, media may require access to media boats with a stable shooting platform for cameras (preferably a catamaran) as well as an area with sun protection. For fun runs and cycling events, cameras generally shoot from the back of motorcycles, and for mass participation events or events with a geographically extended course, photographers and camera operators may need access to a helicopter.

For TV coverage of an event, consider how the footage will be transferred to the relevant TV station. Is there a mobile edit suite? Will footage be uploaded to a website? Will satellite news-gathering equipment (SNG) be required or will the TV stations bring this equipment with them? Onsite meetings and discussion about facilities should be held in a dedicated media centre, prior to the event and then ongoing as a meeting hub to ensure media have what they need.

EVENT MEDIA CENTRES

Major events have dedicated media centres on site as a central point for the distribution of media information. The media centre should be staffed by a public relations professional with a good understanding of the event. Due to the nature of some events, the media centre may be in a marquee, a demountable building or an established office. All media centres should offer high-speed wireless and cabled internet access, ample chairs and desk, access to electricity (with multiple outlets for charging mobile phones/laptop computers/tablets), a printer and photocopier, a computer bank with internet access and the home page set to your event media site, spare stationery, a first-aid kit, a lock-up area for cameras and personal equipment, a message board or personal pigeonholes, ample hard-copy event information, a TV/DVD, non-copyrighted photographs, TV monitors (if your event is being broadcast live) and access to transportation such as boats, motorcycles and helicopters for journalists, photographers and video-camera operators who need to cover the event.

Access will usually be limited to accredited media. This needs to have been sorted out well in advance, with clear identification items, such as a non-transferable pass on a lanyard or a coloured vest to be worn by all accredited media.

The case study following shows the layout of the media centre for the Audi Hamilton Island Race Week.

MEDIA CONFERENCES

During events, media conferences are best used the day prior to the event, especially to peg two rivals against each other and immediately after the event, where winners or participants of prominence can talk to all attending media at once rather than have media scrambling for access to one-on-one interviews. The venue for regular media conferences should be easily accessed by competitors or participants and accredited media.

EXCLUSIVES

A common media tactic for well-managed events is to offer different media an exclusive angle on an event. This may be an exclusive interview with a person of prominence or the right to behind-the-scenes access. In a competitive media environment, it is not realistic to expect competing media (especially magazines and television) to cover your event from the same angle. Channel 7's *Sunrise* and Channel 9's *Today Show* for instance will go to extreme lengths to ensure that their angles and coverage points of major events are vastly different. For example, while covering the 2011 Emirates Melbourne Cup, the *Today Show* had behind-the-scenes access to food preparation in the corporate marquees, while *Sunrise* was given access to the actual Melbourne Cup trophy.

ONLINE MEDIA CENTRES

All media releases and images should be displayed on the event website, in a dedicated 'Media' centre. This area should be easily accessible without any password protected log-ins. The media releases should be displayed in a list in chronological order (newest to oldest), with accompanying images, available for download (again without password protection) in either low or high resolution. Images should be captioned and also stored in a gallery so media can peruse all event images on one screen. The objective of an online media centre is that releases and images are easily available to all media outlets, the information is in one place and no special accreditation or passwords are required to access the information. If information-gathering is easy for the journalist, you will have a greater chance of achieving the coverage you seek.

AUDI HAMILTON ISLAND RACE WEEK

The annual Audi Hamilton Island Race Week is Australia's largest offshore yachting regatta, attracting more than 200 yachts each year in August for a week of sailing and socialising. Hamilton Island is located in the Whitsunday Islands on the Great Barrier Reef. The island's management use the event as an opportunity to showcase the destination to international media by hosting targeted media famils and providing facilities so working media can file stories.

Approximately 100 media individuals visit the island during the event. These media are from sailing publications, local news outlets, targeted lifestyle magazines, and include TV news crews as well as sports, social, property and travel journalists from metropolitan newspapers. The event also attracts a number of freelance photographers who provide imagery to news agencies and publications internationally.

Most media stay on the island for three days to cover the racing and social aspects of the event. They are also exposed to other story angles that are relevant to their outlet for potential coverage at another time during the year (not necessarily associated with Audi Hamilton Island Race Week).

During the event, a dedicated media centre is established. The centre is open daily from 7.00 a.m. until 7.00 p.m., providing all of the resources that the media need in order to file their stories on time. After each day's racing, a media conference is held in a public area of the marina so that event participants can observe. The conference features the top performers in the day's racing as well as skippers of yachts involved in any protests or on-water incidents.

The media centre is divided into three distinct areas. As seen in the figure on the next page, the left-hand side of the room is set up for print media. A bank of tables is in the middle of the room with PC access and room for laptops. There is high-speed wireless access for

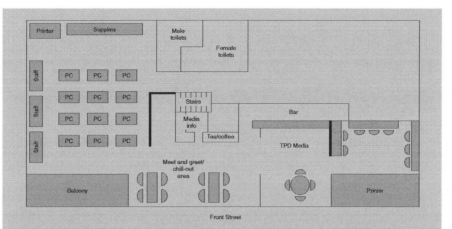

Front Street

laptop computers plus the provision of cabled internet access for photographers, which is sometimes preferable when sending large files.

The centre of the room (divided by doors) is a general lounge area and reception (as it is the entry/exit point of the room). This is an area for meetings and chatting so that working media in the rooms on either side are not distracted. Refreshments are served in this area throughout the day.

The right-hand side represents the area used for TV and radio production. The event utilises the services of Brisbane-based TPD Media, who set up a full edit suite and radio station during the event.

Each day, a TV production team of around fifteen people shoots vision of all on-water and off-water activities, edits it and compiles it into a 15–20 minute feature shown on the big screen in the marina every evening, as well as on a dedicated in-house TV channel throughout the island. The vision is also uploaded to the event website every night.

The team also edits around two to three minutes of vision, which is distributed to the news networks at 2.00 p.m. every afternoon (via an internet link) with a media release summarising the vision. In 2010, the camera crews captured magnificent vision of humpback whales playing in the water on the sailing course, including incredible shots of a large whale propelling into the air with yachts in the background. This vision was broadcast in news bulletins all over the world as well as being featured on feature TV programs like *Good Morning America*.

Another unique communications initiative employed during Audi Hamilton Island Race Week has been the establishment of a radio station. The station operates under a community licence, and Hamilton Island sourced a major sponsor (Club Marine) to cover the operating costs of the station. Race Week Radio operates every morning from 7.00 a.m. until approximately 10.00 a.m., which coincides with the time that crews prepare for their races and start their events. There are live crosses to boats on the starting line, interviews with sailors and visiting celebrities, news bulletins, giveaways and promotions—just like a metropolitan radio station.

In addition to sailing and sporting angles, a number of lifestyle and social reporters are invited to cover the off-water activities, which have included an exclusive Collette Dinnigan collection designed especially for Audi Hamilton Island Race Week, celebrity chef dinners, cocktail parties and long lunches.

The event is also used as opportunity to attract property writers to the island to experience the buzz and excitement during special event time and to report on the island's new developments and real estate opportunities.

The coverage obtained from this media relations activity extends over twelve months, includes various internet reports, blog stories, photographic spreads of social events, TV news stories, magazine features, sports reports, travel stories and, in 2011, a half-hour documentary on the event, which was screened nationally just prior to the Rolex Sydney Hobart Yacht Race.

Source: Case study supplied by Susan Sullivan, Infrontcommunications (2012).

CONCLUSION

Media conferences, famils and special events all have one thing in common: they provide the opportunity to *bring the media to you*. This effectively allows the media relations practitioner to manage the working environment. Media conferences should not be called without careful planning, and you should be sure that a conference is warranted in the first place. This will often result in news coverage of the announcement presented at the media conference. In contrast, famils should not necessarily be equated with news coverage. In many cases, journalists taking part in these will not write about the destination or product immediately, but rather stockpile the information for the future. Sometimes media relations is not so much about getting news into the news hole, but fostering relationships with members of the media with whom you plan to work in the future. Special events can provide great opportunities to work with the media and, generally speaking, the media are positive about special events because they always provide stories and photos.

10 NOT JUST THE NEWS

Up to this point, we have focused largely on media relations' involvement with news and, to some extent, features and current affairs. However, there is a massive field that goes beyond this part of the media within the broader area of popular culture. This chapter will take us beyond news to include alternative formats of the burgeoning fields of satire and parody, panel shows, lifestyle and reality programs, talkback radio and letters to the editor, as well as the role played by celebrity and product placement, as we consider the diverse opportunities for public relations in the wider mass media—particularly the area of entertainment. These alternative media forms and program choices provide opportunities for comment, product and destination exposure beyond the traditional forms of news. Extended print and broadcast formats of feature stories and current affairs are examined in Chapters 11 and 12.

THE RISE IN SATIRE, PARODY AND PANEL SHOWS

What might be considered 'straight' news now shares space with other forms of media coverage that look at issues and events in a more discursive and humorous way, using satire and parody—often in panel shows. Moore argues that 'Crikey, *The Drum*, *Q&A* and hoax-heavy satire like *The Chaser* and *Hungry Beast* . . . have given Australian journalism back its mojo' (2010, p. ix). Add to this *Gruen Planet* (and other Gruen series), *The Project, The Hamster Wheel,* and former successful formats such as *Frontline* and *Good News Week* and we can see journalism firmly positioned in the satire/parody/commentary genres of television.

Deitz (2010) suggests that we should consider 'different, overlapping journalisms' in the make up a modern Australian media ecosystem. This is an excellent way to conceptualise the world of journalism and, to a broader extent, the entertainment media. She explains:

> I don't mean to suggest that political commentators and journalists are irrelevant, but rather that they need to adjust their normative practices. A show like *The 7.30 Report* [now *7.30*] is aesthetically and intellectually out of its time and unable to comment on contemporary life because its agenda is so narrow. (2010, p. 56)

So why have parody and satire become so popular? Perhaps it's the relief they bring from the otherwise serious world of news and opinion—or perhaps fake news, satire and pranks, as Deitz suggests, better enable social and political issues to be critiqued and challenged: 'This approach catches its powerful targets off guard, and does so in a manner that is humorous and therefore arguably more powerful in terms of public engagement and knowledge' (2010, p. 57). Among the best-known Australian satires in recent years has been *The Chaser's War on Everything,* which famously and sometimes outrageously challenged the status quo. *The Chaser* team's most infamous stunt—in which they drove a motorcade through the secured area of the Asia-Pacific Economic Cooperation (APEC) forum in Sydney with a member of the team dressed as Osama Bin Laden—showed that 'there were holes in the security wide enough to drive three trucks, two motorcycles and four secret service cars through' (*The Chaser's War on Everything,* 2007). The stunt drew in 2.3 million viewers on the night it aired in September 2007 (Deitz, 2010, p. 55), and has had tens of thousands of views on YouTube and paid DVDs since.

The Chaser's successor, *The Hamster Wheel,* was subtitled: 'How the week's news is made': it was about news but also about commentary *on* news. A common theme in many of these programs is the use of comedians to front the programs as well as, or instead of, journalists. The nightly panel show *The Project* has settled into prime-time viewing, bringing together a panel of comedians and journalists (and sometimes other celebrities) to discuss the news and current affairs of the day. In a similar way, the panel-based *Gruen* series brings the two together. The various series—most recently *Gruen Planet*—are hosted by comedian Wil Anderson, who leads two advertising executives and two guests through a weekly critique of stunts, campaigns and contemporary issues. In presenting an alternative to mainstream news and current affairs, programs such as this question and parody contemporary politics, business and celebrity, securing positions on prime-time television.

REALITY TV

Comedy, drama and modern-day life are all a part of one of the most pervasive of TV genres: the reality program. But while reality TV may be a contemporary TV success, it is not new. Beginning with *Candid Camera* in 1948, it became a well-entrenched TV genre by the 1990s. In bringing together low-cost production techniques with narrative storylines from dramatic fiction or comedy, reality television provided a genre that captured the imagination of audiences because of the 'realness' and 'ordinariness' of its depictions of life. As Slocum (2005) notes:

> All of these series share a dominant characteristic of the reality-soap genre: they find compelling storylines in hundreds of hours of videotaped life and, through careful writing and editing, shape the real-life subjects into reality-show characters. Documentaries have always done that, but . . . to engage the audience, this genre moves from observation to storytelling in a way traditional documentaries have not.

By using hours of film without the documentary level of editing and rearranging, reality programming provides a window to lives and lifestyles we would not otherwise see—the veterinarian's surgery, the hospital, other people's bedrooms and living rooms, the police station, customs work, the crime lab and so on. Of course, there has been a significant change in reality TV from the *Candid Camera* experience—filming is no longer done covertly. Where *Candid Camera* provided 'unscripted insights into human behaviour and social relationships' (Clissold, 2004, p. 50), newer forms of reality TV are conducted overtly. The rise in reality programming has also brought with it a scepticism about the true reality of what is shown. It is argued that these shows have become scripted and constructed, epitomising some of the concepts raised in Chapter 3. Once filming enters awareness—indeed, people are brought together to act out their own life's experience before a camera—reality TV becomes less 'real':

> One of the biggest criticisms of the recent reality TV craze is that there is actually nothing 'real' about programs such as *Survivor* where camera crews openly move around with the action and where participants directly address the camera in routine asides. (Clissold, 2004, p. 50)

In her account of 'ordinary television', Bonner (2003, p. 24) notes that reality television began at 'the sharp end of public service activities'—in particular, police and emergency workers—and fragmented into different types of docudrama. Nevertheless, police and emergency workers maintain a high presence in reality TV. Police use various reality shows to raise their profile. Research by McGovern and Lee found that:

> policing agencies have become increasingly keen to partner television production companies in producing reality television series of policing—or 'observational documentaries'—as they are somewhat euphemistically known. (2010, p. 109)

Police have been involved in no less than six such 'observational documentaries' (McGovern and Lee, 2010, p. 109). The director of police media relations in Western Australia explained that the unit's objectives were to:

> Demonstrate the professionalism of the police; raise public confidence in policing in our jurisdiction; allow the community to better understand the

challenges that the police face; allow the community to understand the types of decisions that the police have to make. For example, there's been a recent controversy about the use of tasers. Through shows like *The Force*, we're able to show the training that occurs. (McGovern and Lee, 2010, p. 112)

The New South Wales Director of Corporate Affairs explained the targeted approach to each program:

Each show will have a different corporate objective like ... *Crash Investigation Unit* clearly has road safety messages in it so that's why we make that show and because when you're confronted with those investigations you get people thinking about all those sorts of issues. (McGovern and Lee, 2010, p. 111)

For the police, together with other government departments such as customs in *Border Patrol*, there are compelling reasons to be involved in reality programming. Clearly, there are promotional angles in each of these programs. As Bonner (2003) points out, reality TV represents all manner of industries, lifestyles and experiences, and the styles of 'reality television' have become increasingly varied—*Big Brother* is different from *Australia's Top Model* and *Beauty and the Geek*, and different again from *Bondi Rescue, Bondi Vet, Border Security, Biggest Loser* and *Keeping up with the Kardashians*. While all of them bring to the viewer the lives and work of the 'ordinary' and the not so ordinary person, they also bring with them social and political comment, making participants an important part of wider social conversations. Deitz (2010) cites a 2004 episode of *Big Brother* in which evictee Merlin Luck taped 'Free the Refugees' across his mouth while on stage:

Luck later travelled the country speaking on panels with human rights lawyers and politicians. In later media interviews he attempted to increase the public's awareness of Australia's policy of mandatory detention. (2010, p. 13)

This statement shows the power of the reality program when it comes to sending a message.

Other reality show participants also send powerful messages through the way they live their lives. It is argued that *Keeping up with the Kardashians* entrances teenagers because the women in the program are attractive, lead glamorous lives and rub shoulders with celebrities—a far cry from reality for most people. This program has been criticised for its lack of reality and its negative influence on teenagers (McDonald, 2011), with a study of young American women finding that, in the wake of the series, 31 per cent believe they will be famous (*Gruen Planet*, 2011).

Television continues to push the boundaries in trying to create true reality; a recent attempt is SBS's *The Family*—dubbed a 'real' reality program—about the Cardamone family. Reality TV has much in common with other popular genres—notably lifestyle television and competition programs, as well as documentaries.

DOCUMENTARIES

The extended format of documentaries can provide the opportunity to tell longer, more complex stories that deal with content as varied as the evening news, but covered in far greater detail. On the one hand, they are known for their in-depth investigations into big issues—like war, corruption and crime—but documentaries also showcase people, lifestyles and events. Examples are the ABC's *Australian Story* or SBS's *Man vs Wild* (SBS calls the latter a documentary but you could argue it is also a 'reality program').

While they are about aspects of real life, it is argued that they can also be very subjective. Documentary filmmaker Stefan Jarl says that although documentaries usually are associated with *cinéma vérité*— that is, a movie that is both objective and accurate—this is far from an accurate description. He notes that 'there is no such thing as an accurate documentary' because the documentary is filmed through the filmmaker's subjective lens, the scenes are rearranged, and 'a filmmaker is a manipulator' (in Tobias, 1998, p. 149). Once again, this position takes us back to some of the theoretical perspectives suggested in Chapter 3—questions about what is real and what is created. These theories can be revisited in the context of documentaries. It also finds critique in common with the way reality shows are packaged.

Jarl puts a compelling argument for the documentary to remain true to what he calls its 'mission and fate'. By this he means that the documentary is meant to show alternate perspectives, unsanitised—and, if not real, presenting at least a glimmer of reality:

> [D]ocumentaries should be in places like dirty factories, retirement homes, Sarajevo, missing galleries, culverts and hospital corridors. Documentaries should also be in the homes of the hungry and the unemployed, with vagrants and the outcasts, in the dark passages of the neighbourhoods, on the park benches, in prisons, with the downtrodden and the oppressed, the abused, the unjustly rewarded and with those we have deprived of everything and alongside people without a voice. (Jarl, in Tobias, 1998, p. 153)

Some documentaries do push a corporate or political agenda, and are used as tools of advocacy as well as exposé. One example is *An Inconvenient Truth*—the 2006 documentary about former US Vice-President Al Gore's campaign to educate the world about climate change. Others also stay true to their mission while presenting less complex or serious stories. Who could resist the idea of travelling around Vietnam after watching *Luke Nguyen's Vietnam*? Or wouldn't be tempted to dabble in a little archaeology after an episode of *Time Team*? Or want to take to the kitchen to recreate the best of the *River Cottage* dishes? Shapiro (in Tobias, 1998) argues that when people watch non-fiction, news, reality shows, interview shows and documentaries, they expect the truth. 'We owe our audience accuracy, honesty and truthfulness,' he notes (in Tobias, 1998, p. 268). In this regard, documentaries are less likely to have the commercial undercurrent that might be found in reality, lifestyle and game shows, which often use product placement or sponsored items.

In media relations, unless you are a filmmaker the most likely involvement you'll have with documentaries, lifestyle or game shows will be through the supply of talent for interviews, possibly a venue, a product or service. You need to be sure about the context in which your organisation will be portrayed before taking part, and once you have ascertained this, you'll need to consider contracts or written agreements about what is expected of you and your organisation.

LIFESTYLE AND GAME SHOWS

At around the same time as the emergence of reality TV came a boon in lifestyle programs. These are derived from the consumer-driven perspective in which experiences, products and expertise are shown to improve life. According to Bonner: 'Lifestyle television addresses an individual viewer with advice about consumption practices ostensibly designed to improve the quality of life in the area addressed by the program' (2003, p. 104). Where reality programs generally appeal to a younger (under 40) audience, lifestyle programs tend to be watched by an older (over 40) audience (Bonner, 2003).

Like all genres, lifestyle programs have evolved with the times. The late 1990s and early 2000s series of *Burke's Backyard, Better Homes and Gardens* and *The Great Outdoors*—with TV presenters showing how it's done or taking us there—have largely been replaced by alternatives where you do it yourself and hopefully win prizes along the way. These are something of a hybrid of reality TV, lifestyle and game shows, and include *The Block, The Renovators* and *MasterChef. Top Gear* has remained true to the earlier lifestyle format, with specialists in the driver's seat, showing and telling audiences which cars are fastest, safest and coolest—all with the quirky and blokey humour for which the show has become famous. This winning combination is estimated to have around 350 million viewers per week in 170 different countries. As *CBS News* points out: 'No one ranks the most popular television programs on the planet, but if they did, one of them would have to be *Top Gear*':

> The program is ostensibly about cars. But it's really about the adventures of three clever middle-age blokes who travel the world conducting all sorts of elaborate competitions, races and challenges that push the boundaries of television and automotive acceptability. It is part reality show, part buddy movie, part *Monty Python*. (CBS, 2010)

In Australia, the program rates second only to MasterChef (Throng, 2010). Table 10.1 shows the top ten programs, and the average number of viewers, from a 2010 survey of adults aged under 50. The top four programs—*MasterChef, Top Gear, Survivor* and *Bondi Rescue*—are either reality or lifestyle/game shows.

Table 10.1 Top shows for the 18–49 years demographic

Rank	Show	Viewers
1	MasterChef Australia	835 000
2	Top Gear	797 000
3	Survivor: Heroes vs Villains	655 000
4	Bondi Rescue	600 000
5	NCIS	595 000
6	Australia's Got Talent	570 000
7	Grey's Anatomy	549 000
8	Two and a Half Men (Rpt)	531 000
9	The 7pm Project	489 000
10	A Current Affair	477 000

Source: Adapted from Throng (2010).

As with reality programs, characters in these programs often shoot to celebrity status because of their part in the program. This phenomenon is discussed in more detail below. Lifestyle and game shows hold a wealth of opportunities for the media relations practitioner by having products, destinations or events in focus. This therefore has elements of another growing part of the popular and commercial media mix: product placement.

PRODUCT PLACEMENT

A logical extension of the commodity-driven lifestyle program is the use of product placement, also known as product integration, sponsored content or advertising tie-ins, on television and in movies. Early examples of product placement saw Gordon's Gin featured in *The African Queen* in the 1950s and the famous Aston Martin DB5 driven by James Bond in *Goldfinger* in the 1960s. Newell (2003), who has traced product placement through the twentieth century, notes how public relations was involved in the industry very early on. A Columbia Pictures contact list for 'tie-up merchandise' at that time, containing products, names and addresses from 43 companies, placed the responsibility for product placement with public relations rather than advertising: 'About half the companies were represented in Hollywood by public relations firms, with Hill and Knowlton the most frequently appearing source' (2003, p. 19).

Cars, alcoholic and non-alcoholic drinks, chocolate, shoes, underwear, computers—the range of branded products that may be seen these days on television and in movies is as wide as the supermarket shelves. Some movie and TV placements have included:

- Coopers beer in *The Castle*
- Red Stripe beer in *The Firm*
- Pepsi in *Back to the Future*
- Reese's Pieces in *ET*
- Nissan in *Desperate Housewives*
- Apple Powerbook in *Sex and the City*
- Brumby's bakeries in *Kath and Kim*
- Marlboro in *Girl with the Dragon Tattoo.*

Once firmly established in movies in the 1970s and 1980s, product placement moved comfortably to TV sets in homes around the world. The development of video recording devices and remote controls at this time gave TV audiences the power to switch off during advertisements, hence advertisers had to work creatively to place their products within the programs themselves. Although well established in the genres of drama and sit-coms, the growth in lifestyle and reality programs has also seen massive expansion in product placement in these formats. In *American Idol*, for example, Coca-Cola had clearly labelled products on the judges' tables and in the contestant's rooms. Coca-Cola, along with Ford and AT&T wireless, was reported to have paid US$26 million for 'product integration' in this program (Neer, 2006).

Bonner (2003, p. 99) notes that 'consumption is one of the most pervasive of televisual discourses'. Taken to the extreme, this is seen in infomercials, the television equivalent of the print advertorial (discussed in Chapter 11); however, it is also found in lifestyle programs, where products are used to achieve an outcome. Nowhere is this more apparent than in programs that show the viewer how to fix, create and buy things:

In Australia, *The Block* was a world-class entry in the product placement stakes. Tooheys Extra Dry, Toyota, Freedom Furniture, Panasonic, Black & Decker, Masterfoods and the Commonwealth Bank all paid to have their products positioned prominently in the series. (Idato, 2003)

At a less obvious level is the drama or sit-com, in which products are simply used or featured in the script. However, while once it may have been a novelty to pick the product within a program or movie, nowadays named products are the norm. These can amount to dozens of product placements or mentions. *Vanity Fair* magazine conducted what it called an 'unscientific count' of products either seen or 'blatantly mentioned' in the first *Sex and the City* movie (2008), and found the following list of fashion designers (and this does not include other blatant mentions of food or restaurants):

- Manolo Blahnik
- Vivienne Westwood
- Louis Vuitton
- Chanel
- Dior
- Ferragamo
- Roger Vivier
- Diane von Furstenberg
- Hermès
- Christian Louboutin
- Prada
- Escada
- Versace
- Gucci
- Vera Wang
- Oscar de la Renta
- Carolina Herrera
- Christian Lacroix
- Lanvin
- Nike
- Adidas
- Burberry

- Tiffany and Co
- Swarovski
- Hello Kitty.

Product placement has become an industry in its own right, with companies now monitoring what's coming up in television and movies and matching products with productions. In fact, the idea of creating a product simply to fill a role in a movie or on television is not unheard of—in 2004, Audi created the RSQ car for the movie *I Robot*.

While commonplace in Australia and the United States, product placement was restricted in Britain until 2011. In February of that year, the Independent Regulator and Competition Authority for the United Kingdom Communications Industries (Ofcom) changed the laws to allow TV shows and films made in the United Kingdom to include product placement (Ofcom, 2011). *The Guardian* newspaper reported that the new rules would enable commercial broadcasters to access new sources of revenue, while providing protection for audiences:

> Four categories of content—films (which includes dramas and documentaries); TV series including soap operas; entertainment shows; and sports programs—will be free to use product placement. (Robinson, 2010)

THE ROLE OF CELEBRITY

The role of celebrity brings many of these genres together. It is what Poh Ling Yeow, Guy Sebastian and Kim Kardashian have in common—all having been springboarded to fame through competition, lifestyle or reality TV programs. Poh, for instance—the runner-up in season one of *MasterChef*—has moved on to her own cooking series, *Poh's Kitchen*, and has book deals with HarperCollins publishers (Ten Network, 2011). But how do we define 'celebrity' and how can we critically evaluate the concept of what a celebrity actually is?

In their analysis of how celebrities are produced, Turner, Bonner and Marshall (2000) link the notion of celebrity to publicity. They argue that publicity generally describes the central processes through which celebrity is manufactured and traded in the Australian media today (2000, p. 31). As noted in Chapter 1, the term 'publicity' is that part of public relations commonly associated with media relations. Turner, Bonner and Marshall explain that 'publicity is designed to turn advertising into news' (2000, p. 31), and point out that celebrities can do this either through their endorsement of a product or by representing themselves as a commodity (or both).

Boorstin (1961) looks to the creation of celebrity in *The Image*. As explained in Chapter 3, Boorstin identified what he called the 'pseudo-event' in the creation of news. He argues that: 'the celebrity is a person who is known for his [sic] well-knownness . . . He is the human pseudo-event' (1961, p. 57). There are clear synergies between manufacturing celebrity and manufacturing news. The creation of celebrity has resulted in an industry that has grown phenomenally in the past few decades. By the early 1980s, there was a shift towards the commercial production of celebrity, which included the beginning of the promotion of the company CEO as celebrity (Turner et al., 2000). We have seen this in Australia and the United Kingdom with characters such as Richard Branson from Virgin Airlines, and in the United States with Donald Trump—first a businessman then a reality program host. A more recent aspect of the manufacturing of celebrity has been the growth in the reality TV celebrity. At once a paradox due to the ordinariness of reality TV and the extraordinariness that constitutes celebrity, this new breed of stars illustrates how private lives becoming public can change lives—at least for a short time. This shift between the role of ordinary and special is consistent with the idea that the actors in reality TV give up their private (ordinary) lives to become public (special). Indeed, part of the process of creating celebrity is the need to merge the private with the public. Another more recent phenomenom is the rise of the celebrity journalist, with journalists acting as the source of authority.

Celebrities may be viewed on a spectrum. At the one end is the celebrity who is totally managed by specialist agents like Harry M. Miller in Australia. At the more grassroots level is the 'occasional celebrity', like a TV news or weather reader or a local sports personality, who manages their own identity and whose public image may be consistent with a specific theme, organisation or product. In media relations, celebrities may be incorporated into the image of an organisation, product, campaign or event, to provide excitement, endorsement or credibility. However, we need to be aware that the role of celebrity can present a double-edged sword. Celebrities may become commodities to assist with promotions, but they are nevertheless human, and this gives each the potential to change, to do the 'wrong thing' or to present an image that is counter-productive to the image they are employed to represent. Tiger Woods' infidelity scandal in 2009, which saw him dumped by various sponsors, is one of the best-known falls from grace by a celebrity. Management company Accenture, Gatorade and AT&T were said to have dropped Woods' sponsorship because he no longer reflected the companies' ethos (O'Reilly, 2011). Chapter 13 provides illustrations of the issues associated with celebrity and the use of social media.

The concept of celebrity may be very exciting, but public relations practitioners have to be sensible and realistic in their use of this tactic. Restrictions on who you might approach will include budget (Can you afford them?), contracts with other organisations (Are they available?) and physical location (Can they get to where you need them at the right time?). Before any approaches are made to a celebrity or their agent, the first consideration should be about the 'fit' with your organisation, issue or event. Ask yourself:

- Are they well known for a particular position?
- Do they have a certain image?
- Are they identified with a certain section of the community?
- Have they a profile that is consistent with your own?

TALKBACK RADIO

Talkback radio has been called 'dial-in democracy' because of its capacity to let citizens phone radio stations to have their say. It does represent a form of two-way communication, and it does provide a medium with significant reach to a given audience; however, because phone-ins are usually vetted before they go on air and callers are not always representative of the community, talkback cannot necessarily be seen as a true barometer of the community. The opportunity to respond online to radio has expanded this format, so—like all online media—issues can be aired and opinions can be expressed.

In Australia, talkback began on Sydney radio's 2GB in April 1967. It is recounted in this way:

> Suddenly, to the isolated and housebound, human contact was only as far away as their trannie. They could now become involved, articulate their views, air their problems, offer solutions. *They could make a difference.* (Marsden, 1999, p. 7)

But talkback is not restricted to the socially isolated or the home listener. Politicians, corporate spokespeople and community activists can all phone through their opinions on any issue under discussion. Talk radio (as it is summarily known, distinguishing it from music radio), with radio announcers presenting their opinions, received national attention during the 'cash for comment' controversy of the 1990s. The Australian Broadcasting Authority's (ABA) Inquiry into broadcast radio in 2000 saw talkback hosts Alan Jones and John Laws investigated for receiving money in exchange for favourable comment on air. It made the media industry focus closely on the previously blurred lines between news and current affairs, and advertising and sponsorship. The lesson for public relations is simple: if you are providing material to the media for which you are paying for editorial control, make sure it is labelled as such. Similar issues are discussed in Chapter 13.

Following that inquiry, a report found that talkback radio was acknowledged as an agenda-setter among journalists. It discovered that talkback is a 'litmus test' of what citizens are saying, and that community and political leaders use talkback to get their own messages across (Pearson and Brand, 2001). Clearly social media has moved into this space, but talkback still commands major audience share. Moreover, it is widely accepted that radio hosts—particularly those who have achieved celebrity status, like Alan Jones, John Laws, Kyle Sandilands and Jackie O, to name a few—hold significant power as agenda-setters.

LETTERS TO THE EDITOR

Once the litmus test of public opinion in newspapers, letters to the editor pages have undergone some changes in recent times, and also adapted to TV formats. Nowadays, newspaper letters pages can be made up of traditional letters or tweets, and TV talk shows often include emails and tweets from viewers and audience members. Whether as full 'letters', emails or republished tweets, the 'letters' page or section represents public opinion. They can bring a single story into focus if enough people write about it, developing it into a news theme or trend that can last days or even weeks. Like tweets and blogs (which are discussed in more detail in Chapter 13), letters and emails can also put an issue on the news media's agenda.

Letters to the editor can cause a groundswell of pressure. They can also be used by individuals and organisations to 'fly a flag'—that is, to see what the response will be to a letter of a controversial nature. These days, their role overlaps so much with blogging and citizen journalism that it seems likely that letters pages—as distinct entities—might soon become a thing of the past. Trends in consumer-driven media are discussed in Chapter 13.

CONCLUSION

Media relations is not just about 'making' the daily newspaper, radio news or evening TV news bulletin. While these are central to the media relations professional, they are only part of a multi-layered approach to the very complex world of media. The popular media are about entertainment and information, and the wide variety of opportunities that are available can provide a good 'fit' with just about any organisation, industry, issue, event, product or person. In print, letters to the editor are a viable form of making a statement; in television, documentaries, reality TV and lifestyle programs cover a wide range of options; in radio, talkback is about getting heard and setting agendas, often led by celebrity radio hosts. At the same time, popular culture has become more attuned to satire and parody to tell stories, focus attention and create debate—sometimes with journalists doing the storytelling but just as often with entertainers as the anchors or hosts. Within the diverse and extensive melting pot of media choice also come the options of product placement and celebrity—both massive industries in their own right and both feeding into and out of the media relations zone.

11 WORKING WITH NEWSPAPERS AND MAGAZINES

Australia's media industry has emerged out of its print publications. Many of the print-specific terms are still used to describe a more general media—terms like 'press conference' and 'press release', and expressions like 'freedom of the press'. These really refer to the media in general, but the old tags remain. For a long time, though, the newspaper was the only medium available for daily news, and it continues to draw a constant supply of readers. In Chapter 2, we read that newspapers in Australia began with the *Sydney Morning Herald* in 1831. Daily papers in Melbourne, Hobart, Brisbane and Perth were all established by 1860. This history, and the fact that newspapers held the prime share of media for a century before television, established the press as a 'caretaker of democracy'. The idea of the press as the 'Fourth Estate', overseeing the political institutions of government and church, saw its foundations as the voice of and for the people. Newspapers have gone through massive changes since the mid-1800s, with growth and downturns, the demise of 'afternoon' newspapers, the merging of morning dailies, consolidation of ownership, changes to format, style and production practices. Many of these changes have occurred in the face of technological change, new media competition and changing consumption patterns. Moving online represented the biggest change to the newspaper industry in nearly 200 years. Not since the introduction of penny presses in the 1830s have newspapers undergone such radical change to format and availability.

Like the industry itself, the role of the journalist found its genesis in newspapers. The professional association for these workers, the Australian Journalists Association (AJA), founded in 1910, is now part of the Media, Entertainment and Arts Alliance (MEAA). The MEAA still provides guidelines for industry practice and ethics to all journalists, but particularly print media. In addition, the Australian Press Council (APC) is part of the self-regulation of the industry, providing a framework for professional practice by print journalists (as discussed in Chapter 2). This chapter will provide an overview and discussion of print media—newspapers and magazines—both online and in hard copy. While there is clearly a convergence across different media, the chapter will focus on print-specific concepts and ideas in order to inform the media relations practitioner about best practice in this sector.

BENEFITS OF PRINT MEDIA

While the print media have had to adapt and change with electronic media since television was introduced in the 1950s, they nevertheless hold some benefits for the suppliers of news and news audiences that other media do not. The print media are long established within society, and we take it for granted that roundspeople from newspapers will regularly attend parliament, courts, local government meetings, rallies, annual general meetings and so on. The idea of the roundsperson is deeply embedded in newspapers. What this means to us in media relations is the opportunity to form professional relationships with specialist reporters who cover topics relevant to our industry, cause or organisation. Thus we can network with journalists and get to know them and their needs. Specialised magazines and trade journals also provide this opportunity. Because much of media relations is about networking, developing relationships and trust, print publications' dedication to the roundsperson continues to hold opportunities for getting stories to a wide range of audiences. Other major benefits of print are:

- It collectively provides a massive news space, and therefore relies on information and news via media relations professionals.
- The range of publications is incredibly varied, and thus reaches a similarly varied range of audiences.

As we will see throughout this chapter, there are various 'types' of publication targeted to reach widespread, niche or specific audiences. Mainstream publications such as *The Australian* can get stories to people all over the country about politics, corporate developments, trade and so on. Regional or community publications look at more local stories dealing with a geographic location about councils, local developments, events, schools, business and so on. Their news value is proximity—that is, the story must be about the local area. They may include national or international stories, but these will be allocated less space unless there is a local angle, and will likely be based on a standard wire service story. Alternate and trade publications reach very specific, but usually very dedicated, readerships, making them perfect for stories that include minority points of view or specific industries (the latter usually being read in places of business rather than at home). Because there is a wide range of print media available to us in media relations, it is important to target stories to the most effective publication, hence we need to know the media. There is no substitute for reading and monitoring the vast array of print publications available to ultimately target the best newspapers or magazines to reach a desired audience.

In general, the benefits of print media include:

- They are known as the historical record of media.
- They are available in hard copy and online, depending on the publication and personal choice.
- They are portable—you can read a hard-copy newspaper or magazine or an online edition on a portable device anywhere.
- They can be reread—you can store a publication and go back over it.
- They have space for large, complex stories, and are generally considered better for discussion of complicated issues.
- They allow the use of pictures—available in other visual media, but not radio.

- They will run stories that do not have pictures (newspapers in particular), based on news merit, because they are not picture-dependent like television.
- They provide a range of genres in the one edition—news stories, features, letters to the editor, columns, reviews, classified advertising.
- They are cheap and sometimes free—this applies largely to newspapers, but sometimes also to magazines.
- They remain agenda-setters for all media.

While circulation of many printed newspapers has fallen in recent years, analysts say they are still working out metrics to capture sales through smartphones and apps, and calculate all sales. This issue will be discussed further at the end of the chapter.

DAILIES AND WEEKEND PAPERS

News Ltd and Fairfax Media dominate the daily newspapers in Australia. With the exception of Sydney and Melbourne, every capital city in Australia now has only one mainstream daily metropolitan print paper. Sydney has the News Ltd's *Daily Telegraph* and Fairfax's *Sydney Morning Herald*; Melbourne has News Ltd's *Herald Sun* and Fairfax's *The Age*. All these papers run print and online editions. Meanwhile, Brisbane has the print and online *Courier-Mail*, and Fairfax's daily online (only) *Brisbane News*. In addition, there are two national newspapers, News Ltd's *The Australian* and Fairfax's *Financial Review*.

In 2000, Crikey.com was launched on to the Australian news scene. A daily online news service—sometimes called an ezine—Crikey.com is the only national daily publication from an independent publisher, rivalling the traditional online newspapers. What also sets Crikey.com apart is its paid subscription basis and its independence from the mainstream. Crikey is discussed in Chapter 2 and will be discussed further in Chapter 13.

Another addition to the daily newspaper scene in the past decade has been the small-format, print-only metropolitan commuter papers. These papers followed the emergence of international commuter papers like *Metro* in Europe, America and Asia. The best known of these in Australia is News Ltd's *mX*, targeted at 18–39-year-old commuters in Melbourne, Sydney and Brisbane. It is interesting that this target demographic represents the news consumers who tend towards online news rather than hard-copy print. Based on Nielsen Media Research, *mX* reaches around 750 000 people across the three eastern state capital cities (Nielsen Media Research, 2011).

There are distinct differences between tabloids or popular papers (smaller formats) and broadsheets or quality papers (larger formats) whether in hardcopy or online. Tiffen (1989) notes that the popular papers cover more sport, less business, less politics, less features or comment, more cartoons and astrology. While his book *News and Power* was written almost two decades ago, much of his analysis remains relevant today. He notes that the quality papers:

> carry an authority and political relevance the more popular media sometimes lack, partly because of their credibility, partly because they are overwhelmingly the news organs which political elites and participants consume most. (Tiffen, 1989, p. 18)

A trend in recent years has been increased segmentation in newspapers. This has followed the fragmentation of the market and the few broadsheets that are left—*The Age*, the *Sydney Morning Herald* and *The Australian*—have many sections. The *Sydney Morning Herald*, for example, has 20 sections that run either each day, like News, Business Day and Sport, or one day a week, like News Review and Money (Fairfax Media, 2008).

Saturday papers are bigger—intended to provide whole-weekend reading with a focus on features, often including a magazine insert such as *The Australian Magazine* in *The Weekend Australian* and *Good Weekend* in Saturday's *Sydney Morning Herald* and *The Age*. Some cities still produce Sunday papers. Competition between dailies and Sunday papers can be fierce, despite the fact that most Sunday papers are produced out of the same stable of papers (that is, owned by the same group). Sunday papers are compiled throughout the week, and thus they have to compete with their daily stablemates for news.

Regional dailies are another newspaper option. These papers are produced daily, and often compete with the metropolitans for circulation space. Regional dailies tend to fall between the metropolitan dailies and the community newspapers in that they cover local stories and issues but also allocate space for issues of a broader nature and wider significance. Nevertheless, their hybrid qualities—a local paper that also carries national or international stories—make them a good 'one-paper' option for many readers, particularly in rural and regional areas.

WEEKLIES AND COMMUNITY PAPERS

Weekly, community and suburban newspapers are all about providing a form of social cohesion and community connectedness. These papers are argued to be: 'Valued for covering local issues, events and news that really matter to our communities . . . perceived to be without bias, agenda and sensationalism' (News Ltd, 2012). While this is a promotional quote for its advertisers, this comment does sum up the ethos of the local paper. Independent research conducted for News Ltd found that people thought their local newspaper was:

- Honest: 58 per cent
- Trustworthy: 57 per cent
- Friendly or caring: 63 per cent
- Down to earth: 72 per cent
- Informative: 72 per cent
- Relevant: 74 per cent. (News Ltd 2012)

A main strength of community newspapers for media relations is that they represent a different readership. Star News, an independent operator in Victoria, calls itself the 'heart of the community' (Star News, 2012). Small papers such as this provide neighbourhood based stories where locals can tell their stories and see their names and pictures in print.

The content of community newspapers may be divided into two broad areas (or a mixture of both):

- often referred to as the 'parish pump', covering stories such as sixtieth wedding anniversaries, cattle sales, school fetes and community events, and
- local advocate, taking on the role of the voice of the local community, and covering more controversial stories about development and change.

Community papers also service remote, isolated or out-of-the-way communities, which are not well provided for by mainstream papers, although, as the next chapter discusses, may well be serviced by local radio. They are also important for smaller, national communities in developing countries. For example, the Pacific Island nation of Vanuatu has two papers—*The Daily Post* and the weekly *The Independent*. These papers cover news across many of the country's 82 islands. *The Independent*, for instance, publishes news in three languages—English, French and Bislama—and *The Daily* runs news and sport in English and Bislama. These papers must therefore supply not only multiple languages but function as both national and community papers. While *The Independent* runs online and hard-copy editions, many villages in these islands do not have access to computers (or electricity) so the hard copy remains the staple supply of news for most communities.

ALTERNATIVE PRESS

Often independent papers are the most outspoken. One example of this type of paper is the Byron Bay *Echo*, which has become known for its opposition to certain commercial developments in the town. The *Echo* is unusual in Australia's newspaper landscape because it is independently owned and has been in production since 1986. Newspapers like the *Echo* may be both a community and an alternative newspaper—alternative because it represents divergent views; community because it is written for a localised, geographic group. Similarly, we could categorise much multicultural media as a hybrid between community and alternative press, not because they are necessarily counter-culture, but because they are not mainstream. Crikey.com might also see itself as an 'alternative' publication because of its independent ownership and critical perspectives. Clearly, then, not all categories are mutually exclusive.

The alternative press is usually considered to be newspapers that are either radical (left or right wing), counter-culture or divergent from the mainstream. One database of 380 alternative publications notes that these publications 'report and analyse the practices and theories of cultural, economic, political and social change, which includes topics such as the theory and practice of socialism, national liberation, labour, indigenous peoples, gays/lesbians, feminism, ecology, democracy and anarchism (La Trobe Library, 2006). Forde (1998) identifies Australia's alternative press in the 1990s as being committed to 'filling the gaps' in mainstream press and covering issues that the daily papers do not cover:

> The mainstream press in Australia, and indeed most Western nations, claims a strong and romantic history. But our alternative press also has a strong past, harking back to the days of the great general strikes and the anti-conscription movement, which were all captured in detail by the radical working-class press. Similarly, the counter-culture publications of the late 1960s and 1970s recorded and reflected a time of major social change and upheaval in our nation. (1998, p. 120)

It is no coincidence that the emergence of the alternative press over this time coincided with a shrinking of print media outlets and ownership in the mainstream market. While the monopolies of ownership remained strong in the mainstream press, an alternate press began to flourish.

One thing that distinguishes the alternative press is its niche-market audience. Its presence in the market means that small or marginal groups can be reached, and often this is more easily undertaken on the internet, a less expensive option that has been enthusiastically embraced by this sector. These publications represent excellent vehicles to get specific messages out to specific audiences. While their audiences may be smaller than mainstream ones, their readers are generally very committed. The ethos of alternative print has much in common with that of community radio and television, which will be discussed in the following chapter and were also examined in Chapter 2.

TRADE PUBLICATIONS

Also referred to as 'the trades', these publications are often magazine format rather than newspapers. They are generally subscription based, catering to professional and industry groups—hence the name 'trade'. *Margaret Gee's Australian Media Guide* and *Media Monitors Media Directory* include all major media outlets in Australia and list hundreds of trade and specialty magazines—from accounting to welding. One of the main characteristics of these publications is that their audience is very specifically defined. Like the alternative press, trades are read by people who seek them out, and who are members of a particular group—in this case, a professional or industry group. These publications exist for hundreds of industries, informing people from within the industry about what's happening within it and to it—from new laws, market trends, research and development to new products and services, company events and who is working where. They are widely used as a business-to-business tactic, and can assist in keeping up with your own or allied industries or to put your own story out there. Trade magazines on the internet can also be linked to businesses in the same sector as a resource and reference. For example, one hospitality service business has links to *HOTELS Magazine, National Hotel Executive, Association Meetings,* and *Corporate Meetings and Incentives* magazines.

Trade publications are reader-specific, written for an audience that is tuned into industry knowledge and the language that goes with it. Because of this, they include acronyms and jargon. Trade publications in hard copy will often be kept for reference purposes, providing a valuable reference tool. Like the community media, the trades are very receptive to news subsidies such as media releases because of their small editorial staffing levels. This is also the case because trade journals are not hard news breakers; rather, they are information vehicles that, to a large extent, are 'preaching to the converted'— already dedicated audiences—about what is going on in their world of work.

Some trade journals do, however, act as agenda-setters for the wider, mainstream media. One example of this is *B&T* magazine. Stories in this advertising, marketing and media magazine are often referenced in the daily media. So too with journals such as the *Australian* and *British Medical Journals,* which often 'break' news by running stories about research and medical developments that are picked up by the non-trade sector—newspapers, magazines, radio and television.

MAGAZINES

There is therefore an overlap between 'the trades' and magazines more generally, as some magazines—like *Nature*—might fall into both categories because the serve a particular community but also have widespread, general appeal. Australians traditionally have been major magazine consumers and New Zealand has been noted to be among the world's highest consumers of magazines. While most of the 5500 titles in New Zealand are produced in Australia—only 700 are locally produced—those magazines are the biggest sellers (Rosenberg, 2008).

Roy Morgan Research found in 2004–05 that 84 per cent of men and 89 per cent of women regularly read at least one magazine (Magazine Publishers, 2005). While figures from the mid-2000s showed buoyancy in the sector, by the late 2000s the figures were showing signs of waning in some magazine styles. In 2008, the Australian Press Council (APC) reported that mainstream magazine readerships had dropped (particularly for women's magazines); however, this was balanced by an increase in niche magazine publications. The APC suggested that magazine buyers may have been 'cutting back on discretionary spending by sharing copies' of magazines (APC, 2008).

Despite this, the number of magazine titles in Australia remains high. In late 2012, ACP (part of Nine Entertainment Co.) was sold to the Bauer Media Group. Its portfolio of 80 magazines includes long-running, popular titles such as *The Australian Women's Weekly* and *Cleo.* It also includes some that may be described as trades, particularly for the farming sector. Pacific Publications is owned by the Seven Media Group, with 26 titles. Considering the traditional cross-ownership of TV and magazine producers, it is no wonder that many magazines have moved increasingly in two directions: they are celebrity-focused and they cross-promote with television. *Better Homes and Gardens* is probably the best known. In 2008, this magazine was the only one that recorded a significant increase in circulation in the APC study (APC, 2008). Others that have cross-promoted with a TV show over the past decade include *Good Medicine, Burke's Backyard, Money* and *TV Week*. Characters from TV programs like *Australian Idol, Big Brother* and *The Biggest Loser* are often featured in the magazines from the same ownership group.

A growing genre of magazines is the celebrity magazine, which focuses entirely on what celebrities are doing, in pictures, in colour and in large volumes. Titles include (currently) *Famous, Who, NW* and *OK*. In addition, the celebrity focus has found its way into the traditional women's magazines *Woman's Day, Australian Women's Weekly* and *New Idea*, as well as the younger market publications such as *Cleo, Cosmopolitan* and *Dolly*. Probably the best-known celebrity magazine internationally is *People* from the United States. This magazine publishes a mix of celebrity and human-interest stories and its publicists are known to provide exclusives to the magazine. Such strategies are commonplace in the magazine industry.

Media commentator and journalist Mark Day (2006) says celebrity magazines 'are on a roll', based on human curiosity and a need for self-justification. He notes several characteristics of what he calls 'the celebrity phenomenon' (2006, p. 13):

- It has been on the increase for three decades.
- Where once it included longer stories, now it is often picture blocklines.
- More traditional magazines have moved to including 'flip' alternative covers about celebrities.
- Stories are frequently made up, using 'sources' as a catch-all to create facts.
- The next phase of the 'phenomenon' may be based on stories that are stranger than fiction.

Topics of celebrity and reality television were discussed in more detail in Chapter 10.

FEATURE STORIES

These represent the major part of magazines and selected newspaper sections. Where news stories are all about the news of the day, feature stories provide either an extended life to a story or a different perspective—human interest, as noted above, is a common feature style. Sometimes features can even give 'life' to a story that simply would not be considered news. Feature stories allow journalists to dig deeper, and write longer and in more depth about news. Ricketson (2004, p. 2) summarises features as 'articles containing emotion and analysis as well as information, compared to hard news stories that are first and foremost about information'. Features are often seen as the 'softer' approach to news. This is because they do not incorporate 'breaking news' as it is described in Chapter 2. They do include behind-the-scenes stories, the inside story and the personal account. If we consider that news tends to be more about the 'what' aspects of a story, as discussed in Chapter 7, then we might consider that features are about the 'why', 'how' or 'who' aspects of a story. While news values still apply, features include a variety of writing elements not generally associated with news style.

Also under the features banner we might include columns and opinion pieces which now make up a large part of the daily media diet. Columns and opinion pieces are a special type of writing because, as the names suggest, they are about one person's view of an issue and how it relates to society or events in the wider media. These are written by specialist writers—either a specialist who is not a journalist but knows a great deal about a topic (like a doctor or business leader), or a specialist who is an experienced senior journalist. The specialist writer may be a person who has become a known authority on a topic. It is important to know who the key feature writers are and who writes what columns and opinion pieces, as these can provide excellent contacts in media relations. The column or opinion piece is really the forerunner of the blog, and they continue to have much in common. Blogs will be discussed in Chapter 13.

Features can be categorised into two types: controlled and uncontrolled. Both types are frequently used, providing opportunities to tell a story or get a message out. The most important thing to remember is that they are quite different, and should be identified clearly for what they are. It is important to be able to identify a feature story idea to pitch to the media. In media relations, though, you are much more likely to have to write 'advertorial or advertising features'—the controlled feature variety.

CONTROLLED FEATURE STORIES

These include the type of feature story that is paid for—also known as 'advertorials', 'supplements' or 'advertising features'. These feature stories are a hybrid of journalism and advertising. They are written in a feature (or news) style with a lead, body and ending. They will usually include essential elements of a feature story, including quotes from an authority and attribution to this source throughout the feature.

Because advertorials are written in feature style, often either as a single story or as part of a supplement or series that is sponsored by an industry or organisation, they are seen to hold significant weight with the reader. That is, they are viewed as being editorial, and hence are more newsworthy than an advertisement, carrying what is perceived as the endorsement of the publication in which they appear. They can also include the best layout and photography a magazine or newspaper has to offer. For example, during 2011 and 2012, *The Weekend Australian* magazine carried a weekly series of advertorials about Tasmania. These were beautifully presented at the back of the weekly magazine, called *The Ultimate Tasmanian Magazine*. Though they were clearly marked 'advertorial', the features read and looked just like a travel editorial and ran over several months.

Controlled features are a valid public relations tactic that can be used to reinforce an advertising message, or as an alternative to advertising. They should always be identified for what they are—paid material.

PHOTOGRAPHY

The print media are heavily reliant on photographs. Like television, which we will examine in the next chapter, many of the print media need pictures to complete the story. Breaking news might get a run without a photo, but it is a rare soft news story or feature that runs without a photograph. As noted in the previous sections, magazines have moved towards more pictures and fewer words, while smaller format newspapers are also increasingly dedicated to colour photos.

For the media relations professional using online newsrooms or media centres, there are unprecedented opportunities to share photographs with the media. Grahame Long, former senior photographer with News Ltd, says that, as a general rule, newspapers require photographs to be sent as JPEG files because they take less time to access. He points out that firewalls may not let in larger formats such as TIFF or EPS. If the photograph is of a good quality, newspapers will increase the size using photographic software. Long points out that the most important aspect of submitting photographs to newspapers is to begin with a good quality picture. The higher the DPI (dots per inch), the better the quality, so a photograph at 300 DPI can be submitted at a small size of 10 x 15 centimetres. Conversely, a lower resolution of, say, 72 DPI should be submitted at 30 x 36 centimetres. By making sure that either the size is large or the resolution is high, the photographer can increase the image size to fit the space. Photographs should all be sent or available in colour, and newspapers greyscale them if they want a black and white image. The best rule of thumb is to discuss the needs of the particular media outlet with someone in the photographic department, preferably the chief photographer (Long, 2006).

Corporate photographer Michael Crabtree provides some advice for supplying public relations photographs to newspapers. He says picture desks in newspapers see up to 12 000 images a day, so it is important to make yours stand out and that they are clear. Most importantly, they should be captioned using Photoshop, Photomechanic or another software program. A caption is a short description of the photograph, including the left-to-right naming of people in the photograph. Newspapers and magazines call these either captions or blocklines. Crabtree says the JPEGs should be in RGB—red, green and blue—and in 1MB compressed size for newspapers and 2MB compressed size for magazines (Crabtree, 2009). He suggests that as photo editors often need a photograph to fit a particular space the trick is to be able to supply this. For pictures of people, you can provide the following, according to Crabtree:

- A tight headshot is essential because it's the most commonly used picture format.
- Landscape and portrait layouts should include:
  - subject with plain background
  - subject with a background related to their business, and
  - pictures with subtle branding, and some without any branding. (Crabtree, 2009)

In media relations, it might well be our responsibility to monitor or update photography on websites. It might also be our responsibility to outsource and hire professional photographers to take photographs. While these days anyone can take and post a photograph, the role of the professional photographer is still important to us. In our role, we work with professional photographers as employees or freelancers. The work of professional photographers will be subject to copyright. Under Australian copyright law, all photos are covered automatically by copyright. As a general rule, if a photograph is taken during the course of employment, the employer will own the photograph; if it is taken on a commission basis, the photographer will own the copyright, unless otherwise stated in a contract—such as for domestic purposes like weddings.

In addition, copyright has another layer of acknowledgement required under what is called 'moral rights' legislation. While copyright itself can be assigned—that is, you can license it to another—moral rights always exist with the creator, and therefore photographers should be acknowledged even if they are not the copyright owner of a photograph.

Where photographs are placed on a website, they will usually include details of copyright and may only allow access to the photographs after the user agrees to sign a contract. If you are commissioning a photographer to take photographs, you need to be sure you have an agreement in writing, outlining exactly where these images can be used and reproduced. The photographs that accompany the media kit for Mt Buller ski resort in Chapter 8 provide an example of the terms and uses of copyright of its media photo gallery, restricting the photographs' usage for any purpose other than the promotion of Mt Buller. For more information on copyright, see Chapter 4.

Newspapers also include video in their online editions because they have moved to multi-platform delivery. The supply of video is discussed in the next chapter.

CHALLENGES AND CHANGES TO NEWSPAPERS

Changes to technology, media delivery and reader habits have given rise to a host of challenges for the print media. Newspaper analyst Julianne Schultz (2002) explains that the press has been a resilient form of media because of two distinguishing characteristics:

1. a central and enduring role in public life, notably as the Fourth Estate, and
2. the monopolistic nature of newspapers owned by large conglomerates. (2002, p. 102)

In addition, it can be observed that the press has adapted and changed when faced with the challenges of new media—first television, and most recently the internet.

One of the biggest shifts in recent years has been the adoption of 'paywalls' for 'premium' online content. This signalled a significant change in thinking about online news—newspapers had been struggling with charging for copy, but how were they to reverse years of access to free internet news? One of the earliest adopters of the paywall, *The Australian Financial Review* (AFR), began using the system in 2006 but altered it in 2011 to combine print and online subscriptions, and reduce the cost of web-only access to below the print price (Jackson, 2011). Financial Review Group chief executive and publisher Brett Clegg announced that *The Financial Review* would launch its iPad app in 2012 and flagged a return to syndication of the paper's content (which means it will share more copy with other Fairfax Media publications) (Jackson, 2011). Both these moves are also part of the strategy of the news organisation to retain market share and cut costs.

In late 2011, *The Australian* was the first general newspaper to apply a paywall to its premium news. The strategy was described as 'an evolution in news' by the newspaper's editor, Clive Mathieson (Christensen, 2011a). *The Australian*'s digital subscription uses what it calls a 'freemium model' that provides some free stories but charges for analysis, opinion and more specialist material (Christensen, 2011b). The move to adopt online paywalls is not universal in daily newspaper publishing, but a 2011 Citigroup report titled *Paywall: A Necessary Evil* concluded the move was 'more a question of when (not if)':

> Newspaper publishers worldwide are grappling with issues related to online content, what to charge and how to charge it, as circulation and advertising revenues continue to fall, leading to a crisis in the funding of journalism. (Leys, 2011)

However, since advertising accounts for the majority of revenue, some newspapers are not rushing into the paywall option. Fairfax Media have suggested that:

> We get 85 per cent of our revenue from advertising, so we aren't particularly enamoured about paywalls . . . We produce journalism, in the same way BHP might produce minerals . . . and we distribute that journalism in print, online, through smartphones, through iPads and newfangled smart TVs. It's not just newspapers anymore. (Leys, 2011)

Newspapers have moved into other formats to retain market share. In a three-month audit period in 2011, Fairfax alone released figures showing more than 200 000 apps had been downloaded for its *Age* and *Sydney Morning Herald* newspapers, and it was estimated that more than three million newspaper-branded apps were downloaded to tablets and smartphones during 2011 (AAP, 2011b). Another way in which print newspapers have taken on the challenge of a changed media environment has been to move from broadsheet paper size to smaller formats, either the popular tabloid or the slightly larger Berliner or 'midi' size. When Brisbane's *Courier-Mail* moved to this format in 2006, it dropped the broadsheet format it had used for 160 years. In 2013, *The Age* and the *Sydney Morning Herald* also moved to 'compact' formats. This move reflected changes worldwide, with other moves to smaller or narrower formats by *The Times* (in the United

Kingdom), *The Guardian* (across Europe), *The Wall Street Journal* (in the United States), *Le Monde* (in France), *La Vanguardia* (in Spain) and *La Repubblica* (in Italy) to name a few.

Newspapers have also moved to consolidating their production to centralised locations. When this occurred in community papers, some argued that it would have negative effects because community newspapers are, by their nature, part of the local community.

Nevertheless, it is a trend that is likely to continue, and one that has gained momentum in Australia. The highly successful arm of Australian Associated Press (AAP), Pagemasters, has taken on the role of sub-editing and laying out pages for many Australian newspapers. Described as 'one of [AAP's] biggest success stories' (AAP, 2010, p. 24), Pagemasters announced in 2011 that it would expand its existing operations to: 'subediting of general news, business and sport for the *Sydney Morning Herald*, the *Sun-Herald*, *The Age* and *The Sunday Age*' (AAP, 2011a). This means of course that the newspaper will be sub-edited and produced in a central location.

This outsourcing has occurred in the face of major economic challenges for newspapers. One of the biggest outcomes has been staff cuts, or 'journalist shedding'. In 2008, Fairfax Media cut 550 jobs in Australia and New Zealand (Steffens, 2008), and in the same year News Corporation announced it would shed an undisclosed number of jobs from its Australian and British newsrooms (McLennan, 2008). Further shedding followed in 2009. In late 2011, APN News and Media announced the closure of several regional newspapers and the scaling back to either online-only or Saturday-only in others. Axed were the *Gold Coast Mail* and *Robina Mail*, with *The Daily News* and the *Coffs Coast Advocate* being scaled back, resulting in journalists' job losses.

The changes to newspapers have been described as the need to 'differentiate or die' (Phillips, 2012, p. 139) in the increasingly homogenised and pressured world of journalism. Phillips suggests one way will be that: 'As businesses seek an audience, a certain proportion will simply give in to the gravitational pull of pure entertainment and seek to provide a bigger, flashier way of offering it' (2012, p. 139). New models have emerged, and will continue to develop, in the evolution of the newspaper. The *Huffington Post* represents an example of one such new model, based on fewer full-time journalists and more full-time (unpaid) bloggers. This model will be discussed further in Chapter 13.

Finally, while newspaper sales in traditional forms are definitely on the decline in some countries, it is interesting to note that this is not a universal trend. Research from the World Newspaper Congress and World Editors Forum which surveyed 69 countries in 2010/11 found the following:

- In the Asia Pacific region, circulations increased 7 per cent from 2009 to 2010, and 16 per cent over five years.
- Latin America also saw significant circulation increases—2 per cent last year and 4.5 per cent over the past five years.
- Falls occurred in Europe—2.5 per cent year-on-year and 11.8 per cent over five years in Western Europe and 12 per cent in 2010 and 10 per cent over five years in Eastern and Central Europe.
- Decreases were greatest in North America, where newspapers lost 11 per cent of circulation year-on-year and 17 per cent over five years. (Moos, 2011)

CONCLUSION

Despite changes and a general global downsizing of traditional print media, print continues to remain an agenda-setter in the Australian media environment; and, while its sales have declined in western countries, this is not a universal trend. It is an extremely diverse and varied form of media—from the daily paper to weekend, regional, weekly and community papers, alternative and trade papers, and magazines. These all cater to a wide variety of topics, community and individual needs and social trends. Print has been challenged by change probably more than any other single medium, and it has responded by changing itself and developing new models. This has included the burgeoning growth in titles to cater for fragmented and niche audiences, but also the segmentation of publications, smaller formats and adaptation into the multimedia internet environment, notably adopting phone and tablet applications. These changes have allowed this medium to maintain a market share (as auditors update their calculations frameworks), and in media relations it remains a hugely important medium to reach a wide range of audiences.

In researching the news of the day, media monitor other media. None works in isolation. In this context, print is inextricably bound up with the other media—television, radio, social media and the internet—which form the basis of our next two chapters.

12 WORKING WITH RADIO AND TELEVISION

Radio and television have responded in different ways to changed technology and lifestyle. Both mediums are embedded in our culture, and while television is well known as a very pervasive medium, radio is also an integral part of our daily lives—in our cars, on our stereo systems and beside our beds. In Australia, radio was first publicly broadcast in 1919, while television was launched in 1956. Just as the radio was the centre of the living room by the 1930s, so television became the focal point of the family room by the 1960s. These media have strengths that are not available in their print counterparts of newspapers and magazines, or of internet-only options. In particular, radio's immediacy and reach are significant benefits, while television's visuals and its sheer pervasiveness within most cultures set it apart. Radio can get a message to a wide audience quickly, and is a strong medium for short, direct messages. Television's impact is profound because it can be so selective with its combination of vision and audio, and because it is in virtually every household in the country.

Like print media, radio and TV sectors have codes of practice that govern their conduct, content and overall activity. Broadcasting sectors have specific codes of practice and conduct registered with the Australian Communications and Media Authority (ACMA), which is the governing body that oversees broadcasting activity in Australia. In addition, ACMA has policies relating to broadcast and internet standards, with the most recent new guidelines relating to privacy (as discussed in Chapter 4).

RADIO

DEVELOPMENT AND OVERVIEW

In Australia, radio was developed by the Amalgamated Wireless Company Ltd (AWA). Two types of licence were issued by the government: 'A' licences funded by subscription and 'B' licences funded by on-air advertising. In 1932, this two-tier system of radio was made up of the national broadcaster—the ABC—with twelve stations, and the commercial sector with 43 stations. The ABC initially was funded by radio listeners' licence fees, but these were discontinued in the 1970s while the commercial stations were funded by advertising.

Because bandwidths were restricted, the government—through the Australian Broadcasting Control Board (ABCB)—could control the expansion of radio. It was restricted to the AM band because television had been allocated the FM band, and this remained the case until the Whitlam era of the 1970s when the Very High Frequency (VHF) band of television was shared with FM radio. By 1978, there were in excess of 200 AM and five FM radio stations (Miller and Turner, 2002). The move to the FM band opened up space for a third tier of broadcasting: community or public broadcasting. As a result, Australia now has the commercials, the ABC and SBS (public broadcasters), and the community sector. The *Broadcasting Services Act 1992* moved towards deregulating the industry, bringing in industry-based self-regulation (Langdon, 1995; Miller and Turner, 2002).

The transformation from AM to FM was a very expensive one. Only certain AM stations were allowed to make the change, and it came at a huge cost. For example, Victoria's 3KZ paid $30 million to convert from AM to FM and South Australia's 5DN paid $6 million (Langdon, 1995). The major expenditure resulted in downsizing of the internal workings of radio stations, and this has remained a legacy of the era (Miller and Turner, 2002). The range of music has shrunk, and news is now often networked out of shared newsrooms. Talkback emerged as a response to the downsizing of music, news and current affairs.

In 2009, Australia began the shift to digital. Digital Audio Broadcasting+ (DAB+) was introduced to most Australian capital cities, with 60 per cent of the population able to access digital broadcasting by 2011. The Commercial Radio Australia (CRA) association explains the differences between DAB+ and FM and AM:

> DAB+ uses a transmission system similar to digital TV, broadcasting in VHF Band III (174–235MHz), a higher frequency than both AM and FM resulting in even shorter wave lengths. This spectrum efficient technology allows broadcasters to offer their listeners new digital only stations using less spectrum. DAB+ uses a robust modulation which is designed for radio reception in mobile environments such as vehicles and trains. DAB+ also provides new features such as scrolling text, EPG, slideshow and in some receivers, animation. (CRA, 2011a)

In addition, DAB+ offers:

- more choice of stations, with up to 22 digital-only stations available, including chill, comedy, dance and country
- tuning by station name, not frequency, making it easy to find favourite stations
- scrolling text on screen with artist and song information, weather and news updates, and
- additional features on some digital radio models, including the ability to pause and rewind live radio and broadcast slideshow images. The technology has the provision in the future for downloadable music direct to the radio's memory and electronic program guides. (CRA, 2011a)

In November 2011, Nielson radio figures showed that the number of people listening to digital radio each week was at 940 000 (CRA, 2011b). Based on uptake between 2009 and 2010, it was predicted that digital radio adoption would be around 16 per cent by 2014 (CRA, 2011c). Meanwhile, some countries have predicted they will switch off their FM radio bands within a few years—the United Kingdom by 2015 and Norway in 2017. Other countries, including New Zealand, have been trialling DAB+

while some countries are still only expressing interest in its adoption (CRA, 2011c).

COMMERCIAL SECTOR

In Australia, there are 261 commercial radio stations (registered with Commercial Radio Australia)—151 FM and 110 AM stations (CRA, 2011c). This includes the three new FM commercial radio licences issued over the past few years—Vega Sydney, which launched on air in 2005, and Nova Brisbane and Vega Melbourne, which launched in 2005. Eighty per cent of Australia's radio stations are owned by thirteen radio networks, with some of the big names being the Macquarie Network, Austereo Network, Australian Capital Network, V Group, Fox Radio Network, Southern Cross Broadcasting and DMG Radio (CRA, 2011c). According to the Commercial Radio Network:

- Popularity has increased in some sectors since the rise of the internet.
- Commercial radio reaches 77 per cent of Australians aged over 10 each week.
- Australians spend a daily average of 2.5 hours listening to radio (higher among 55+ years).
- Almost half of regional Australians talk about what they hear on radio.
- More than half of people aged 25–54 always listen to radio on the way to work. (CRA, 2007)

FM radio news tends to be 'harvested' from other sources. A study by Raward and Johnston (2009) found the FM news-gatherer tended to work alone, produce news for more than one station, and did not have the time or the resources to perform traditional Fourth Estate journalistic functions (2009). They concluded that the FM radio journalist had become a 'harvester' or a news-gatherer of information from a range of sources, predominantly other media (2009). Table 12.1 shows the sources of news in Raward and Johnston's study of a newsroom operated by one of Australia's largest commercial radio operators.

Table 12.1 Sources of news

Source*	Number of stories	Percentage
AAP	115	61.1
FM Network	23	12.2
Sky News	14	7.4
Other TV news	3	1.5
Media release	4	2.1
Local TV news sharing agreement	4	2.1
Newspaper	5	2.9
Self-sourced	21	11.1

* Twenty stories were deemed to have multiple sources and are counted more than once. Stories with multiple sources were most commonly those derived from AAP copy accompanied by audio sourced from Sky News. These are counted in both the AAP and Sky News categories.

Raward and Johnston (2009) argue that FM radio news had moved towards a process of what Davies (2008) called 'churnalism'—that is, the recycling and reusing of news. In this context, the high use of AAP copy went along with a rewriting into a more relaxed, informal and shorter FM style of story. In addition, the newsroom they looked at was also a 'news hub', responsible for sourcing and preparing bulletins for a wide network of stations within its ownership group. In this case, it was one of four news hubs providing news for 86 stations across six Australian states. The idea of 'hubbing' has clear implications for the media relations practitioner: it is not enough to know who's who in your local radio newsrooms, you also need to know where your local news is produced. For example, Raward and Johnston (2009) noted news for several West Australian FM stations was compiled in a radio newsroom on the east coast of Australia—4000 kilometres away.

Another issue that emerged from the study was the relatively low use of media releases. This does not take into account, however, the use of media releases which may have been used to generate the AAP, Sky, networked and other TV news copy and then was recycled in the FM news. Studies have shown that wire services (or news agents) are major users of media releases (Lewis, Williams and Franklin, 2008; Forde and Johnston, 2012).

THE ABC AND SBS

The Australian Broadcasting Corporation (ABC) was based on the British model of the British Broadcasting Commission (BBC). It was established by the *Australian Broadcasting Commission Act* in 1932 and currently operates a range of radio services. Its website describes these as follows:

- JJJ—enemy of average (youth music)
- ABC Classic FM—come alive with the classics (classical music)
- Dig FM—music with depth (jazz, soul and country)
- ABC Radio National—explore a world of ideas (current affairs/ issues/talk)
- ABC Local Radio—the world from your backyard (local stories Australia-wide)
- ABC News Radio—continuous news as it happens (news, sport and features).

The ABC is quite different from commercial media because it is funded by the federal government. The ABC is considered an institution and an icon within the Australian media environment, a subject discussed in more detail in the TV analysis. Radio programs such as *AM* (the morning current affairs program) and *PM* (the afternoon equivalent) are industry leaders and agenda-setters in the news and current affairs media. Many of its radio policies of non-commercialism apply across ABC television and its internet site—for example, its style restricts journalists from using commercial names and endorsements wherever possible. This means that sponsorship names are often dropped. Thus Suncorp Stadium in Brisbane is known as Lang Park (its previous name before being renamed for the sponsor), the Pura Milk Cup is the interstate cricket competition. News and current affairs on the ABC are, along with those on the Special Broadcasting Service (SBS), usually considered the 'serious' news and current affairs, with a more traditional information focus and longer stories rather than the entertainment approach more commonly ascribed to the ABC's commercial counterparts. Due to its Fourth Estate role, it does, however, sometimes receive criticism for anti-government, anti-authoritarian bias. For example, it came under criticism for its news and current affairs coverage of the war in Iraq under the Howard government. However, it was also charged with bias in reportage of the Gulf War under the previous Labor government (Walters, 2004).

SBS radio and television are unique because they broadcast in more languages than any other single network in the world (SBS, 2011). The SBS radio network was established as multilingual radio stations 2EA Sydney and 3EA Melbourne in 1975, originally to inform ethnic communities about Medicare (Langdon, 1995). Since then, SBS has expanded to a five-signal network that is available in all capital cities and across much of regional Australia. It is the world's most linguistically diverse broadcaster, producing more than 13 500 hours of language-specific programs each year, in 68 languages (60 in television and 50 online), changing language each hour. The network broadcasts 36 news bulletins a week and each weekday, at 6.30 a.m. and 5.00 p.m., the English-language news and current affairs program *World View* provides a multicultural perspective on national and international events (SBS, 2011). For media relations, SBS radio provides an opportunity to reach a diverse range of listeners and internet viewers.

COMMUNITY RADIO

Community radio has emerged to provide a third tier of radio choice, alongside the commercials, the ABC and SBS. It first emerged the 1970s to fill a gap in the radio market, under limited licences. Community broadcasting is based on two models: special-interest (such as language or ethnic group) and geographic (based in specific locations). These two types originally formed the basis for the community broadcasters that now exist with either full or partial licences.

Community radio stations in Australia now represent a significant part of the broadcast media sector. There are currently 350 fully licensed community broadcasters, with the majority of these located in non-metropolitan areas (Community Broadcasting Foundation, 2011). These radio stations are seen as sites of 'cultural empower-ment' or 'cultural citizenship' (Forde, Meadows and Foxwell, 2002, p. 17). While this is undoubtedly the case in terms of programming and content, they also provide unique opportunities to get news messages out to very specific and targeted communities. In addition, their reliance on volunteers—about 23 000 Australians regularly volunteer in community broadcasting (Community Broadcasting Foundation, 2011)—can mean they are very receptive to supplied information. In fact, many community radio stations rely on the 'rip'n'read' approach to news. (This approach refers to ready-written news, easily accessed and read as provided.) While audiences may not be as widespread or as large as those for mainstream media, they can provide avenues of focused publicity and exposure that should not be overlooked.

Audience research has shown about 27 per cent of Australians tune into community radio at least once a week, and about 57 per cent tune in at least once a month. This is partly because, in many regional and rural areas, community radio is the only service available following the withdrawal of many local commercial radio stations from regional areas in the past five to ten years (Forde, 2011). Community radio caters to localised or niche markets or audience groups. In this way, audience reach extends to specific minorities: Indigenous groups; ethnic or language groups; activist or political groups; religious groups; print disabled listeners; listeners in a specific geographic location. Community radio has become a key place for communications professionals (like media relations) to get their messages across to niche audiences, and is also a media training ground for the competitive commercial, ABC or SBS networks. While it does provide paid work, this represents only a small proportion of its workers, and it relies heavily on volunteers.

RADIO NEWS

The use of radio to get news out represents a range of conflicting possibilities. On the one hand, radio is an extremely immediate medium with a wide reach. On the other hand, news and current affairs on radio have shrunk as the industry has had to rationalise its spending against new media, licence restrictions, shrinking and fragmenting audiences, and increasing budget demands. As noted above, the reality of commercial radio news is that the large radio networks operate news and programming 'hubs' to service the needs of clusters of stations within their ownership groups. This contraction of news services reflects general reductions in radio newsroom staffing. Where radio newsrooms once employed journalists to locate stories in person, this ultimately has contracted to many journalists locating stories by phone, or from the internet, email or other media.

Network material is produced in central newsrooms or production studios and generally transmitted via satellite. Thus, sending news releases to a targeted local station or geographical area can often be a futile exercise. It is therefore best to make contact with radio stations and determine the point of news production. For some stations, broadcasting may be in-house for only a brief part of the day, often during 'breakfast' and sometimes morning shifts before they revert to networked programming until the next morning. For media releases targeting these local segments, the material should be available for use at 4 a.m. when breakfast shifts generally start. To send a media release at the start of business at 9.00 a.m. renders it virtually useless to that station unless it is also directed to the station's network hub where it must compete with a much greater volume of material for exposure. One busy Brisbane public relations manager advises that if you make can make a radio interviewee available by phone before 7.00 a.m., you have a stronger chance of getting your client interviewed and a story run.

Many commercial radio newsrooms routinely use contributed interview grabs pre-cut to lengths of between 10 to 30 seconds and supplied with suggested intros. These can be sent directly to the newsroom as either MP3 or WAV files or released, for a fee, through media distribution services. Veteran radio journalist Rod McLeod from the Southern Cross Austereo network cautions against directing journalists to their websites to download audio or retrieve releases (Raward, 2012). Commercial radio newsrooms are pressurised work environments with journalists often required to produce news bulletins for multiple stations in their networks. Coupled with the avalanche of material received on a daily basis, adding another step in the newsgathering process almost guarantees its failure. He estimates he receives up to 300 emails a day of unsolicited material and would have time for little else if he was to follow up telephone calls from each sender. It also underscores the necessity for the material to be ready to use immediately (Raward, 2012).

McLeod says he chooses contributed audio on the basis of 'good talent', brevity and relevance, particularly to wider network audiences.

'Good talent' is the somewhat intangible measure of a speaker's suitability for broadcast. It can be loosely defined as a dynamic, engaging, knowledgeable speaker whose comments add value to the written material being sent.

As a matter of policy, ABC stations do not use supplied, pre-cut audio in their news bulletins but may consider the material as a lead for pursuing their own stories. To be considered for radio coverage on the ABC, always supply the contact details of your talent so journalists can conduct their own interviews, most often by telephone. The talent should be readily accessible on the day of the media release and well versed on what is required in telephone interviews, namely concise, conversational answers that deliver the message. Anything that is obviously read from a prepared release or statement will not be considered. In many cases, journalists or producers will prefer to speak to the head of an organisation or a key player rather than a media relations spokesperson. For all journalists though, particularly on radio, the good talent requirement can be an overriding factor (Raward, 2012).

Radio also offers other opportunities beyond news to get a message out or have your organisation's name mentioned. These include sponsorships and promotions (in commercial radio) as well as community service announcements (CSAs) and talkback (in all sectors).

WORKING WITH RADIO

As with all media, you need to know the product you are working with—so get to know what radio stations use, when they use it and how they use it. Tips on getting a message well received in a radio newsroom include developing an understanding of radio style and the following points:

- Broadcast news stories are two to four paragraphs in length with (an optional) 30 seconds of audio.
- Every three words accounts for one second—for example, a 20-second news story is roughly 60 words in length.
- Broadcast style uses present tense, with attributions at the beginning of the sentences rather than at the end.

- There is little room for background information or complicated explanations.
- The same story is generally rewritten into two or three different versions to avoid repetition through the day.
- Media releases need to be written clearly and succinctly, and to reach the newsroom at the optimum time of day for your message.
- Use talent—that is, someone who can talk authoritatively on your topic.
- Have that person ready to talk and coach them to know how to get a message across in 'grabs' or 'sound bites' (ten to 25 seconds).
- Consider any controversial angles and be prepared for 'tricky' questions.
- If supplying audio, ensure it is of good quality with two to three 'grabs' ranging in length from ten to 25 seconds. Send it directly to the newsroom or put it on your media web link.
- Work fast because radio won't wait! (Raward, 2012)

In addition to these points, there are some simple methods to maximise the effectiveness of radio interviews. Most radio interviews are done over the phone. Usually a radio producer will have researched the story and you may not even talk to the radio host until the actual interview. The producer will either take your call or call you for the interview, put the call on hold and then the radio host will commence the interview. In the case of a long interview, you may be put on hold for a song or a commercial break; stay alert during this time as they will quickly return to resume the interview.

Here are some radio interview tips:

- Make (or receive) your phone call in a quiet area, free of any distractions.
- Disable call waiting and use a landline if possible.
- Don't turn on the radio to listen to yourself.
- Find out how much time is allocated to the interview before you start.
- Know your subject and key messages.
- Speak in simple terms and be prepared to discuss current events or trends.

- Avoid sounding too commercial.
- Never read from a script but keep key words handy for prompts.
- Answer the question and then stop talking—do not try to fill the gaps—that is the journalist's job.

BENEFITS OF RADIO

Despite the competition that has arisen during the past several decades, radio has continued to grow in all sectors, with an 'explosion' in the past 25 years (Canberra Media Research, n.d.). Some of this growth is due to radio's adaptation to the internet environment, which provides an alternative mode of delivery for this traditional medium.

Next to newspapers, radio is the oldest of the daily news media. It has been through major changes in its response to government policies and the new media of television and the internet. Radio's ongoing 'claim to fame', however, is its immediacy, frequency and accessibility. Radio is arguably the best medium in an emergency or crisis. For example, during the 2010/11 Queensland floods, radio—particularly the ABC—was found to have been of prime importance in providing information on conditions, road closures and other emergency news. The Queensland Floods Royal Commission noted that the floods demonstrated the importance of radio as a means of communicating natural disaster information to the community:

> The community relies on radio as a source of information about local conditions during a disaster. During the floods, radio stations broadcast information from members of the community about road closures, unofficial evacuation centres, where to go, and what to do in their particular area. Radio stations in Ipswich and Moreton Bay gave accounts of their telephone lines being overwhelmed with calls from listeners seeking, and wanting to provide, information. (Queensland Government Commission of Inquiry, 2011, p. 131)

While social media were identified as of high importance, it was radio that warranted the greatest mention and praise from the commission (Queensland Government Commission of Inquiry, 2011).

Talkback is a major part of all radio sectors, as discussed in Chapter 9, and this can be tapped into not only to get a message across but also to use as a form of environmental scanning in gauging public opinion. Talkback and current affairs on radio provide for longer time on air than news, allowing for issues to be discussed in some detail and for topics to be treated in more depth. Thus radio can be an excellent medium for complex topics if you can secure time for a lengthy interview.

In general, radio provides a range of benefits, including the following:

- It is easily accessed for the listener.
- It is available in a range of venues and locations.
- It can be listened live or in delayed time on the internet.
- It is portable—and can be battery operated (which works in blackouts).
- It is immediate.
- It has a range of programs to suit different messages.
- It can be two-way, with talkback.
- It doesn't require 100 per cent attention and can be listened to while doing something else.
- After purchase, it requires little upkeep or expense.
- It is familiar—you 'get to know' announcers.
- It is not picture-dependent.

TELEVISION

DEVELOPMENT AND OVERVIEW

Television first went to air in Australia on 16 September 1956, when Bruce Gyngell announced 'Good evening and welcome to television' on TCN9 Sydney. The broadcast was restricted to New South Wales and Victoria, and other states and territories were to receive television between the years of 1959 and 1971 (ABA, 2005). Within eight years, 80 per cent of Australia's households had a television. Colour television was introduced in 1975. By 2005, 99 per cent of households had one television and 55 per cent had two (ABA, 2005).

In Australia today, there are four types of television:

- commercial—three networks, Nine, Seven and Ten
- ABC—offers more serious programs as well as entertainment
- SBS—presents foreign language programs along with documentaries and minor sports, and
- pay TV—three networks, Foxtel, Austar and Optus.

Digital television was launched in Australia in January 2002, and was originally planned for a full transition over an eight- to ten-year period (ABA, 2005). This was later revised for a complete switchover by the end of 2013. One of the major changes that came with the move from analogue to digital was the rollout of more free-to-air television channels called 'freeview', which currently totals sixteen channels (Australian Government, 2011d).

Research shows that consumers are watching more television than ever before, using TV sets, the internet, mobile phones, in-home and out-of-home, live and time-shifted, free and paid, rebroadcasts and original program streams. Nielsen Media Research (2012a) reports that households have greater choice and access to digital terrestrial television (DTT):

- 95 per cent of all homes have at least one DTT-enabled TV set (up from 90 per cent in 2011)
- 70 per cent of homes can receive DTT on every working TV set in the home (up from 55 per cent 2011), and
- 44 per cent of households have access to time-shifting devices, such as personal video recorders (up from 37 per cent in 2011)

While the report found that TV viewing on smartphones and tablets was increasing, when viewed on a TV screen, biggest was best. 'There is a strong and positive relationship between screen size and propensity to view, with people demonstrating a preference to watch content on the largest screen available' (Nielsen Media Research, 2012a).

COMMERCIAL TELEVISION

While commercial television was first broadcast in Australia by TCN9 Sydney in September 1956, network Seven launched later that year, followed by the Ten Network in 1965 (Televisionau.com, n.d.). Though its introduction had been considered during the 1940s, World War II delayed television's launch in Australia (Televisionau.com, n.d.). The commercial TV environment in Australia is made up of three national networks—Nine, Seven and Ten—plus a number of regional networks. Some regionals still compile local news; however, there has been a trend for some time to close or down-size regional news offices. Regional television covers the areas outside the capital cities of Sydney, Melbourne, Brisbane, Adelaide and Perth.

Commercial TV ratings are based on how many people view the station at a given time. Ratings are key to advertising and audience reach. In Australia, ratings are dominated by the Nine and Seven Networks. Nielsen Media Research (2012b) notes that TV ratings are used by programming, statistics, sales teams, publicity and promotions to:

- provide a sales tool for marketing their advertising strengths
- evaluate the effectiveness of programming
- establish the value of commercial air time
- rank the top-rating programs and look at their audience loyalty over time
- produce demographic information on the size and profile of TV audiences, and
- assist with scheduling programs and promotions, and
- research changes and trends in TV viewing behaviour.

THE ABC AND SBS

The ABC and SBS, receive federal government funding, and for that reason are known as 'public' broadcasters, but to date only SBS has also incorporated advertising.

ABC TV came on air in Australia one month after the first broadcast by its commercial counterpart (Channel 9) in Sydney in 1956. The first broadcast from Melbourne's studios took place two weeks later, in time for ABC TV's coverage of the 1956 Olympic Games. ABC TV came online in most states and territories through 1959 and 1960. The idea behind the ABC—both television and radio—was that it would provide quality programming across the nation, not driven by commercial or parochial pressures. As the national broadcaster, it took on the slogan 'Our ABC', through which it clearly aimed to present a sense of ownership in its national presence. Part of the ABC's iconic nature is its colloquial name of 'Aunty', which has characterised it as part of the national identity.

Several things distinguish the news and current affairs of the ABC. It is known as a quality broadcaster—much like the broadsheet version of the newspaper, pitched to an educated market. It has a long history of serious current affairs, with *Four Corners* having been a cornerstone of investigative journalism. *Foreign Correspondent* is its flagship international current affairs program and *Australian Story* combines human interest with profiles and newsworthiness. Its news coverage is generally considered a leader, differing subtly from the commercials with slightly longer news stories and a clear non-commercial policy, which means organisational names are rarely used.

SBS was launched in April 1979, originally as the Independent and Multicultural Broadcasting Corporation. The new TV channel was to provide for Australians who spoke a language other than English, and also reflected Australia's broader multicultural society. Currently it broadcasts in 60 languages. Much of its programming was, and remains, imported—largely due to its commitment to multicultural and multilingual television. Like the ABC, it leans towards serious news and current affairs. Its one-hour evening news tends to focus more heavily on international and overseas content than others (not surprisingly), and it runs foreign-language news services in the mornings. Its current affairs program *Dateline* presents serious current affairs, and is a news agenda-setter, similar to the ABC. SBS is also known for its range of world movies, sport and documentaries. Its slogan 'Seven Billion Stories' (which also creates the SBS acronym) is based on the global 'feel' of the station—that everyone in the world has a story to tell.

COMMUNITY TELEVISION

Community (previously known as public) television in Australia began in the early 1980s when Imparja TV in Alice Springs, followed by RMITV in Melbourne, sought licences to broadcast (Australian Government, 2006a). In 1992, the Australian Broadcasting

Authority (ABA)—now the Australian Communications and Media Authority (ACMA)—began licensing community TV operators on a trial basis using UHF31 as their frequency. The first permanent licences were issued in 2004 to community TV stations in four states. These were:

- MCTC in Melbourne
- TVS in Sydney
- Briz 31 in Brisbane, and
- Perth 31 in Perth. (Australian Government, 2006a)

In 2006, Adelaide's C31 came on board and all five capital city services have now gone digital. In addition, there are 78 Indigenous community licences, which cover regional and remote Indigenous communities (CBAA, 2010). The Community Broadcasting Association of Australia (CBAA) predicts that more services will go live with the advent of as digital technology. Currently around 80 per cent of community broadcasting services reach rural, remote or regional viewers, with 20 per cent in the cities (CBAA, 2010).

Like community radio, community television provides another level of broadcasting to compete with commercials and national broadcasters, with licences issued by the ACMA to provide community and educational services.

Community television is funded by sponsorship, which is governed by the Community Television Code of Practice. Nevertheless, the community television (CTV) sector argues that it should receive some funding to maintain diversity in its operations, catering to 3.7 million viewers across non-English speakers, hearing-impaired, youth, Aboriginal and Torres Strait Islanders, social justice and religious groups, and gay and lesbian communities (CBAA, 2010). Community television provides access to anyone through its 'open access' policy. Thus educational institutions, ethnic groups, independent filmmakers and minority groups have access to broadcast on the sector. Like radio, community television relies on volunteers to operate, and provides a solid training ground for the industry. One-third of community television is devoted to news and current affairs, 'presenting views and discussing issues not covered by other media sectors' (CBAA, 2010, p. 16).

PAY TV

Pay TV (or subscription TV, STV) was introduced into Australia in 1995, and Australia's two major telcos, Telstra and Optus, became early participants in the industry. In its initial transmissions, pay TV did not include advertising; however, this soon crept in. Pay TV moved early to digital (by Australian standards), completing the changeover by 2007. The move to digital has meant the adoption of interactive programming and video-on-demand channels.

The two main retail pay TV service providers in Australia are Foxtel and Austar:

- Foxtel delivers its services to mainland capital cities and major regional centres over Telstra's broadband cable network and via satellite. Foxtel provides its customers with a fully digital pay TV service with over 200 channels across multiple platforms: cable, satellite, mobile and PC. As at 31 December 2010, Foxtel had approximately 1.63 million subscribers.
- Austar delivers its services to regional areas, primarily via satellite. Austar does not offer its pay TV service to Western Australia, Canberra or within 50 kilometres of mainland state capitals. As at October 2010, Austar had over 761 000 subscribers. (Australian Government, 2011a)

There are also a number of smaller pay TV operators throughout Australia, including Neighbourhood Cable, UBI World TV and TransACT Communications. These operators deliver subscription broadcasting and bundled services to niche and regional markets (Australian Government, 2011a).

TV NEWS AND CURRENT AFFAIRS

For years, studies have shown that television is the most trusted news source for all media, and while the internet is growing rapidly in popularity among the 18–25-year-old age group, television continues to be the preferred source of news and current affairs across most age groups. Table 12.2 shows that most Australians report watching

Table 12.2 Media use by age, 2010

Media use	18–24 years	25–34 years	35–49 years	50–64 years	65+ years
	Percentage of Australians				
Use at least weekly:					
Television for news and current affairs	85	92	93	95	95
Radio for news and current affairs	71	67	77	76	72
Online social media sites	88	67	37	19	5
Never use:					
Television for news and current affairs	5	4	2	2	2
Radio for news and current affairs	11	14	9	17	18
Online social media sites	8	20	49	72	91

Survey sample: n = 1200 weighted to the Australian population.
Source: ACMA (2011a).

TV news and current affairs programs at least once a week, followed by radio use.

This report shows that while online social media sites are important media for finding about news and current affairs, television is still overall the most important medium. The National Film and Sound Archive (2008) sums up the role of news and current affairs on television:

> News and current affairs programs have traditionally been the flagship programs of television stations around Australia. Since television began in 1956, news broadcasts have grown from short, mostly-live reads to 24 hour coverage of local, national and international stories.

Television news is characterised by three distinctive features—brevity, simplicity and moving pictures:

- *Brevity:* The words of a half-hour commercial news bulletin would not fill the front page of a broadsheet newspaper (Tiffen, 1989). In fact, if you tallied news stories in a commercial bulletin, you would find several minutes of advertisements and a total of around fifteen stories, each between one and two minutes long.

- *Simplicity:* Like radio news, TV news has to cater to audiences who may be doing other things, like cooking the dinner or helping the kids with homework. In addition, stories must be kept short to cover a range of issues in such a brief space of time and the limitations involved in writing for the ear. These factors combine to keep news bulletins simple.
- *Moving pictures:* Television is about pictures, and while it is important for sound and vision to work together, vision takes the lead.

Current affairs, on the other hand, includes moving pictures but traditionally has not included either brevity or simplicity. Rather, current affairs traditionally has called for extended and more in-depth examinations of the news, providing explanation and analysis of the issues of the day. These programs often follow the nightly news programs on television, with extended discussion, interviews, expert sources and commentary. However, analysts have noted a decline in current affairs since the early 2000s. Graeme Turner wrote in 2005 of the decline of current affairs in Australia, noting how audiences were no longer engaged by traditional current affairs and extended interviews. Deitz (2010) illustrates this, comparing the ratings for the ABC's *7.30 Report* (now *7.30*) with those for *The Chaser's War on Everything*—800 000 compared with 2.3 million: 'A show like *The 7.30 Report* is aesthetically and intellectually out of its time and therefore unable to comment on contemporary life because its agenda is so narrow' (Deitz, 2010, p. 55). While newer formats like the ABC's *Q&A* have emerged to bring current affairs and entertainment together, traditional current affairs programs would appear to be seriously under threat. Media relations' role in current affairs will certainly continue, however, in preparing people for interviews and providing background materials for journalists. As models of programs evolve and new ones emerge, this role may become more critical than ever.

WORKING WITH TELEVISION

Just as pre-cut interview grabs are used daily in radio newsrooms, TV news services routinely consider vision contributed by government and private sources. It has been a long-standing practice for organisations to supply moving pictures as a visual accompaniment to written media releases.

Video news releases

The VNR is a TV version of the media release, complete with visuals, scripted audio and talent, or interview grab. There are various ways to create and distribute VNRs. Australian Associated Press's (AAP) Medianet explain how it works with them:

> Targeting broadcast media outlets has never been easier with the help of AAP Medianet's Video News Release (VNR) capabilities. The technology used by Medianet converts your video tape (4:3 or 16:9 format) into insertions of three seconds to a minute in length, creating a storyboard of clips for news professionals to preview, select, download and insert into their newscasts, programs and websites . . . your content is distributed in its original, unedited form. Your organisation's video is simply transformed into a professional, digital format available to download in a series of clips. Your VNR can then be posted on the Medianet . . . and delivered via email alert to television stations, producers, program directors and other relevant recipients. (AAP, 2009)

Development of VNRs is a specialty field. In Australia, companies such as VnR and Medialink Productions both include examples of their VNRs on their websites. VNRs have come under criticism in the United States due to their prevalence and the lack of disclosure that surrounds their airing. A ten-month study by the Centre for Media and Democracy tracked 36 VNRs issued by three broadcast PR firms. Their key findings included:

- VNR use is widespread.
- VNRs are aired in TV markets of all sizes.
- TV stations don't disclose VNRs to viewers.
- TV stations disguise VNRs as their own reporting.

- TV stations don't supplement VNR footage or verify VNR claims.
- The vast majority of VNRs are produced for corporate clients. (Farsetta and Price, 2006)

This widespread use of pre-packaged VNRs is not so common in Australia, however. Media relations practitioners have found much greater success with a softer approach, using sequences of vision which can be readily incorporated into stories being prepared by TV journalists. As noted by AAP, above, VNRs can be supplied in 4:3 and 16:9 formats, with highly professional filming and loose editing to allow journalists maximum flexibility to create their own stories. Most VNRs in Australia contain general overlay footage, a selection of interview grabs and, sometimes, specialised graphics or animated 3D vision. They are accompanied by supporting text containing selected information journalists may need in writing their own scripts. The vision is also generally supplied in Windows Media Player and Quicktime to cover all information systems, including those of web broadcasters.

Another alternative is the option of placing audio-video materials on organisational websites. Web streaming allows an organisation to control what materials they make available but not the selections that are made by the media in putting a story together. This trend has increasingly been adopted by various sectors of the government and corporate sectors, which see the need to get their messages out via audio and video to both the media and the wider community. For example, some courts in Australia use their websites in this manner, which has meant radio and television can include judge's voices for a more authentic news presentation and members of the public can also hear judge's decisions.

Journalist-Producer from the Nine Network Petrina Zaphir (2012) says as newsrooms diversify and there is more pressure to produce quick turnaround stories for the internet, supplied vision will always have a place in modern newsgathering. She says well shot footage with multiple angles, good graphics and a selection of informative, unbiased grabs has the best chance of making it to air. Material that is overtly branded or blatantly one-sided stamps itself as being unworkable. Zaphir says once a PR outfit gains a reputation for peddling such material, it casts future releases from the organisation in a bad light (Zaphir, 2012).

Television interviews

Television is the form of media that makes people most anxious about interviews. Interviews may be conducted on location or in a studio. In most cases, the interview will be pre-recorded, although for breaking news or in times of crisis management the interview may be live, especially in the case of Australian breakfast TV programs like *Sunrise* or *Today*.

Here are some tips for TV interviews:

* Know the interviewer—or at least know their style.
* Run through things with the journalist before you go to camera and don't be afraid to set some ground rules.
* Always assume that the microphone is on.
* Be excited about what you have to say—enthusiasm (or lack of it) shows on television.
* Speak in simple terms and adjust your messaging for the time allocated.
* Practise your response to likely questions in 20-second grabs.
* Try to stay calm and composed—nervous habits will be amplified on the camera.
* Look at the interviewer (not the camera) but relate to the viewer.
* Use the reporter's name and remain friendly.
* Use silences, mentally prepare your answer before giving it and don't rush.
* Repeat important words and messages.
* After the interview is over, stay in your seat until the interviewer stands.
* In a studio, ask for makeup and don't be put off by lights and technical activity.
* Clothing tips for television:
    - Do not wear white.
    - Do not wear stripes.
    - Make sure your dress style suits the theme and setting.
    - Know the media training techniques described in Chapter 5.

BENEFITS OF TELEVISION

Television presents a range of programming styles and opportunities beyond the ambit of TV news. As noted in Chapter 9, documentaries allow for more in-depth coverage of issues and happenings, while lifestyle and reality programs are part of the entertainment mix of television—rather like the human-interest features of print productions and often cross-promoted with magazines. Then there are chat shows, akin to radio's talkback. In TV news and current affairs, there are benefits available to us, the information provider and the audience. These include the following:

- Pictures create impact.
- Television has widespread reach.
- Television can get messages out immediately—programming can be interrupted for breaking news.
- Television is the most commonly used media for news.
- Television is highly trusted for news.
- Television provides a range of opportunities for exposure because of the range of programs.
- Once purchased, television is cheap to access (free-to-air, rather than cable).
- Television doesn't require 100 per cent attention, and can be watched while doing something else (in other words, it is passive—which can also be seen as a negative aspect).
- Television is not messy, does not use paper or require tidying up, like print.
- Television can be taped and re-run at your leisure or, increasingly, available on demand.
- Television can be accessed on a range of formats—e.g. TV sets, mobile phone, computers—and time and space shifted.

CONCLUSION

Radio and television hold overlapping but separate places in the media mix. Each includes elements of immediacy and reach, and together they are a formidable team to get a message to a wide and varied range of audiences. Separately, they can be used to get messages to very specialised groups across the commercial, public and community broadcaster sectors. When we consider the range of media opportunities overviewed in this chapter, it is clear just how pervasive the broadcast media are, especially in their capacity to be accessed by traditional means as well as mobile technology, live or time-shifted and on-demand. Learning about the development and reach of the broadcast media within the Australian context provides us with a clearer understanding of them as a whole, and it is from this position that we can make informed and clever choices about working with broadcast media in our media relations role.

WORKING WITH THE INTERNET AND SOCIAL MEDIA 13

This chapter looks at the intersection between media relations, the internet and social media, and the news. It does not focus on social media's use by the public relations industry in a broad sense—there are dozens of books that do this. Instead, it analyses how the news (and sometimes entertainment) media use the internet and social media so that we can understand this orientation in our dealings with them. It also focuses on how we in media relations use various non-traditional media channels in distributing news. Since news is no longer the sole preserve of journalists, we need an expanded understanding of media relations to function most effectively. So we consider contemporary ideas of journalism, including the role of the professional blogger and the rise of the 'citizen journalist'.

In this chapter we expand some earlier themes in the book and provide further examples, research and insights. We also look at the merging of traditional and social media—or, to put it another way, the merging of mass and interpersonal communication to new versions of what has been called 'masspersonal' communication (Wu et al., 2011). As discussed in Chapter 2, the Australian government continues to update policies and laws for governing the digital environment. One of the approaches has been to revise the way we look at media as a collection of layers rather than silos because media no longer work via single formats; a silo suggests that newspapers are accessed through hard copy or that television is watched on televisions when we know they are now accessed through phones, tablets and computers, and stored and used on demand anywhere, anytime. So as news and entertainment now use multi-platforms, we need to think laterally and broadly about our relationship with the media, whoever they may be. But rather than look at the technology behind these media, this chapter is about information, messages and communication—the building blocks of the media relations professional.

As we have seen in earlier chapters, the news media is in a state of major change—an evolution that is happening at revolutionary pace. Adaptation is key. During the time this edition of the book was being written, apps for downloading newspapers became commonplace; newspapers shut down hard-copy editions and moved to internet-only editions; mainstream newspapers followed the example of their business counterparts (*The Australian Financial Review* and *Wall Street Journal*) and introduced 'paywalls'; bloggers broke major news stories that were followed up by mainstream media and Twitter grew from 300 million to 500 million users (between May 2011 and January 2012).

ONLINE NEWS, CITIZEN JOURNALISTS AND READER PARTICIPATION

In previous chapters, we analysed online news insofar as it applies to newspapers, radio and television. Much has been made of the recycling of news in various formats. Dwyer and Martin (2010) note the patterns for the re-use of news:

- re-use of the same story across co-owned publications on the same platform
- re-versioning, including updates and localisation, for co-owned publications
- re-purposing for different platforms, e.g. from radio to web, mobiles, personal digital assistants and e-readers
- licensing and syndication, including to aggregator services like Yahoo! News

- archiving in digital repositories
- the use of unlicensed news aggregation, such as *Google News*, and
- curation or content farming, such as *Answers.com* and *Demand Media*.

The recycling of existing stories is a criticism that is levelled at some internet-only news organisations that arguably grew and thrived from the freely accessible news published elsewhere. It is said that *The Huffington Post*, for instance, sources the vast majority of its stories from either other published media or citizen journalism contributions (Alterman, 2011). It has 46 full-time employees and more than 1800 unpaid bloggers (Alterman, 2011), and works on a model that has 'capitalised on the problems confronting newspapers in the Internet era' (Alterman, 2011, p. 6). The paper began as a website alternative to the *Drudge Report*, which aggregated political news and gossip, coupled with a group blog. This capitalisation has clearly worked for this paper (and others like it); *The Huffington Post* has grown into one of the most successful papers in the United States—reportedly more popular than all but eight other newspaper sites (Alterman, 2011, p. 7).

Online-only and independent models of news delivery have burgeoned globally in recent years. In Australia, Crikey.com began in 2005 and remains notable in the Australian news environment because of its independence and tendency to act as a watchdog on other, mainstream media. One of the other elements which sets it apart is its adaptability and enthusiasm for using non-traditional news sources. In 2010, it linked up with the University of Technology Sydney (UTS) Journalism Department to research and write the 'Spinning the News' project, which looked at public relations' impact on the media (discussed elsewhere in this book). Crikey also worked with Melbourne's Swinburne University in 2010 and 2011 on what were known as 'The Brumby' and 'The Baillieu Dump' series, which utilised student power to locate stories from hundreds of 'dumped' annual reports and documents from the Victorian government. As one of the reporters explained, the investigation dug into pile of reports that otherwise had overwhelmed mainstream media's capacity for follow-up:

The overwhelming majority of the reports were ignored. The media outlets were still unable to process so much information and the news cycle ensured that very few reports were looked at after the day of their release. (Dodd and Green, 2011)

In 2012, Crikey again linked up with a university—this time Bond University in Queensland—for an investigation into carbon tax, the economy and Australia's biggest polluters. Crikey also regularly features articles written by university academics. This model of university collaboration clearly is gaining momentum. The inclusion of knowledge banks and skill centres beyond its own staff shows an openness that we now associate with online and new media organisations. The ABC's *The Drum* and the independent *The Conversation* are also expert-opinion news programs or online sites.

In an era in which investigative journalism has been affected seriously by staff cuts and resource issues, readers, bloggers and citizen journalists (or student journalists in Crikey's case) represent a vast resource to online news outlets, and it is no surprise that they are used widely. *TPM* (Talking Points Memo) is a New York- and Washington DC-based online newspaper that, like Crikey, covers breaking news, original reporting and investigative journalism. It also uses its readers when it needs to—crowd sourcing has become common practice in online media. Major traditional publications like *The Los Angeles Times, The New York Times,* the *Columbia Journalism Review, The New York Observer* and others have sung the praises of this news organisation's use of readers as news producers. One feature article on it explains:

> The bloggers used the usual tools of good journalists everywhere—determination, insight, ingenuity—plus a powerful new force that was not available to reporters until blogging came along: the ability to communicate almost instantaneously with readers via the Internet and to deputize those readers as editorial researchers, in effect multiplying the reporting power by an order of magnitude. (McDermot, 2007)

Such deputising took the form of calling on readers to help sift through a 3000-page document dump from the White House in 2007.

The headline and call to action from the newspaper was unambiguous: 'TPM Needs YOU to Comb Through Thousands of Pages' (Kiel, 2007). The result is an exceptionally long blog from readers around the world, analysing the complex documents and contributing to the blog thread.

Some long-established print publications have also adapted well to the digital environment and embraced citizen journalists and bloggers, with these sources breaking important news stories that the news media then follow up. For example, in 2009 *The New York Times* ran a front-page story on the CIA's waterboarding torture at Abu Zubaydah, acknowledging its source: 'The new information on the number of waterboarding episodes came out over the weekend when a number of bloggers, including Marcy Wheeler of the blog emptywheel, discovered it in the May 30, 2005, memo' (Shane, 2009).

Brown (2009) notes that the British *Guardian* newspaper was one of the earliest to expand to include bloggers, and this has worked well for the newspaper. In many cases, Brown explains, there will be 'individuals closer to the action than journalists' (2009, p. 14), and this has meant relinquishing total control at the most fundamental level—the writing and publishing of news by non-journalists. Part of the changed model has been some changed conventions:

> In digital news environments the conventions are quite different. Postings are regarded generally as sacrosanct. They may be deleted altogether if they are deemed to be illegal or, for example, if they promote hatred, but they are very rarely edited. This ceding of control exhibited by major news organizations clearly means that PR people need to extend their contacts beyond those with conventional journalists. (2009, p. 14)

Among the paper's most recent initiatives was the decision to publish its *upcoming* stories in order to receive and monitor reader feedback from readers—*before they were published*. One blogger noted:

> Using readers as a resource is one thing, but revealing what stories are planned and offering to let readers affect that process is another. In the not-too-distant past most newspapers were almost as secretive as government

agencies; the processes involved in producing journalism day-to-day were only revealed to members of the priesthood, and things like story lists were kept under virtual lock and key. (Roberts, 2011)

Clearly the idea of including readers is driving change. This two-way communication flow, which is responsive to consumer choice, is symmetrical communication in action. Media relations practitioners need to work in much the same way with the media—supplying what they need, facilitating news and information both directly to the media and within the blogosphere.

SOCIAL MEDIA IN THE NEWS MIX

Crowd sourcing is also used by the media to confirm information. Foreign correspondent Jess Hill explains how this occurs:

Social media is perhaps the best verification tool journalists have ever had. The number of sources that you can access in any given area, that may not be directly connected, enables you to triangulate in ways you can't do on the ground. On Twitter you can do it. This blows the source field wide open. (cited in Knight, 2011)

Thus Twitter has become an invaluable tool for media to both attract and locate news. It also offers news websites an alternate way to disseminate news stories. Because of this, news organisations have begun a race for followers (Christensen, 2011a). In late 2011, these Australian news media had the following Twitter followers:

- News.com.au (@newscomau): 17 000 followers
- the *Daily Telegraph* (@dailytelegraph): 14 000 followers
- the *Herald Sun* (@theheraldsun): 11 000 followers
- the *Sydney Morning Herald* (@smh): 40 000 followers
- *The Australian* (@australian): 37 000 followers
- *The Age* (@theage): 34 000 followers
- *ABC News* (@abcnews): 88 000 followers. (Christensen, 2011)

The ABC's social media coordinator, Gary Kemble, explains that *ABC News* integrates the tweeting duties with the main news desk. The main benefits of this are:

- *Speed:* Rather than Twitter being the optional extra at the end of the process, it is the first thing producers do in a breaking news situation. By having the senior producers send the tweets, there are minimal barriers between the audience and the news.
- *Engagement:* Because ABC producers are sending tweets, they are also monitoring Twitter for breaking news, tip-offs and feedback. While @abcnews is not a 'talkative' account, it does respond to audience concerns over inaccuracies in its coverage.
- *Relevance:* Sending tweets manually means full control of what is sent, and can make full use of the medium by adding hashtags.
- *Human touch:* People appreciate knowing there's a real person behind the account. Each morning the ABC's early producer sends a 'Good morning' tweet and these human touches make a difference. (Kemble, 2011)

In summary, Twitter can be used by journalists to:

- identify and cultivate sources
- verify information
- maintain a continuum of reports on a major story
- update fellow reporters
- alert the audience to new developments
- encourage interactivity
- publicise reports, and
- grow audience. (Knight, 2011)

Much Twitter media activity is also synthesised and siphoned through other people. This is an important interpretive level which is also about aggregating types of tweets together. In the sea of tweets, people follow conversations about topics, themes and issues. A study based on the Twitter activity of 42 million users, which looked at 260 million tweets over 223 days in 2009–10 (including only tweets containing URLs), found that:

> . . . half the information that originates from the media passes to the masses via a diffuse intermediate layer of opinion leaders who, although classified as ordinary users, are more connected and exposed to the media than their followers. (Wu et al., 2011, p. 14)

Such bloggers are people like media law professor Mark Pearson, whose journlaw blog and Twitter handle focus on media law issues. Pearson—like others in this category—acts as a commentator and analyst, synthesising news stories in his specialty field.

Wu and colleagues (2011) note that the top ten international Twitter sites are individual people—mostly celebrities—but the microblog had also developed a new list of 'semi-public' individuals made up of bloggers, authors and journalists. The use of Twitter—strong in both mass and inter-personal communication—has made it a 'masspersonal' communication (Wu et al., 2011, p. 2). The study also found that like followed like: it was 'homophilous'—celebrities followed celebrities, media followed media, bloggers followed bloggers. This confirms our knowledge of media.

It seems that Twitter is the social media of choice for most news media. Wu and colleagues (2011, p. 13) describe it 'as a subset of a much larger media ecosystem in which content exists and is repeatedly rediscovered by Twitter users'. However, it is also argued that 'amid the Twitter race for followers most Australian news sites remain reliant on sites such as Facebook for the lion's share of their social media referrals' (Christensen, 2011b).

While Facebook may not achieve the same level of 'referrals' (the news media's suggestions about what to read), it is nevertheless up there with Twitter as an information source for the media. A 2011 study on digital journalism, in which nearly 500 journalists from fifteen countries were polled, found that 47 per cent of them used Twitter as a source (up from just 33 per cent in 2010), and the use of Facebook as a source went up to 35 per cent (from 25 per cent in 2010) (Gunter, 2011). The study also found that an increasing number of journalists were turning to social media to verify information, with a third using Twitter and a quarter Facebook. A response to an article published about the findings sums up the media relations position: 'Great article! And it really highlights the fact the business owners have the potential to be seen as an expert if they are posting relevant, time-sensitive, factual information' (Gunter, 2011).

In the news media, Facebook has become a standard tool for contacting individuals. This is no surprise, given its dominance in social networking across the younger population. As one social media commentator puts it: 'Facebook is and will continue to be the way that individuals communicate, inform, and influence others for the foreseeable future'—especially for the 25–45-year-olds (Socialmediatoday, 2011).

YouTube has also found an important niche in the news media for the media relations professional. Burgess and Green (2009) explain that as YouTube has evolved, so has its role in the cycles of news reporting, changing from a novelty, to a threat to media dominance and civil order, to its contemporary position as a bona fide medium. Launched in 2005, the original concept of YouTube was to provide a simple, integrated interface for users to upload, publish and view streaming videos without high-tech knowledge. For the news and entertainment media, YouTube has settled into a space that is a quick visual reference, an easy filler for TV talk and panel shows, a repository for news stories, providing third-party support for a claim or to illustrate a point. In 2009, YouTube Direct was launched, enabling media organisations to request and rebroadcast clips directly from YouTube users. YouTube's head of news and current affairs Steve Grove said the move was about creating 'an ecosystem between the news audience and YouTube', making it simple for media to upload videos and fact-check their authenticity (Grove, in Bunz, 2009):

> As the role of news organisations transforms from gatekeepers to gate-watchers, this open-source application lets media organisations use customised versions of YouTube's upload platform on their own websites. In addition, the tool offers a virtual assignment desk in which news and media organisations can ask YouTube users to submit breaking news videos, user-generated reports, or reactions to questions or news events of the day. (Bunz, 2009)

As it has moved into a commercial environment, YouTube has come to represent something of a paradox for many media organisations.

Keen to have their material available on the site, they are also conscious of revenue losses to YouTube's advertising. YouTube (and its owner, Google) have been sued by media companies from several continents for copyright breaches (Burgess and Green, 2009). One plaintiff, Viacom, argued that YouTube legitimates the uploading of content that infringes the copyrights of Viacom and others (Burgess and Green, 2009). Possibly the best illustration of this paradox lies within the internal conflict of marketers and lawyers over its importance: 'Marketing divisions upload content to the service only to have unaware legal departments request to have the same content removed' (Burgess and Green, 2009, p. 31). And while YouTube can be a boon for publicity purposes, it can also be disastrous. Chapter 9 considered this in the context of media conferences and interviews.

MEDIA RELATIONS AND THE WEB

So far, this chapter has focused on the development of news stories in online media and the role of social media in news production. Implicit in this has been the need for media relations professionals to know about news development and production in order to link into this and become actively involved. An active online and social media presence will allow us to capitalise on what the media need, when they want it and how they want it delivered.

Twitter, Facebook and YouTube have moved into prominent use by all organisations wanting to communicate with their relevant publics. For example, these were primary tools used by local councils in the 2011 floods in south-east Queensland:

> An independent review of the Brisbane City Council's response to the January 2011 floods determined that Facebook and Twitter were used extensively to access information about the 2010/2011 floods. Many of the councils that do not currently use social media to provide information to residents have indicated an intention to do so in future disaster events. (Knight, 2011)

Likewise, police have found them useful during natural disasters in Queensland:

During Tropical Cyclone Yasi and Tropical Cyclone Tasha, the Queensland Police Service (QPS) took to their newly created Facebook and Twitter accounts to inform the public about weather patterns and impending threats, safety measures and tips, public transport closures, emergency services responses and, most importantly, 'mythbusting' information aimed at quashing widespread rumours and community concerns. (McGovern and Lee, 2012 p. 166)

McGovern and Lee (2012) note that police across all states now use social media, including Facebook, Twitter and YouTube. As with all organisational communication, there is now a significant crossover between targeting and using social and traditional media. Like many organisations, the Queensland Police Service's Media and Public Affairs Departments now incorporate their social media platforms into their media communication. For example, their email signatures include:

Follow us on Twitter—http://twitter.com/QPSmedia.
Like us on Facebook—http://www.facebook.com/QueenslandPolice.
Watch us on YouTube—http://www.youtube.com/QueenslandPolice.

In Chapter 8, we looked at using online newsrooms, media kits and centres. These provide an immediate go-to point for the media, who often have to access material in a hurry and without personal communication. The importance of up-to-date top-quality online materials for the media has emerged as a high priority in the last decade. In the first edition of this book, published only five years ago, we looked at a study of 170 online newsrooms in eight countries conducted by IBM in 2004. The study focused on big-name businesses—such as Wal-Mart, Ford Motors, Boeing and Time Warner in the United States, Singapore Airlines, Hewlett-Packard and Hitachi Asia in Singapore and the like (González-Herrero et al., 2005, p. 97). The findings showed that:

- media were considered the second most important audience after clients
- only eighteen companies (out of 170) did not have an online media room

- nearly 70 per cent of inquiries made by journalists were not answered at all, and those that did took too long to get an adequate response
- nearly 40 per cent of all countries updated their media material daily—the highest per cent was in the United Kingdom (more than 57 per cent updated daily), the lowest was Spain (with only 14.7 per cent updating daily), and
- 13.5 per cent never updated online media materials.

The IBM study showed that major companies worldwide had embraced the internet as a means for communicating with the media, and valued the media as one of their key publics. However it seemed that, while all companies used the internet as an *information-out* tool, it was still not being really utilised as an interactive tool between organisations and media. The findings indicated that 'there is still a lot to be done to take advantage of the full potential that the internet offers as a Corporate Communications tool' (González-Herrero et al., 2005, p. 97). It is not surprising that online media relations has moved on from this—imagine 13.5 per cent of organisations never updating their online media materials and 70 per cent of inquiries not being answered today!

A greater focus on supplying online news now exists. Online newsrooms have also become a specialised service, sometimes outsourced to organisations such as Wieck online newsrooms (www.wieck.com.au). These newsrooms can be integrated into existing online properties, managing digital files for organisations that do not have the time or specialisation to do it themselves. They also provide 'dark site' development, which is a useful tool in crisis communication, as discussed in Chapter 5. The company Airservices Australia—the government-owned provider of air traffic control and airport fire and rescue services—used an online newsroom during the 2011 volcanic ash cloud crisis in south-east Australia. During 21–25 June, at the peak of disruption to air traffic, it recorded the following activity:

- 5732 media releases were viewed (105 downloads)
- 2251 images were viewed (26 downloads)

- 1283 videos were viewed (27 downloads), and
- 2432 press kits were viewed.

Airservices Australia said the benefits of the online newsroom were the ability to provide material as the news media wanted it in the quality they needed for reproduction (Wieck, 2011).

Another tool for both the news media and bloggers is RSS (Really Simple Syndication) feeds which were first introduced in the late 1990s (Lewin, 2003) and have become a standard tools for syndicating content and metadata over the Internet. RSS is commonly used to share headlines and links to news articles, and it is an important tool for publishers because feeds can be used to syndicate content, and to integrate third-party content into your site (Lewin, 2003). Here's a typical example of how RSS is used:

- A publisher has some content that they want to publicise.
- They create an RSS channel for their content.
- On this channel, they include items for web pages they want to promote.
- This channel can be read by remote applications, and converted to headlines and links. These links can be incorporated into new web pages, or read in dedicated readers.
- People see the links on various sites, click on them, and go to the original publisher's site. (Lewin, 2003)

RSS readers enable internet users to display and subscribe to the RSS feeds in which they are interested. They include: Newz Crawler, Feed Newz Crawler, Awasu, SharpReader, NetNewsWire, Newsfire, Bloglines, NewsGator, Amphetadesk, Straw (for a list of readers, go to any news website such as News.com and follow the prompts at the RSS site).

Lewin (2003) points out that RSS has contributed to the explosion of blogs. It provides the opportunity to tag your information and stories so that others can locate them—this is central to the mission of the social media release (SMR). These were discussed in Chapter 7, where we looked at their format and benefits. Essentially, SMRs have the best of the traditional media release but they are value added. They need a catchy headline and a news angle, like a traditional release, but they will also include:

- links within the text to direct journalists elsewhere within your site, such as a YouTube story or media kit
- search engine optimisation, such as keyword use
- links to audio or video sites (both your own and others that are related)
- multimedia links like audio files or embedded videos, and
- 'add to' widgets for bookmarking sites like Digg or Del.icio.us.

YouTube and Google are full of sites on how to write and distribute social media releases. (Zoe DeLuca has an excellent site at <www.youtube.com/watch?v=hyCbXYJA4zc> that leads you through how to integrate social media and position yourself as an opinion leader and commentator.)

WORKING WITH BLOGGERS AND THE RISE IN BLOGGER RELATIONS

The rise of the 'citizen journalist', as well as alternative and community journalism, has led to a far greater diversity in news. Who would have thought that 'mummy bloggers' (women who blog about home issues and activities) would become major trend-setters? British mummy blogger network Britmums alone has 3000 members and its 2011 conference attracted more than just members, as the following commentary illustrates:

> Alongside the bloggers, the event has attracted dozens of PRs and brand representatives, keen to forge commercial relationships with these influential voices, as a new channel into the lucrative parents' market. (Katz, 2011)

STUDIES OF BLOGGERS

Unsolicited approaches to bloggers have become commonplace, but care should be taken to confirm that bloggers are open to public relations communication, including offers of sponsorship or advertising. When you develop your blogger lists—either by developing your own or using a professionally developed list from somewhere like PostRank—you should make sure any approaches are welcome. It is important to find out:

- what information and visuals they can use
- when it is wanted
- how to send it (email message, Twitter, phone, media release or direct pitch), and
- (importantly) whether the blogger is open to media pitches.

A survey of bloggers by communications and public relations company Brumfield, Bird and Sandford (BBS) (Edwards and Newbury, 2011) sought information about the role of the blogger in the media landscape, developing some important profile information about the sector. After surveying print, TV and radio journalists each year since 2003, the company turned its attention to new media by surveying national bloggers for the first time, looking at issues that ranged from what bloggers wrote about to whether they received advertising income, how they generated content, when they started, why they blog, their likes and dislikes regarding the public relations industry, how often they received PR-generated material and what types they received, and whether they ever used it. Of the 50 bloggers they surveyed, BBS found:

- 70 per cent classed their blogs as 'professional'
- 55 per cent said blogging was either part of their profession or related to it
- 22 per cent had 10 000 followers or more (6 per cent of these had more than 100 000 followers)
- 34 per cent were paid for their blog
- 30 per cent said they wished they were paid for their blog
- 40 per cent received advertising income from their blog
- 24 per cent said they would like to receive advertising from their blog, and
- 76 per cent had been blogging for five years or less.

The main reasons many bloggers began blogging was to share their experiences and ideas (28 per cent), as a hobby (20 per cent) or to develop their professional profile (20 per cent). And food was the most popular topic for blogging, followed by life (in general), popular culture, health, arts and fashion.

What was also interesting was the source of their content and what sorts of information bloggers wanted to receive. By far the most bloggers wrote from life experience, professional experience and using other blogs/websites, as shown in Figure 13.1. What they wanted to receive were facts, prizes and photos, as shown in Figure 13.2.

The BBS findings revealed important information for the media relations practitioner, not least of which was the openness of many bloggers to receiving information. The survey also highlighted relevant factors that contribute to our knowledge of the blogosphere and why bloggers blog. As we become more systematic about working with bloggers and expand our understanding of blogger relations, as we have with journalists for decades, it is extremely important to learn about this sector and develop a knowledge of bloggers as publics.

Figure 13.1 Where do you generate your content from?

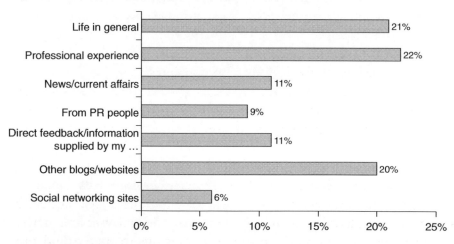

Source: BBS Blogger Survey.

Figure 13.2 What sort of information do you want to receive?

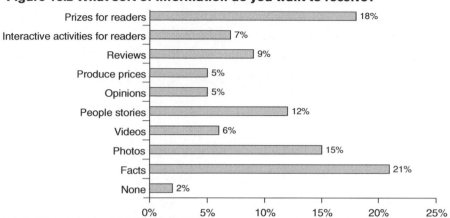

Source: BBS Blogger Survey.

A study by Park and Jeong (2011) developed this concept of getting to know bloggers and examining them within a public relations framework as a new public, or series of publics. They note that bloggers do perform 'journalistic communication', carrying out six primary functions:

1. Blogs have the power to mobilise people.
2. Blogs mediate and filter news and information, and therefore act in a citizen journalism role.
3. Errors are corrected because of the continuous nature of the role.
4. Facts are checked due to this, guaranteeing credibility.
5. Bloggers report as eyewitnesses.
6. Bloggers monitor the media (especially when their reports appear to be biased or unfair) and ultimately can bring about change through rallying readers and fellow bloggers. (Park and Jeong, 2011, p. 393)

The last point—monitoring the media—therefore puts bloggers in a somewhat different role from that of journalists; arguably more like a columnist who comments on and analyses the news. Park and Jeong's approach to blogging helps us to understand the growing, disparate field of blogging. They argue that for bloggers to be most influential and effective, they will be both involved in an issue and have a high degree of self-efficacy (the latter is defined as each blogger's relative desire to influence issues and their level of confidence in their ability to do so). In effect, the idea of self-efficacy in blogging is about being able to problem-solve. 'This means that active involvement with issues in the blogosphere will depend on blogger's capacities—blog self-efficacy—which carries the issues into the public arena of the blogosphere' (Park and Jeong, 2011, p. 395). Park and Jeong then took this idea one step further and developed typologies of four blogger publics, suggesting what they call a 'Blogger Public Segmentation Model' (BPSM). This segmentation breaks bloggers down into four categories:

1. *Active blogger publics:* bloggers who have high levels of issue involvement and blog self-efficacy. Those in this group work as 'journalistic communicators', and include opinion leaders, agenda-setters and commentators. They have the ability to frame situations as issues.
2. *Constrained blogger publics:* bloggers with high issue involvement but low self-efficacy concerning a problem or how to resolve it. While they recognise an issue and have motivation, they lack the conviction or confidence to move into a 'journalistic communicator' role.
3. *Latent blogger publics:* those who have high confidence in using their blogs to solve a problem but are not personally involved in the problem. They are confident in their blogs' ability to effect change.
4. *Routine blogger publics:* represent an inactive public that lacks motivation or communication in a journalistic way. They tend to be personal bloggers, using their blog as a diary. (Park and Jeong, 2011)

In this model, each individual blogger's level of journalistic communication behaviour is a crucial yardstick for determining whether bloggers are influential publics. Thus the media relations practitioner's connection with bloggers will be much the same as it is with (other) journalists—that is, we should work towards developing relationships with bloggers who work in fields that can impact and affect our industries, particularly active and latent blogger publics, described above. This involves looking at blogging patterns and communicating with bloggers as an ongoing tactic, rather than letting issues evolve into crisis and then starting communication. Compiling and updating blogger lists is a major part of this process.

While we target appropriate bloggers as part of our media relations role, the other way in which we can use blogs is to recommend that clients develop their own blogs, and in doing so become opinion leaders, commentators and agenda-setters. An entire professional industry has developed around blogging. While plenty of people write their own blogs, others seek out 'ghost writers' or pay communications staff to either research and write their blogs, or start them in the process. For those of us in media relations, blogs are a valuable part of an overall strategic communications approach to achieving our goals and objectives.

THE WIKIPEDIA PHENOMENON

Wikipedia has become a quick point of reference for all those who use the internet for research. While it might be frowned upon in academic circles, and generally students are not allowed to quote from it, it is widely used—with a *New York Times* report noting that 100 US judicial court rulings have relied on Wikipedia (Cohen, 2007). Whichever way you look at it, Wikipedia provides a solid stepping-off point for investigation and fact finding—and that includes for the news media as well as social media and recreational internet users.

Founded in 2001, Wikipedia is an open-sourced online encyclopedia, ranked #6 on the world's most-visited websites. It has been described as 'Everybody's Encyclopedia' (Ayers et al., 2008) because everyone is able to make contributions. It runs on only 30 paid staff (Zetlin, 2010) and contributions from volunteers. As of May 2012, Wikipedia existed in 285 languages, with 3 949 314 content articles in English alone. It had over 85 000 active contributors and 400 million unique visitors monthly (Wikipedia, 2012a).

Lih (2008) describes Wikipedia as playing an important role in filling the 'knowledge gap' in the period between when the news is published and the history books are written. Unlike traditional encyclopedias, one of the benefits of Wikipedia is the fact that knowledge can quickly be uploaded and updated on to Wikipedia pages (Lih, 2008). Ayers, Matthews and Yates (2008) cite several core policies for Wikipedia entries:

1. *Verifiability:* You should always be able to verify that the content of a Wikipedia article is factual, using reliable outside sources that are cited within the article.
2. *No original research:* All concepts and theories in Wikipedia articles should be based on previously published accounts and ideas.
3. *Neutral point of view:* This attempts to present ideas and facts in such a way that both supporters and opponents can agree.

Although anyone is able to contribute to Wikipedia, it has strict rules on self-promotion and conflicts of interest. Thus its fourth core principle is:

4. *Conflict of interest:* This involves contributing to Wikipedia in order to promote your own interests or those of other individuals, companies, or groups. Where advancing outside interests is more important to an editor than advancing the aims of Wikipedia, that editor stands in a conflict of interest. (Ayers et al., 2008)

As part of Wikipedia's guiding policies for writing and editing articles, it has a 'Law of Unintended Consequences' that states:

> If you write in Wikipedia about yourself, your group, your company, or your pet idea, once the article is created, you have no rights to control its content, and no right to delete it outside our normal channels. Content is irrevocably added with every edit, and once added will not be deleted just because the author doesn't like it anymore . . .
>
> In addition, if your article is found to not be worthy of inclusion in the first place, it *will* be deleted, as per our deletion policies. Therefore, do not create promotional or other articles lightly, especially on subjects you care about. (Wikipedia, 2012b)

However, while the guidelines and policies presented above discourage public relations and marketing professionals from self-promotion, there are ways to maximise your chances of inclusion on the Wikipedia site, as the following process explains.

HOW TO GET INVOLVED IN WIKIPEDIA

- *Get noticed elsewhere.* The more mentions you have in the media and the more visibility you have in social media and blogs, the more likely you are to seem legitimate and 'notable'—a precondition for inclusion. Make sure your website is up to date and offers complete information on your organisation, issue or event so others can access it.
- *Be a Wikipedia volunteer.* Invest time in adding information to those subjects where you have expertise—professionally, socially, culturally or politically. Or if you find any errors, point these out. This will both win friends at Wikipedia and give you a valuable inside view of how it works.
- *Search your organisation, issue or event.* You may find your organisation, issue or event is mentioned in a different article. If it is, add information.
- *Find out whether you have in-house expertise.* Check to see if anyone already working in your organisation is a Wikipedia volunteer. If so, that person can be a valuable resource to help you find your best strategy for getting included.
- *Learn from Wikipedia.* There are hundreds of articles on Wikipedia (as well as a wizard) that explain to users how to create articles and what the rules are. If you still have questions, make an inquiry via info@wikimedia.org. You can also ask for help on the discussion page of your article.
- *Keep it short.* Don't write long entries straight away, as they're more likely to get removed. Instead, start with a 'stub'—an article of only a sentence or two. Wikipedians see this as a challenge.
- *Include links to third-party sites.* Everything that is included in a Wikipedia article should be referenced to a previous publication. It

> may work best to begin with these external links first so those links are already established.
>
> - *Use the discussion page.* Every Wikipedia article comes with a discussion page so use this to explain that you'll be adding more information or links, as well as asking for advice.
> - *Grow a thick skin.* Remember that anyone can write anything about you on Wikipedia. If faced with an unwarranted attack, your best strategy is to appeal to the Wikipedia community for help. Editing the article yourself can look like an attempt at censorship.
>
> Source: Adapted from Zetlin (2010).

Staying well clear of commercially driven contributions (such as your employer) is the best advice. One company that tried to upload its own entry and was found out was computer software company PacketTrap. PacketTrap began writing and posting pages about itself just after launching in 2006, but it was removed with the feedback that it was a 'candidate for speedy deletion' (Zetlin, 2010). Several months later, a Wikipedia entry about PacketTrap was put up by a user. Organisations might see themselves as important enough to have a Wikipedia entry but they should not post it themselves.

In another incident, Microsoft created controversy by attempting to pay a blogger to edit a Wikipedia article on the company in 2007 (Elsworth, 2007). Defending the action, Microsoft's senior technical ambassador Dough Mahugh explained: 'We feel that it would be best if a non-Microsoft person were the source of any corrections . . . Our goal is simply to get more informed voices into the debate' (Elsworth, 2007). The incident sparked controversy in the online community, with Wikipedia's general counsel arguing that: 'Microsoft wanting to soften the edges on an entry raises concerns about the perceived independence of both Wikipedia and Microsoft' (Elsworth, 2007).

Finally, it is important to consider the sources on which many Wikipedia entries and facts are based—published articles and news stories. These are clearly identified by Wikipedia as historically, legitimate documents, confirming the value placed on the veracity of fact-checking by the news media. (Alternatively, it might be a challenge to find a Facebook or Twitter link as a reference within its pages.) Since the news media undoubtedly use Wikipedia from time to time, we can see this as illustrating the point made early in the book—news will be used to develop more news, in this case it is simply filtered through this online encyclopedia.

MANAGING SOCIAL MEDIA AND DEVELOPING SOCIAL MEDIA POLICIES

Social media presents unparalleled challenges when it comes to managing the conversations of individuals, conversations that the media use regularly as the basis for news stories, magnified many times from the first, ill-conceived utterance. As we noted in Chapter 4, social media can be unforgiving when it comes to slip-ups in public conversations.

When swimmer Stephanie Rice tweeted a now-famous anti-gay tweet following the Wallabies' Rugby Union win over South Africa in 2010, she could not have imagined the negative fallout. Rice apologised for the comment and removed the tweet, but the story remains on record. Within a day of the tweet, Rice was reportedly dropped by her sponsor, Jaguar (News.com, 2010). Like it or not, an inappropriate tweet has potential to stick for a long time—especially if it includes that favourite news value, 'conflict'.

Most organisations across all sectors—corporate, government and the third sector—are developing social media policies or codes of conduct that help everyone to know what to do and what not to do in this field. As the lines between personal and professional lives are blurring, these are becoming increasingly important so they need to explain that you do not discuss work issues on social media or comment as a professional (or an employee) in your private communications. A good example is the Victorian Department of Justice's code of conduct, which can be found on <www.youtube.com/watch?v=8iQLkt5CG8I> and includes a link to a catchy video. Another is IBM's twelve-point social media guidelines, which are clear and comprehensive: <www.ibm.com/blogs/zz/en/guidelines.html>. These incorporate points that would apply across most, if not all, organisations—for example (in clause 2):

IBMers are personally responsible for the content they publish on-line, whether in a blog, social computing site or any other form of user-generated media. Be mindful that what you publish will be public for a long time— protect your privacy and take care to understand a site's terms of service. (IBM, 2010)

All organisations know the value of positive conversations generated by their staff, but this needs to be balanced with an understanding of where the lines are drawn and the damage that can be done by inappropriate tweets or comments on Facebook, especially if the news media pick up on them. Working with high-profile people or celebrities can be especially challenging for the media relations professional, and social media etiquette should be spelled out clearly in contracts and staff and clients regularly reminded about it. We can also learn from the mistakes of others as social media protocols continue to be developed.

At the end of 2011, TV journalist Peter Harvey ran a news story of the 'Worst Tweets for 2011', noting how 'Twitter gives celebrities the opportunities to bypass their publicist to interact with the public'— sometimes with disastrous results. Here are some of the tweets that Harvey dubbed 'the worst':

- American politician Anthony Weiner was forced to resign after he tweeted an inappropriate image.
- Actor Ashton Kutcher decided to stop tweeting after he posted a message defending an alleged paedophile.
- Actress Tori Spelling was undoubtedly furious when her husband tweeted an image of her topless.
- Comedian Gilbert Gottfried outraged many when he posted the following after the 2011 Japanese tsunami: 'Japan is really advanced. They don't go to the beaches the beaches come to them.'
- Designer Kenneth Cole was forced to apologise after posting an inappropriate tweet during the revolution in Egypt: 'Millions are in uproar in Cairo. Rumor is they heard our new spring collection is available online.'
- Rapper Kanye West was forced to apologise after tweeting an 'expletive-laden' message about abortion. (Harvey, 2011)

Ill-conceived tweets like these can have embarrassing—and potentially career-changing—outcomes. It will remain increasingly important for media relations and other communications advisers to counsel clients on keeping clear of controversial issues on social media and thinking twice before commenting private thoughts in public spaces. This will increasingly call on organisations to have clear, well-articulated social media policies.

CONCLUSION

The internet and social media have changed the way the media does business—and the way we do business with the media. Members of the public now enthusiastically join the media in breaking and contributing to stories, and the media just as enthusiastically have developed strategies to enable these citizen journalists and bloggers to be part of the news conversation. Tapping into this reader expertise is now a major function of daily news and much entertainment media, which have to cover vast spaces with limited staff. In media relations, we need to work proactively within this model of news production, establishing ourselves, our senior managers and our organisations as opinion leaders and contributors to news and online discussions

At the same time, we need to work with the new ranks of agenda-setters—bloggers who are passionate about and interested in a vast range of niche issues and topics—supplying them with stories, information and materials that are engaging and relevant. Media relations needs to be able to 'do it all' across the diverse media spaces of the internet and social media, but as daunting as that may sound, there are strategies and practices that can manage the challenge. Working systematically and to a plan is the best way to achieve our outcomes. Carefully considered objectives, strategies, tactic selection and professional implementation of these are the key. Moreover, even in the world of mobile devices and external communications, we should not lose sight of the fact that relationships and the management of these relationships still matter—whether face to face, computer to computer, phone to phone or whatever else technology throws our way.

REFERENCES

ABC (2010) 'Research Finds PR Spinning Most Newspaper Stories', *ABC News*, 16 March, <www.abc.net.au/news/2010-03-16/research-finds-pr-spinning-most-newspaper-stories/366356>, accessed 18 March 2010.

ABC (2012) 'WA Labor calls for inquiry into Government media advisers', *PM with Mark Colvin*, 31 January, http://www.abc.net.au/pm/content/2012/s3419887.htm, accessed 5 February 2012.

Alterman, E. (2011) 'Out of Print: The Death and Life of the American Newspaper', in R. McChesney and V. Pickard (eds), *Will the Last Reporter Turn the Lights Out*, New York University Press, New York.

Australian Associated Press (AAP) (2009) VNRs, Medianet, <www.aapmedianet.com.au/video-news-releases.aspx>, accessed 21 December 2011.

—— (2010) *On the Wire: The story of Australian Associated Press*, AAP, Sydney.

—— (2011a) *About AAP*, <http://aap.com.au/about-aap>, accessed 21 November 2011.

—— (2011b) 'Newspaper circulation falls 3.5 per cent', *The Australian*, 11 November, <www.theaustralian.com.au/news/breaking-news/newspaper-circulation-falls-35-per-cent/story-fn3dxity-1226191993883>, accessed 13 December 2011.

Australian Broadcasting Authority (ABA) (2002) *Sources of News and Current Affairs*, <www.aba.gov.au/tv/research/projects/sources/stage2/exec_summary2.htm>, accessed 20 November 2011.

—— (2005) *Australian Television History and Trivia*, <www.aba.au/tv/overview/FAQs/AusTVhistory.shtml#top>, accessed 30 January 2007.

Australian Communications and Media Authority (ACMA) (2011a) *Broken*

273

Concepts: Old Rules Struggling with New Technology, Commonwealth of Australia, Canberra, <http://engage.acma.gov.au/broken-concepts>, accessed 1 December 2011.

—— (2011b) *Broken concepts: The Australian Communications Legislative Landscape, Commonwealth of Australia*, <http://engage.acma.gov.au/wp-content/uploads/2011/08/ACMA_Broken-Concepts_Final_29Aug1.pdf>, accessed 1 December 2011.

—— (2011c) *Australians' Views on Privacy in Broadcast News and Current Affairs*, Commonwealth of Australia, Canberra, August.

Australian Film Commission (2003) *What Australians are Watching: Pay Television in Australia*, <www.afc.gov.au/gtp/wptvanalysis.html#Ray25399>, accessed 20 November 2011.

Australian Government (2006a) 'Community Television', Culture and Recreation Portal, <www.cultureandrecreation.gov.au/articles/community television>, accessed 22 November 2011.

—— (2006b) 'Meeting the Digital Challenge: Reforming Australia's Media in the Digital Age', <www.archive.dcita.gov.au/__data/assets/pdf_file/0006/37572/Media_consultation_paper_Final_.pdf>, accessed 20 January 2012.

—— (2011a) *Convergence Review: Interim Report*, Department of Broadband, Communications and the Digital Economy, Canberra, <www.dbcde.gov.au/__data/assets/pdf_file/0007/143836/Convergence-Review-Interim-Report-web.pdf>, accessed 20 January 2012.

—— (2011b) *Convergence Review*, Department of Broadband, Communications and the Digital Economy, Canberra, <www.dbcde.gov.au/digital_economy/convergence_review>, accessed 1 December 2011.

—— (2011c) *Independent Media Inquiry*, Department of Broadband, Communications and the Digital Economy, Canberra, <www.dbcde.gov.au/digital_economy/independent_media_inquiry>, accessed 1 December 2011.

—— (2011d) *Digital Television Switchover*, Department of Broadband, Communications and the Digital Economy, Canberra, <www.dbcde.gov.au/television/digital_televison_switchover>, accessed 19 December 2011.

—— (2011e) *Pay TV*, Department of Broadband, Communications and the Digital Economy, Canberra, <www.dbcde.gov.au/television/pay_tv>, accessed 20 December 2011.

—— (2011f) *Media Kits*, Australian Taxation Office, <www.ato.gov.au/corporate/pathway.aspx?sid=42&pc=001/001/017/012&mfp=001&mnu=43478#001_001_017_012>, accessed 10 January 2012.

Australian Press Council (APC) (2005) *About the Council*, <www.presscouncil. org.au/pcsite/apc.html>, accessed 20 September 2011.

—— (2008) *State of the News Print Media 2008*, <http://www.presscouncil. org.au/uploads/52321/state-of-the-news-print-media-2008.pdf>, viewed 1 December 2011.

—— (2011a) *Statement of Principles*, <www.presscouncil.org.au/statements-of-principles>, accessed 20 June 2011.

—— (2011b) *Welcome to the Australian Press Council*, <www.presscouncil. org.au>, accessed 18 December 2011.

Ayers, P., Matthews, C. and Yates, B. (2008) *How Wikipedia Works: And How You Can Be Part of It*, No Starch Press, San Francisco.

Bacon, W. and Pavey, S. (2010) 'Who's Really Controlling the Media Message?', *Crikey*, 15 March, <www.crikey.com.au/2010/03/15/whos-really-controlling-the-media-message>, accessed 1 December 2011.

BBC (5 July 2000) 'McLibel Pair Get Police Payout', *BBC News*, <http:// news.bbc.co.uk/2/hi/uk_news/820786.stm>, accessed 25 December 2011.

Berg C. (2011) 'Communications regulation is a dog's breakfast', *The Drum*, <http://www.abc.net.au/unleashed/2867188.html>, accessed 1 March 2012.

Bivins, T. (2011) *Public Relations Writing*, 7th ed., McGraw-Hill, New York.

Bonner, F. (2003) *Ordinary TV: Analysing Popular TV*, Sage, London.

Boorstin, D. (1961) *The Image: A Guide to Pseudo-Events in America*, Atheneum, New York.

Brown, R. (2009) *Public relations and the social web: How to use web 2.0 in communications*, Kogan Page, Philadelphia.

Brown, S. (2003) *Crime and Law in Media Culture*, Open University Press, Maidenhead.

Bunz, M. (2009) 'YouTube Direct Service to Link Citizen Reporters and News Organisations', *The Guardian*, 17 November, <www.guardian. co.uk/media/pda/2009/nov/16/digital-media-youtube-direct-local-news>, accessed 17 January 2012.

Burgess, J. and Green, J. (2009) *YouTube Online Video and Participatory Culture*, Polity Press, Cambridge.

Butler, D. and Rodrick, S. (2007) *Australian Media Law*, Law Book Co., Sydney.

Carpignano, P., Anderson, R., Aronowitz, S. and DiFazio, W. (1993) 'Chatter in the Age of Electronic Reproduction: Talk, Television and the "Public Mind"', in B. Robbins (ed.), *The Phantom Public Sphere*, University of Minnesota Press, Minneapolis, MN.

Carrick, D. (2010) 'Trade Mark Disputes', *The Law Report*, 2 February, <http://www.abc.net.au/radionational/programs/lawreport/trademark-disputes/3101484>, accessed 2 February 2012.

CBS *News* (2010) 'The Secret Behind the Hit TV Car Show *Top Gear*', *60 Minutes*, 25 October, <www.cbsnews.com/stories/2010/10/21/60minutes/main6978679.shtml>, accessed 9 November 2011.

Chapman, C. (2011) *The 'Convergence Phenomena' from a Regulator's Perspective*, Communications and Media Lawyers Association, Sydney.

The Chaser's War on Everything (2007) '*The Chaser's War on Everything*— APEC Motorcade', ABC TV, 12 September, <www.youtube.com/watch?v=NvH3YQGQwLM>, accessed 8 November 2011.

Christensen, N. (2011a) 'The Australian to Launch Paid Content on Monday', *The Australian, Media*, 20 October, <www.theaustralian.com.au/media/the-australian-paywall-to-launch-monday/story-e6frg996-1226171691697>, accessed 13 December 2011.

—— (2011b) 'It's click-through that counts in news race', *The Australian, Media*, <www.theaustralian.com.au/media/monday-section/its-click-through-that-counts-in-news-race/story-fna1k39o-1226167954222>, accessed 17 January 2012.

—— (2011c) 'Stricter privacy laws hamper news investigation', *The Australian, Media*, 20 December, <http://www.theaustralian.com.au/media/stricter-privacy-laws-hamper-news-gathering/story-e6frg996-1226229733719>, accessed 20 January 2012.

Clissold, B. (2004) '*Candid Camera* and the Origins of Reality TV: Contextualising a Historical Precedent', in S. Holmes and D. Jermy (eds), *Understanding Reality Television*, Routledge, London.

Cohen, H. (2011) 'Don't Trust the Web', *Background Briefing*, 18 September, <www.abc.net.au/radionational/programs/backgroundbriefing/dont-trust-the-web/3582912>, accessed 25 December 2011.

Cohen, N. (2007) 'Courts Turn to Wikipedia, but Selectively', *The New York Times*, 29 January, <http://www.nytimes.com/2007/01/29/technology/29wikipedia.html?_r=1>, accessed 1 March 2012.

Commercial Radio Australia (CRA) (2007) *Commercial Radio: A Snapshot*, December, <www.commercialradio.com.au/files/uploaded/file/Advertising%20on%20Radio/Snapshots%202007_forweb_amended.pdf>, accessed 18 December 2011.

—— (2011a) *About Digital Radio*, <www.digitalradioplus.com.au/index.cfm?page_id=1002>, accessed 18 December 2011.

—— (2011b) 'Big Jump in Digital Radio Sales', News Archive, <www.digitalradioplus.com.au/index.cfm?page_id=1026&news_display_year_1785=2011&display_news_id_1785=1099>, accessed 18 December 2011.

—— (2011c) *Digital Radio Report 2011*, <www.commercialradio.com.au/files/news/Digital%20Radio%20Industry%20Report%202011.pdf>, accessed 18 December 2011.

Communications Law Centre (CLC) (2011) *Media Ownership Factsheet*, University of Technology Sydney, <www.law.uts.edu.au/comslaw/fact sheets/media-ownership.html>, accessed 1 December 2011.

Community Broadcasting Association of Australia (CBAA) (2010) *Voices and Vision: Community Broadcasting in Australia*, <www.cbaa.org.au/sites/default/files/Voices%20%26%20Vision%20-%20All%20About%20Community%20Broadcasting.pdf>, accessed 20 December 2011.

Community Broadcasting Foundation (2011) *Australian Community Broadcasting Snapshot*, <www.cbf.com.au/Content/templates/sector.asp?articleid=31&zoneid=13>, accessed 1 December 2011.

—— (2012) 'About Australian community broadcasting', <http://www.cbf.com.au/Content/templates/sector.asp?articleid=30&zoneid=13>, accessed 10 March 2012.

Community Broadcasting Online (2007) *Community Broadcasting Database: Survey of the Community Radio Sector, 2005–06 Financial Period*, Community Broadcasting Association of Australia (CBAA), Sydney, <www.cbonline.org.au/index.cfm?pageId=37,0,1,0>, accessed 1 August 2009.

Conley, D. and Lamble, S. (2006) *The Daily Miracle*, Oxford University Press, Melbourne.

Crabtree, M. (2009) *Michel Crabtree Portraits*, <http://www.michaelcrabtree.co.uk/corporate/corporatePRabout.html>, accessed 22 March 2012.

Craig, G. (2004) *The Media and Public Life*, Allen & Unwin, Sydney.

Crane, T. (2004) *What is Issue Management?* Issue Management Council, Leesberg, <www.issuemanagement.org/documents/im_details.html>, accessed 20 June 2011.

Crikey (2010) 'The Spin Cycle: How Your Newspaper Fared', <http://www.crikey.com.au>, accessed 15 March 2012.

—— (2011) 'About Crikey: Crikey is Australian for Independent Journalism', <http://www.crikey.com.au/about/>, accessed 10 March 2012.

Cropp, F. and Pincus, D. (2001) 'The Mystery of Public Relations: Unravelling Its Past, Unmasking Its Future', in R. Heath (ed.), *Handbook of Public Relations*, Sage, London.

Davies, N. (2008) *Flat Earth News*, Chatto & Windus, London.

Davis, A. (2000) 'Public Relations, Source Production and Changing Patterns of Source Access in the British National Media', *Media, Culture and Society*, no. 22, pp. 39–59.

Davis, L. (1999) 'Scandal Management 101—Excerpt from "Truth to Tell"',

Washington Monthly, <http://findarticles. com/p/articles/mi_m1316/is_5_31/ai_54644718>, accessed 1 December 2011.

Day, M. (2006) 'Celebrity Magazines', *The Australian: Media Section*, June 10.

Deitz, M. (2010) *Watch This Space: The Future of Australian Journalism*, Cambridge University Press, Melbourne.

Devereux, E. (2003) *Understanding the Media*, Sage, London.

Dodd, A. and Green, S. (2011) 'The Baillieu Dump: More Accountability, but Same Tactics from Ted', Crikey.com, 24 November, <www.crikey.com.au/2011/10/24/the-baillieu-dump-more-accountability-but-same-tactics-from-ted>, accessed 18 January 2012.

Downie, C. and Macintosh, A. (2006) *New Media or More of the Same?*, Australian Institute, <http://72.14.203.104/search?q=cache:DFV2kIZCs6gJwww.tai.org.au/Publications_Files/Papers%26Sub_Files/Cross-media%2520ownership%2520Owebpaper%2520_May%25202006_pdf+%22media+ownership+laws%22+2006&hl=en&gl=au&ct=clnk&cd=7>, accessed 20 August 2011.

Downie, L. and Schudson, M. (2009) 'The Reconstruction of American Journalism', in R. McChesney and V. Pickard (eds), *Will the Last Reporter Please Turn Out the Lights*, The New Press, New York.

Drechsel, R. (1983) *News Making in the Trial Courts*, Longman, New York.

Dwyer, T. (2011) 'Australian Media Monitor, September 2011', *Global Media Journal: Australian Edition*, 5 (1) <www.commarts.uws.edu.au/gmjau/mm.html>, accessed 1 December 2011.

Dwyer T. and Martin F. (2010) 'Updating Diversity of Voice Arguments for Online News Media', *Global Media Journal: Australian Edition*, 4 (2), <http://www.commarts.uws.edu.au/gmjau/v4_2010_1/dwyer_martin_RA.html>, accessed 1 December 2011.

Edwards, J. and Newbury, A. (2007) *BBS 2007 Media Survey*, Brumfield, Bird and Sandford Communications, Brisbane.

—— (2011) *BBS 2011 Media Survey*, Brumfield, Bird and Sandford Communications, Brisbane.

Electoral and Administrative Review Commission (EARC) (1993) *Report on Review of Government and Information Services*, Queensland Government, Brisbane.

Elsworth, C. (2007) 'Microsoft Under Fire in Wiki Edit War', *The Telegraph*, 26 January, <www.telegraph.co.uk/news/worldnews/1540669/Microsoft-under-fire-in-Wiki-edit-war.html>, accessed 20 August 2011.

Entman, R.M. (1993) 'Framing: Toward Clarification of a Fractured Paradigm', *Journal of Communication*, vol. 43, no. 4, pp. 52–8.

Ericson, R., Baranek, P. and Chan, J. (1987) *Visualizing Deviance: A Study of News Organization*, University of Toronto Press, Toronto.

Errico, M. (1996) 'The Evolution of the Summary Lead', *Media History Monographs,* vol. 1, no. 1, pp. 1–18.

Fairfax Media (2006) *Merger of Fairfax Media and Rural Press,* <www.fxj. com.au/shareholders/FairfaxRuralMergerAnalystPresentationv1.0.pdf>, accessed 16 November 2011.

—— (2008) 'Sydney Morning Herald—Sections', *Fairfax Publications,* <http://www.adcentre.com.au/the-sydney-morning-herald.aspx? show=sections>, accessed 20 January 2012.

Falls, J. (2010) 'Postrank Makes Online Media Relations Easier With Top Blogs Lists', *Social Media Explorer,* 14 January, <www.socialmediaexplorer. com/online-public-relations/postrank-makes-online-media-relations-easier-with-top-blogs-lists>, accessed 18 January 2012.

Farsetta, D. and Price, D. (2006) 'Fake TV News: Widespread and Undisclosed', Centre for Media and Democracy's PR Watch, <www. prwatch.org/fakenews/execsummary>, accessed 20 December 2011.

Finkelstein, R. (2012) 'Report of the Independent Inquiry into the Media and Media Regulation', Commonwealth of Australia, <http://www. dbcde.gov.au/digital_economy/independent_media_inquiry>, accessed 17 March 2012.

Fisher, A. (2005) 'Hot Careers for the Next 10 Years', *Fortune Magazine,* 21 March, <http://money.cnn.com/magazines/fortune/fortune_archive/ 2005/03/21/8254853/index.htm>, accessed 1 December 2011.

Fishman, M. (1980) *Manufacturing the News,* University of Texas Press, Austin, TX.

Fleishman-Hillard (2001) *Fleishman-Hillard Media Training Manual,* <www.appanet.org/eweb/Resources/National_Branding/AFORCE_ MediaTrainingManual.pdf>, accessed 2 November 2011.

Forde, S. (1998) 'Monitoring the establishment: The development of the alternative press in Australia', *Media International Australia,* no. 87, pp. 114–33.

—— (2011) *Challenging the News: The Journalism of Alternative and Community Media,* Palgrave Macmillan, London.

Forde, S. and Johnston, J. (2012, forthcoming) 'The News Triumvirate: Public Relations, Wire Agencies and Online Copy', *Journalism Studies.*

Forde, S., Meadows, M. and Foxwell, K. (2002) *Culture Commitment, Community: The Australian Community Radio Sector,* Griffith University, Brisbane.

Foster, C. (1995) *The Crowe Communications Report*, Crowe Communications, Sydney.

Fox, L. (2003) *Enron: the rise and fall*, John Wiley & sons, New Jersey.

Galtung, J and Ruge, M.H. (1965) 'The Structure of Foreign News: The Presentation of the Congo, Cuba and Cyprus Crises in Four Norwegian Newspapers', *Journal of Peace Research*, vol. 2, no. 1, pp. 64–90.

Gandy, O.H. (1982) *Beyond Agenda Setting: Information Subsidies and Public Policy*, Ablex Publishing, Norwood, NJ.

Golin, A. (2002) 'Trust: Hard to Earn, Easy to Lose', <www.ameinfo.com/16891-more2.html>, accessed 3 November 2011.

González-Herrero, A., Ruiz de Valbuena, M. and Ruiz San Román, J.A., (2005) *Best Practices in Public Relations: An Analysis of Online Press Rooms in Leading Company's Around the World*, IBM, Madrid.

Gruen Planet (2011), ABC TV, 9 November.

Grunig, J. (2001) 'Two-way Symmetrical Public Relations: Past, Present and Future', in R. Heath (ed.), *Handbook of Public Relations*, Sage, Thousand Oaks, CA, pp. 11–30.

Grunig, J. and Hunt, T. (1984) *Managing Public Relations*, Holt, Rinehart & Winston, New York.

Gunter, J. (2011) 'Journalists Increasingly Using Social Media as News Source, Finds Study', Journalism.com.uk, 18 May, <www.journalism.co.uk/news/journalists-increasingly-using-social-media-as-news-source-finds-study/s2/a544193>, accessed 18 January 2012.

Habermas, J. (1962, translated 1989) *The Structural Transformation of the Public Sphere: An inquiry into a category of bourgeois society*, Polity, Cambridge.

—— (1998) *On the Pragmatics of Communication*, MIT Press, Boston, MA.

Haltom, W. (1998) *Reporting on the Courts*, Nelson-Hall, Chicago.

Harris, L. (2011) 'When Your Communication Gets in a Spin: The Battle of Policy versus Populism', paper delivered to the Public Relations Institute of Australia annual conference PR Directions 2011, October, Sydney.

Hartley, J. (1992) *The Politics of Pictures*, Routledge, London.

Harvey, P. (2011) 'Worst Celebrity Tweets 2011', Ninemsn, 21 December, <http://news.ninemsn.com.au/viralvacuum/glance/208468/worst-celebrity-tweets-of-2011.glance>, accessed 22 December 2011.

Hayes, A. (2011) email communication, Queensland Tourism, 1 December.

Hendrix, J.A. (1998) *Public Relations Cases*, 4th ed., Wadsworth, Belmont, CA.

Holub, R. (1991) *Jürgen Habermas: Critic in the Public Sphere*, Routledge, London.

Hurst, D. (2011) 'Book Bungle: Award Winners Out of the Bag, as Hicks Misses Out', *Sydney Morning Herald*, 6 September, <www.smh.com.au/entertainment/books/book-bungle-award-winners-out-of-the-bag-as-hicks-misses-out-20110906-1jvd6.html>, accessed 3 November 2011.

IBM (2010) *Social Computing Guidelines*, <www.ibm.com/blogs/zz/en/guidelines.html>, accessed 20 January 2012.

Idato, M. (2003) *Great Moments in Product Placement*, <www.mediaman.com.au/articles/great_moments.html>, accessed 20 August 2011.

Jack, I. (2006) *The Granta Book of Reportage*, 3rd ed., Granta Books, London.

Jackson, S. (2011) '*Australian Financial Review* Lowers Its Paywall', *The Australian, Media*, 1 December, <www.theaustralian.com.au/media/financial-review-lowers-its-paywall/story-e6frg996-1226210302448>, accessed 13 December 2011.

Johnston, J. and Forde, S. (2009) '"Not Wrong for Long": The Role and Penetration of News Wire Agencies in the 24/7 News Landscape', *Global Media Journal* (Australian Edition), vol. 3, no. 2, <www.commarts.uws.edu.au/gmjau/v3_2009_2/johnson_forde_RA.html>, accessed 20 January 2012.

Johnston, J. and Zawawi, C. (eds) (2009) *Public Relations: Theory and Practice*, 3rd ed., Allen & Unwin, Sydney.

Katz, L. (2011) 'Cybermummy—a Blogging Conference Like No Other', *The Guardian*, 28 June, <www.guardian.co.uk/media/2011/jun/28/cybermummy-blogging-conference>, accessed 15 November 2011.

Kelly, K.S. (2001) 'Stewardship: The fifth step in the public relations process', in R.L. Heath (ed.), *Handbook of Public Relations*, Sage, Thousand Oaks, CA.

Kemble, G. (2011) 'Clicks no substitute for engagement', *ABC News*, <http://blogs.abc.net.au/newseditors/gary-kemble/>, accessed 13 May 2012.

Kenny, M. (2012) 'Gillard staffer sacked over tip to tent embassy protesters', *Adelaide Now*, 27 January, <http://www.adelaidenow.com.au/gillard-and-abbott-run-protest-gauntlet/story-e6frea6u-1226254435221>, accessed 5 February 2012.

Kiel, P. (2007) 'TPM Needs YOU to Comb Through Thousands of Pages', *TPM*, 20 March, <http://tpmmuckraker.talkingpointsmemo.com/archives/002809.php>, accessed 26 December 2011.

Killoran, M. (2011) 'Coast Mayoral Race's Dirty Tricks', *Gold Coast Bulletin*, 3 August, <www.goldcoast.com.au/article/2011/08/03/338005_gold-coast-news.html>, accessed 5 August 2011.

Knight, A. (2011) 'How to Tweet the News', *Online Journalism*, 30 November, <http://alanknight.wordpress.com/category/the-abc>, accessed 17 January 2012.

La Trobe Library (2006) *Database: Alternative Press Index*, <www.lib.latrobe.edu.au/databases/info.php?i=17> accessed 1 June 2011.

Lamme, M.O. and Russell, K.M. (2010) 'Removing the Spin: Toward a New Theory of Public Relations History', *Journalism and Communication Monographs*, vol. 11, no. 4, pp. 281–362.

Langdon, J. (1995) 'The Social and Political Forces that Led to the Development of Public Radio in the 1960s', Australian Centre for the Moving Image, <http://www.acmi.net.au/AIC/PUB_RAD_OZ_LANGDON.html>, accessed 30 May 2007.

Ledingham, J. (2003) 'Explicating Relationship Management as a General Theory of Public Relations', *Journal of Public Relations Research*, vol. 15, no. 2, pp. 181–98, <www.leaonline.com/doi/pdf/10.1207/S1532754XJPRR1502_4>, accessed 20 December 2011.

Lee-Wright, P., Phillips, A. and Witschge, T. (2012) *Changing Journalism*, Routledge, London.

Lewin, J. (2003) 'Content Feeds with RSS 2.0: Syndication Goes Mainstream, *IBM Developer Works*, 23 December, <www.ibm.com/developerworks/xml/library/x-rss20>, accessed 18 January 2012.

Lewis, J., Williams, A. and Franklin, B. (2008) 'A Compromised Fourth Estate?', *Journalism Studies*, vol. 9, no. 1, pp. 1–20.

Leys, N. (2011) 'Paywalls an "Inevitable Reality"', *The Australian, Media*, 16 November, <www.theaustralian.com.au/media/paywalls-an-inevitable-reality/story-e6frg996-1226196081013>, accessed 13 December 2011.

Lidberg, J. (2005) 'FOI as a Journalistic Tool', *Scoop* (Australian Journalism Association, WA, Magazine), 16 November.

Lih, A. (2008) 'Wikipedia as Participatory Journalism: Reliable Sources? Metrics for Evaluating Collaborative Media as a News Resource', paper presented to the fifth International Symposium on Online Journalism, University of Texas, Austin, 16–17 April, <http://jmsc.hku.hk/faculty/alih/publications/utaustin-2004-wikipedia-rc2.pdf>, accessed 20 October 2011.

Long, G. (2006) Personal Interview, Gold Coast.

Lurie, I. (2007) 'Social Media Press Release: The Next Step, HTML, Conversation Marketing', <www.conversationmarketing.com/2007/12/social_media_press_release_the.htm>, accessed 7 November 2011.

Magazine Publishers (2005) 'Readership', <www.magazines.org.au>, accessed 20 October 2011.

Maloney, K. (2006) *Rethinking Public Relations: PR Propaganda and Democracy*, 2nd ed., Routledge, London.

Marsden, S. (1999) *Talkback: Trash and Treasure*, R&R Publications, Melbourne.

Marston, J.E. (1963) *Nature of Public Relations*, McGraw-Hill, New York.

Macnamara, J. (2001) 'The Impact of PR on the Media', <www.pria.com. au/sitebuilder/resources/knowledge/files/1172/primpactmedia.pdf>, accessed 1 May 2011.

McCarthy, T. (1981) *The Critical Theory of Jürgen Habermas*, MIT Press, Boston, MA.

McChesney, R. (2008) *The Political Economy of the Media*, Monthly Review Press, New York.

McChesney, R. and Pickard, V. (eds) (2011) *Will the Last Reporter Please Turn Out the Lights: The Collapse of Journalism and What Can Be Done to Fix It*, The New Press, New York.

McCombs, M. (2004) *Setting the Agenda: The Mass Media and Public Opinion*, Polity Press, Cambridge.

McCombs, M., Shaw, D.L. and Weaver, D. (1997) *Communication and Democracy: Exploring the Intellectual Frontiers in Agenda-setting Theory*, Lawrence Erlbaum, Mahwah, NJ.

McCoy, L. (2009) 'Ethical Practice', in J. Johnston and C. Zawawi (eds), *Public Relations: Theory and Practice*, Allen & Unwin, Sydney.

McDermot, T. (2007) 'Blogs Can Top the Presses', *Los Angeles Times*, 17 March, <http://articles.latimes.com/2007/mar/17/nation/na-blogs17>, accessed 26 December 2011.

McDonald, E. (2011) 'Girls and the Impact of Reality TV', *Life Matters*, ABC Radio National, 8 November, <www.abc.net.au/rn/lifematters/ stories/2011/3358514.htm>, accessed 8 November 2011.

McGuirk, R. (2006) 'Australia Relaxes Media Ownership Laws', Associated Press, 18 October, <www.boston.com/ae/media/articles/2006/10/18/ australia_relaxes_media_ownership_laws>, accessed 20 October 2011.

McGovern, A. and Lee, M. (2011) 'Cop[ying] it Sweet: Police Media Units and the Making of News', *The Australian and New Zealand Journal of Criminology*, vol. 43, no. 3, pp. 444–64.

—— (2012) 'Police Communications in the Social Media Age', in P. Keyzer, J. Johnston and M. Pearson (eds), *The Courts and the Media: Challenges in the era of digital and social media*, Halstead Press, Sydney.

McLean, H. (2011) Personal Communication, Gold Coast.

McLennan, L. (2008) 'Murdoch to cut jobs at papers', *The Age*, News, 7 November, <http://search.ebscohost.com/login.aspx?direct=true&db= n5h&AN=SYD-5MIUKMW93EG14QK4R8O4&site=ehost-live>, accessed 2 March 2011.

McNair Ingenuity (2008) *Community Broadcasting Audience Survey*, <www.cbonline.org.au/media/McNairListners2008/FullNationalListener Survey2008.pdf>, accessed 20 October 2011.

McQueen, H. (1977) *Australia's Media Monopolies*, Widescope, Melbourne.

Medialink Productions (2012) <http://medialinkproductions.com/>, accessed 22 March 2012.

Media Entertainment and Arts Alliance (2012) 'Code of Ethics', <http://www.alliance.org.au/code-of-ethics.html>, accessed 10 January 2012.

Media Standards Trust (2011) 'Churnalism.com', <http://mediastandardstrust.org>, accessed 1 May 2011.

Meetings Industry Association of Australia (MIAA) (2001) 'Comments on . . . Goods and Services Tax', <www.miaanet.com.au/members/pdfs/contraGSTruling.pdf>, accessed 20 June 2004.

Meyer, P. (2004) *The Vanishing Newspaper: Saving Journalism in the Information Age*, University of Missouri Press, Missouri.

Meyer, P.J. (2003) *Attitude is Everything: If You Want to Succeed Above and Beyond*, Meyer Resource Group, Waco, TX.

Miller, T. and Turner, G. (2002) 'Radio', in S. Cunningham and G. Turner (eds), *The Media and Communications in Australia*, Allen & Unwin, Sydney.

Mindframe (2011) 'Reporting Suicide and Mental Illness', <www.mindframe-media.info/site/index.cfm?display=82652>, accessed 10 January 2012.

Moore, T. (2010) 'Encountering Australian Journalism', in M. Deitz (ed.), *Watch This Space: The Future of Australian Journalism*, Cambridge University Press, Melbourne.

Moos, J. (2011) 'Worldwide, newspapers reach more people than the Internet, WAN-IFRA survey shows', The Poynter Institute, <http://www.poynter.org/latest-news/mediawire/149516/worldwide-newspapers-reach-more-people-than-the-internet-wan-ifra-survey-shows/#.Tw9wjz7vJvM.email>, accessed 23 March 2012.

National Film and Sound Archives (2008) 'News and Current Affairs', <http://nfsa.gov.au/collection/television/news-and-current-affairs/>, accessed 2 January 2012.

Neer, K. (2006) 'How Product Placement Works', *How Stuff Works*, <http://money.howstuffworks.com/product-placement6.htm>, accessed 20 September 2011.

Nielsen Media Research (2011) 'MX: Readership and circulation', <http://www.mxnet.com.au/>, accessed 13 May 2012.

—— (2012a) 'Australia's first ever multi-screen report reveals evolution in television viewing', Press Release, <http://nielsen.com/content/dam/

corporate/au/en/reports/2012/Australia-Multi-Screen-Report-Q411-press-releaseL.pdf>, accessed 25 March 2012.

—— (2012b) 'TV Ratings: Free to Air', <http://203.11.170.41/product. asp?ProductID=27>, accessed 25 March 2012.

Newell, J. (2003) *Product Placement 1896–1982*, <http://mediatown. org/ articles/PPHistAEJMC6-031.pdf>, accessed 20 September 2011.

News Ltd (2012) 'News Community Media,' News Space, <http://www. newsspace.com.au/communitynews/>, accessed 21 March 2012.

News.com (2010) 'Stephanie Rice Loses Sponsor Jaguar After Anti-gay Tweet', September, <www.news.com.au/business/stephanie-rice-loses-sponsor-jaguar-after-anti-gay-tweet/story-e6frfm1i-1225915098261#ixzz1hIxWBmop>, accessed 23 December 2011.

Ofcom (Independent Regulator and Competition Authority for the UK Communications Industries) (2011) 'Product Placement on TV', <http:// consumers.ofcom.org.uk/2011/02/product-placement-on-tv>, accessed 8 November 2011.

O'Reilly, L. (2011) 'Tiger Woods is Riskiest Brank Ambassador', *Marketing Week*, 21 August, <http://www.marketingweek.co.uk/tiger-woods-is-riskiest-brand-ambassador/3029636.article>, accessed 23 November 2011.

O'Sullivan, M. (2011) 'Virgin Basks in the Glow as Brand Qantas Crashes and Burns', *Sydney Morning Herald*, 2 November, <www.smh.com.au/business/virgin-basks-in-the-glow-as-brand-qantas-crashes-and-burns-20111102-1mv8n.html>, accessed 3 November 2011.

Outhwaite, W. (1994) *Habermas: A Critical Introduction*, Polity Press, Cambridge.

Park N. and Jeong J.Y. (2011) 'Why Do Bloggers Behave Journalistically in the Blogosphere? Bloggers' Journalistic Communication Behavior Model', paper delivered at the *International Association of Media and Communication Research conference*, Istanbul.

Patching, R. (2012) 'The *News of the World* scandal and the Australian privacy debate', in P. Keyzer, J. Johnston and M. Pearson (eds), *The Courts and the Media: Challenges in the era of digital and social media*, Halstead Press, Sydney.

Pearson, M. (2012) *Blogging and Tweeting Without Getting Sued*, Allen & Unwin, Sydney. .

Pearson, M. and Brand, J. (2001) *Sources of News and Current Affairs*, epublications@Bond, Bond University, <http://epublications.bond.edu. au/hss_pubs/96>, accessed 1 February 2011.

Pearson, M. and Polden, M. (2011) *The Journalist's Guide to Media Law*, Allen & Unwin, Sydney.

Pew Center Project for Excellence in Journalism (2008) *The State of the News Media: An Annual Report on American Journalism*, The Pew Center, <www.stateofthemedia.org/2008>, accessed 20 June 2008.

Pfeffer, R., Evans, T., Dore, M., Morgan, M., Gilmore, L., Sembach, S. and Shearer, A. (2004) *The History of the News Media*, <www.personal.psu.edu/users/r/j/rjp210/newspaper.html>, accessed 20 September 2011.

Phillips, A. (2012) 'Transparency and the ethics of news journalism', in P.H. Lee-Wright, A. Phillips, and T. Witschge, *Changing Journalism*, Routledge, London.

Public Relations Institute of Australia (2012) 'Code of Ethics', <http://www.pria.com.au/membercentre/members-code-of-ethics>, accessed 10 January 2012.

Putnis, P. (1994) *Recut, Reused and Re-visioned*, Bond University, Gold Coast.

Queensland Government Commission of Inquiry (2011) 'Forecasts, Warnings and Information', <www.floodcommission.qld.gov.au/__data/assets/pdf_file/0010/8785/QFCI-Interim-Report-Chapter-4-Forecasts,-warnings-and-information.pdf>, accessed 10 January 2012.

Raward, D. (2012) Personal Interview, Gold Coast.

Raward, D. and Johnston, J. (2009) 'FM radio news: Spreading the news or spread too thin?' *Australian Journalism Review*, vol. 31, no. 1, pp. 63–76.

Readfearn, G. (2001) 'Nice Bit of Gas-powered Journalism', Crikey.com.au, 25 March, <http://blogs.crikey.com.au/rooted/2011/03/25/nice-bit-of-gas-powered-churnalism>, accessed 1 May 2011.

Register, M. and Larkin, J. (2008) *Risk Issues and Crisis Management in Public Relations: A Casebook of Best Practice*, Kogan Page, London.

Reich, Z. (2010) 'Measuring the Impact of PR on Published News in Increasingly Fragmented News Environments', *Journalism Studies*, vol. 11, no. 6, pp. 799–816.

Ricketson, M. (2004) *Telling Feature Stories*, Allen & Unwin, Sydney.

Roberts, D. (2011) 'Lessons from Our Open News Trial', *The Guardian Blog*, 17 October, <www.guardian.co.uk/help/insideguardian/2011/oct/17/guardian-newslist>, accessed 17 January 2012.

Robinson, J. (2010) 'Ofcom Confirms Product Placement on UK TV', *The Guardian*, 20 December, <www.guardian.co.uk/media/2010/dec/20/ofcom-product-placement-uk-tv>, accessed 8 November 2011.

Rogers, E.M. and Dearing, J.W. (1988) 'Agenda-setting Research: Where Has It Been, Where is It Going?' in J.A. Anderson (ed.), *Communication Yearbook 11*, Sage, Newbury Park, CA, pp. 555–94.

Rolfe, P. and Kearney, S. (2010) 'John Brumby the Spin King of Australia', *Herald Sun*, 17 October, <www.heraldsun.com.au/news/victoria/john-

brumby-the-spin-king-of-australia/story-e6frf7kx-1225939651938>, accessed 28 April 2011.

Rosenberg, B. (2008) 'News Media Ownership in New Zealand', *Cyber Place*, <http://www.converge.org.nz/watchdog/15/05.htm>, accessed 22 March 2012.

Roy Morgan Research (2006) 'Australian Media Viewed With Scepticism: TV Remains Our First Stop When Chasing the News', Roy Morgan Research, 16 December, <www.roymorgan.com/news/polls/2006/4117>, accessed 1 December 2011.

Rusbridger (2011) '*The Guardian*'s iPad Edition Goes Live', *The Guardian Blog*, 13 October, <www.guardian.co.uk/help/insideguardian/2011/oct/13/guardian-ipad-edition-newsstand-app>, accessed 17 January 2012.

Saul, S. (2008) 'Claim Over Red Cross Symbol is Settled', *New York Times*, 18 June, <www.nytimes.com/2008/06/18/business/18cross.html>, accessed 10 December 2011.

Scheufele, D. (1999) 'Framing as a Theory of Media Effects', *International Journal of Communication*, no. 49, pp. 103–22.

Schlesinger, P. and Tumber, H. (1994) *Reporting Crime: The Media Politics of Criminal Justice*, Oxford University Press, New York.

Schultz, J. (1994) *Not Just Another Business: Journalists, Citizens and the Media*, Pluto Press, Sydney.

—— (1998) *Reviving the Fourth Estate*, Cambridge University Press, Melbourne.

—— (2002) 'The Press', in S. Cunningham and G. Turner (eds), *The Media and Communications in Australia*, Allen & Unwin, Sydney.

Sedorkin, G. (2003) 'Television Journalism: The Cultural Politics of Contemporary Current Affairs Reporting', unpublished PhD thesis, Deakin University.

Siebert, F., Peterson, T. and Shramm, W. (1956) *Four Theories of the Press*, University of Illinois Press, Urbana, IL.

Shane, S. (2009) 'Waterboarding Used 266 Times on 2 Suspects', *The New York Times*, 19 April, <www.nytimes.com/2009/04/20/world/20detain.html>, accessed 26 December 2011.

Shirky, C. (2009) 'How Social Media Can Make History', *Ted*, June, <www.ted.com/talks/clay_shirky_how_cellphones_twitter_facebook_can_make_history.html>, accessed 18 January 2012.

Simmons, P. and Spence, E. (2006) 'The Practice and Ethics of Media Release Journalism', *Australian Journalism Review*, vol. 28, no. 1, pp. 215–29.

Simons, M. (2007) *The Content Makers: Understanding the Media in Australia*, Penguin, Ringwood.

Slocum, C. (2005) *The Real History of Reality TV or, How Alan Funt Won the Cold War*, <www.wga.org/organizesub.aspx?id=1099>, accessed 20 September 2011.

Smith, R. (2002) *Strategic Planning for Public Relations*, Lawrence Erlbaum, Mahwah, NJ.

Socialmediatoday (2011) 'Who Uses Facebook, Twitter, LinkedIn, & MySpace?', 13 April, <http://socialmediatoday.com/paulkiser/285851/who-uses-facebook-twitter-linkedin-myspace-4thq-1stq-stats-and-analysis>, accessed 18 January 2012.

Soley, L. (1992) *The News Shapers: The Sources Who Explain the News*, Praeger, New York.

Solis, B. (2008) 'The Definitive Guide to Social Media Releases', <www.briansolis.com/2008/02/definitive-guide-to-social-media>, accessed 7 November 2011.

Special Broadcasting Service (SBS) (2011) 'About Us', <http://www.sbs.com.au/aboutus/our-story/>, accessed 26 March 2012.

Stacks, D. (2011) *Primer of Public Relations Research*, 2nd ed., Guildford Press, New York.

Stanton, R. (2007) *Media Relations*, Oxford University Press, Sydney.

Star News (2012) *Star News Group*, <http://www.starnewsgroup.com.au/about/>, accessed 22 March 2012.

Steffens, M. (2008) 'Fairfax Media to Cut 550 Jobs in Australia, NZ', *Sydney Morning Herald*, Edition 1, Business, 27 August, p. 18, <http://search.ebscohost.com/login.aspx?direct=true&db=n5h&AN=SYD-5LHVDIJV778UM2O58XH&site=ehost-live>, accessed 2 March 2011.

Sullivan, S. (2012) 'Infrontcommunication', Personal interview, 15 October, Bond University, Gold Coast.

Sussman, B. (2004) *Why Watch Dog? And Why Question?*, Neiman Foundation of Journalism at Harvard University, <www.niemanwatchdog.org/index.cfm?fuseaction=about.mission_statement&stoplayout=true&print=true>, accessed 20 September 2011.

Televisionau.com (no date) *The History of Australian Television*, <http://www.televisionau.com/sixties.htm>, accessed 22 March 2012.

Ten Network (2011) 'Where is Poh Now?', *Junior MasterChef*, <www.masterchef.com.au/where-is-poh-now-.htm>, accessed 10 November 2011.

Thompson, J. (2011) 'Government Flags Wide-ranging Media Inquiry', ABC Online, 13 September, <www.abc.net.au/news/2011-09-13/media-inquiry-launched-in-australia/2897136>, accessed 1 December 2011.

Throng: Australia's TV Watching Community (2010) '16–39 and 18–49 Demographic Top Shows Tuesday April 27, 2010', <www.throng.com.au/

ratings/1639-and-1849-demographic-top-shows-tuesday-april-27-2010>, accessed 9 November 2011.

Tiffen, R. (1989) *News and Power*, Allen & Unwin, Sydney.

Tobias, M. (1998) *The Search for 'Reality': The Art of Documentary Making*, Michael Weise Productions, Studio City, CA.

Tourism Western Australia (2012) *Familiarisations*, <www.tourism.wa.gov.au/marketing/Familiarisations/Pages/Familiarisations_Overview.aspx>, accessed 20 March 2012.

Tuchman, G. (1978) *Making News: A Study in the Construction of Reality*, The Free Press, New York.

Turner, G. (2005) *Ending the Affair: The Decline of Television Current Affairs in Australia*. UNSW Press, Sydney.

Turner, G., Bonner, F. and Marshall, D. (2000) *Fame Games: The Production of Celebrity in Australia*, Cambridge University Press, Melbourne.

Underwood, L.J. (2003) *The Mass Media as the Fourth Estate*, <www.cultsock.ndirect.co.uk/MUHome?cshtml/media/4estate.html>.

Vanity Fair (2008) '*Sex and the City*: A Product-Placement Roundup', *Vanity Fair*, <www.vanityfair.com/online/daily/2008/05/sex-and-the-city>, accessed 8 November 2011.

Walters, B. (2004) 'An attempt to Restrict Free Speech', *The Age*, 23 June, <www.theage.com.au/articles/2004/06/22/1087844934216.html?from=storylhs>, accessed 1 July 2007.

Waterford, J. (2002) 'Journalism for the Real World', *The Media Report*, ABC Radio National, 15 August.

Weaver, D.H. (2007) 'Thoughts on Agenda-setting, Framing, and Priming', *Journal of Communication*, vol. 57, no. 1, pp. 142–7.

Weiss, D.C. (2010) '"Attack Dog" Group Buys Newspaper Copyrights, Sues 86 Websites', *ABA Journal: Law News Now*, 4 August, <www.abajournal.com/news/article/attack_dog_group_buys_newspaper_copyrights_sues_86_websites>, accessed 10 December 2011.

Wieck Australasia online newsrooms (2011) *Information Kit*, distributed at 2011 PRIA conference, Sydney, <www.wieck.com.au>, accessed 20 January 2012.

Wikipedia (2012a) *About Wikipedia*, <http://en.wikipedia.org/wiki/Wikipedia:About>, accessed 13 May 2012.

—— (2012b) *Unintended Consequences*, <http://en.wikipedia.org/wiki/Unintended_consequences>, accessed 20 January 2012.

—— (2012c) *Conflict of Interest*, <http://en.wikipedia.org/wiki/Conflict_of_Interest>, accessed 20 January 2012.

Wong (2011) 'Government will Continue Negotiations to Pass MRRT', *AM*, ABC Radio, 2 November, <www.abc.net.au/am/content/2011/s3353745.htm>, accessed 20 November 2011.

Wu, S., Mason, W., Hofman, J. and Watts, D. (2011) 'Who Says What to Whom on Twitter', International World Wide Web Conference Committee, 28 March–1 April, Hyderabad, India.

Zaphir, P. (2012) Personal Interview, Gold Coast.

Zawawi, C (1994) 'Source of News: Who Feeds the Watchdogs?', *Australian Journalism Review*, no. 16, pp. 67–72.

Zetlin, M. (2010) 'Using Wikipedia as a Marketing Tool', *Inc.*, 18 January, <www.inc.com/managing/articles/201001/wikipedia.html>.

INDEX

4112941R00169

Printed in Great Britain
by Amazon.co.uk, Ltd.,
Marston Gate.